THE ACTIVIST'S HANDBOOK

THE
ACTIVIST'S
HANDBOOK

A PRIMER

UPDATED EDITION
WITH A NEW PREFACE

Randy Shaw

UNIVERSITY OF CALIFORNIA PRESS
BERKELEY   LOS ANGELES   LONDON

University of California Press
Berkeley and Los Angeles, California

University of California Press, Ltd.
London, England
© 1996 by The Regents of the University of California

Preface to the Second Edition
© 2001 by The Regents of the University of California

Library of Congress Cataloging-in-Publication Data

Shaw, Randy, 1956–
    The activist's handbook : a primer / Randy Shaw.
        p.   cm.
    Includes bibliographic references and index.
    ISBN 0-520-22928-2 (pbk).
    1. Social action—United States.   2. Community organization—United
States.   3. Political activists—United States.   4. Political participation—United
States.   5. Social reformers—United States.   I. Title.
HN65.S48   1996
361.2—dc20   95-33113
                                                                              CIP

Printed in the United States of America

10   09   08   07   06   05   04   03   02
9   8   7   6   5   4   3

The paper used in this publication is both acid-free and totally chlorine-free (TCF).
It meets the minimum requirements of ANSI/NISO Z39.48-1992 (R 1997)
(*Permanence of Paper*). ∞

To Lainey

Contents

Preface to the Paperback Edition

In the wake of the Seattle protests against the World Trade Organization, the Million Mom March for stricter gun controls, and nationwide student sit-ins to protest sweatshops, the power of activism to achieve social change has gained renewed respect. As new campaigns have emerged around such issues as globalization, a living wage, genetically engineered "Frankenfoods," gay marriage, and a ban on logging in national forests, grassroots activism is increasingly recognized as the most potent counterbalance to a political system dominated by corporations and big money. These ongoing struggles have reaffirmed the lessons of this book. Once-invulnerable targets ranging from the National Rifle Association to the World Bank are taking citizen action more seriously; it is therefore imperative that activists choose their strategies and tactics wisely.

I wrote this book to assist those actively engaged in trying to improve their neighborhood, their nation, and the world. By profiling activist campaigns, I tried to convince readers that grassroots action could prevail as long as activists relied upon the strategies and tactics necessary for success. Many of the successful campaigns described in this book—such as the defeat of a proposed incinerator at the Brooklyn Navy Yard by an unusual coalition of Hasidic Jews and Puerto Rican Catholics (chapter 3) and the lowering of citywide rent increases by tenant activists in San Francisco (chapter 4)—represented tremendous grassroots victories over powerful politicians and wealthy special interests. *The problem was that few activists across the country ever learned of such victories, and certainly had no "behind the scenes" information regarding the keys to success. Activists thus continued to lack the confidence that they too could succeed against similar odds.* I hoped that chronicling these successful struggles would provide activists a road map for victory and inspire readers to believe that they could also triumph.

My hopes for this book have repeatedly borne fruit since its first publication. Among the many people who have contacted me was Thuyen Nguyen, a Vietnamese American upset about a television show he saw on the mistreatment of young Vietnamese women making sneakers for Nike. Nguyen told me he wanted to fight these abuses and was carefully reading my book to learn how to become a successful activist. Six months later the national media and broader public were galvanized by shocking new revelations of abuses in Nike's production facilities in Vietnam. The author of the report was Nguyen, who told me that my book had given him the confidence to believe he could succeed.

I have been gratified to hear from many other activists and organizations who have benefited from the book. Adoptee-rights activist Helen Hill became so persuaded by chapter 4's strategy for winning ballot initiatives that she used much of her inheritance to fund a landmark "open records" measure for Oregon's November 1998 ballot. The initiative won a sweeping upset victory, paving the way for the passage of similar measures in other states

While it is important to highlight success stories, I also wanted readers to recognize the most common strategic errors that doom winnable grassroots campaigns. Chief among these is activists' failure to hold politicians at all levels accountable for their campaign promises. As I discuss in chapter 2, national environmental groups thought they had a friend in the Clinton-Gore administration and refused to publicly criticize their "allies" when, soon after taking office, the administration broke its promise to close down a dangerous waste incinerator in East Liverpool, Ohio. Environmentalists' failure to hold the administration accountable paved the way for future betrayals. It was not until the Sierra Club and other national groups reinvigorated their grassroots mobilizing base and adopted what I describe as the necessary "fear and loathing" relationship to elected officials that the environmental gains of the Clinton era were achieved.

Activists also err when they allow their adversaries to set the terms of the debate. In chapter 1 I discuss how conservatives launched a major public relations campaign in the 1990s to blame the rise of widespread visible homelessness in America on individual behavior rather than on a lack of affordable housing. The goal was to shift attention away from cutbacks in federal housing assistance and society's failure to address homelessness and to redefine the problem as one of aggressive panhandling and problem street behavior Unfortunately, many homeless advocates accepted their opponents' reframing of the issue and made the strategic error of fighting a battle on their opponents' terms. Instead of continuing to emphasize federal cutbacks in funding for affordable housing and the paltry federal allocations to combat homelessness, advocates became zealous defenders of the right to camp and beg in public places. Both public support for homeless persons and federal funding for affordable housing subsequently declined.

A central theme of this book is that activists must be proactive. It is only by creating and implementing our own agendas, rather than fighting defensive battles, that social change is achieved. Support for this fundamental principle has been repeatedly reaffirmed since the book's publication. For example, at the community level, I describe in chapter 1 how those trying to curb development within cities must act proactively to rezone entire neighborhoods rather than try to defeat specific projects. This proactive strategy is now being used from New Jersey to California to combat urban and suburban sprawl. By enacting growth boundaries, acquiring strategically situated land for open space, endorsing in-fill housing, and redefining their agenda as "smart growth" (rather than the politically losing "no growth"), antisprawl advocates have avoided project-by-project battles and outmaneuvered their opponents.

The value of activists fighting proactively has been even more greatly affirmed in the national arena. For example, in advising activists on using the media, I discuss how "supply-side" economics governed American fiscal policy throughout the 1980s by being aggressively marketed by Ronald Reagan and his allies in the press as a cure for the nation's economic ills. Although Democrats argued that supply-side's massive tax cuts would primarily enrich the wealthy, they did not mobilize the public to support a more equitable alternative. In a contest between a new idea and an untenable status quo, supply-side easily prevailed.

Contrast the campaign for supply-side economics to ongoing efforts to allocate federal budget surpluses for massive tax cuts. Rather than simply attack such proposals, education and health-care activists, labor unions, and community groups are pushing to use the record sur-

plus for serving human needs. These groups only advocate tax cuts targeted to address specific social problems. By creating a choice between
tax cuts for the rich and the need to build schools, expand health care,
and enhance environmental protection, activists shifted public support
toward a more progressive agenda. The siren song of steep income-tax
cuts no longer resonates with most Americans.

The need to switch from a defensive to a proactive stance described
in *The Activist's Handbook* has also been reaffirmed during the ongoing battle over globalization. During the Congressional battle over the
North America Free Trade Agreement, the Clinton administration and
its corporate allies successfully tarred their opponents as antitrade,
fearful of the future, and unwilling to accept the globalization of the
economy. It took only a few years for the framing of the trade debate
to change. As I discuss in my second book, *Reclaiming America: Nike,
Clean Air and the New National Activism,* labor, students, and human
rights activists succeeded in putting a human face on the free trade debate by publicizing the plight of the young women making garments
for American import in overseas sweatshops. Meanwhile, environmental groups highlighted the harm done to the ever-popular sea turtles by
free trade agreements that undermined environmental protections.
Those opposed to unrestricted free trade now had a proactive agenda:
fair trade. Faced with a choice between trade with or without labor
and environmental protections, the public favored the latter. It became
clear during the WTO protests in Seattle that activists' proactive
agenda setting had changed the terms of the global trade debate.

The myriad campaigns described in this book have a common
thread: a positive process for developing proactive agendas and strategies. For many organizations, particularly ACORN (Association of
Community Organizations for Reform Now) and those affiliated with
US Action, National People's Action, and the Industrial Areas Foundation, the vesting of decision making in the hands of low-income and
working-class people is central to the group's identity and mission. As
campaigns increasingly require building coalitions among diverse, multi-
issue constituencies, the skill of ensuring good process both internally
and externally is even more vital.

This book describes strategies for ensuring sound decision making
in several contexts: when activists ally with former adversaries (chapter
3), create ballot initiatives (chapter 4), work with the media (chapter
5), deal with attorneys (chapter 6), engage in direct action (chapter 7),
and set their own agendas (chapter 8). It is encouraging to see that

activist groups that rely on students, such as the state- and campus-based Public Interest Research Groups (PIRGs), train students in agenda setting and make strategizing a centerpiece of their organizing and recruitment. The PIRGs give students a crucial vehicle for participating in state and national campaigns, particularly on environmental and consumer issues. Organized labor's creation of Union Summer student internships has similarly built student activists' agenda-setting skills both on campuses (through the involvement of its graduates in the United Students Against Sweatshops) and through local and national campaigns for workers' rights.

Protests, rallies, strategy sessions, press releases, membership events, fundraising, accountability meetings—working for social change can become so consuming that organizations often forget that activists need to have fun. Anyone who does not enjoy working with a group or campaign will drop out. In this book I describe how campaigns can maintain activists' participation by using tactics that are both fun and effective—the use of rat costumes to protest failed housing-code enforcement, the "Put People First, Not Polluters" bus tour whose participants carried "Arkansas Chickens" to symbolize Bill Clinton, or ACT UP's brilliantly choreographed nonviolent direct action to bring critical AIDS issues to a national audience. Organizations or campaigns that help to foster close friendships—a particular strength of the affinity groups used by many antiglobalization activists—also help ensure that activists stay involved over the long haul.

As the legendary early-twentieth-century anarchist Emma Goldman is reputed to have said, "If I can't dance I don't want to be part of your revolution." I hope that new generations of activists will take Goldman's spirit to heart as they use the suggestions in this book to improve their neighborhood, city, nation, or the world.

Acknowledgments

I have learned much about social change from my fellow activists. Whether through one-time meetings or common struggles, my discussions with fellow activists have been essential to the insights expressed in this book.

My organization, the Tenderloin Housing Clinic, has provided me with a perfect environment and vehicle for implementing my ideas for achieving social change. I could not have written this book without the encouragement and support of the entire Clinic staff. I am particularly grateful to Tim Lee for his steadfast friendship and professional encouragement and support throughout my career, and to my longtime colleague Steve Collier. Richard Hack provided important clerical and editorial assistance. Jamie Sanbonmatsu, the Clinic's longtime organizer, assisted me greatly by serving as a sounding board for many of the ideas discussed in this book.

In addition to Clinic staff, several other activists have particularly influenced my thoughts about social-change activism over the years. Leroy Looper, owner of San Francisco's historic Cadillac Hotel, has long served as a model of integrity and street-smart strategic savvy. Grateful for the opportunity to exchange ideas with Leroy in his back office at the hotel, I have always tried to live up to his ideals in my work. My strategic analysis has also benefited from my discussions with Margaret Brodkin, Calvin Welch, Jim Shoch, and Erik Schapiro. Chris Tiedemann has both influenced my thinking and provided valuable feedback on portions of this work. Larry Shapiro has not only shaped my overall thinking on strategy, but greatly assisted my understanding of environmental issues. Shapiro and his NYPIRG colleagues, Arthur Kell and Martin Brennan, helped to ensure the accuracy of my account of the Brooklyn Navy Yard incinerator battle.

I am also indebted to Robert Peterson for my material on the New Fratney School, and to Kitty Cone and Judy Heumann for their perspectives on the Section 504 campaign. Rick Hind generously contributed feedback to my analysis of national environmental issues and provided key material on the Greenpeace struggle against the East Liverpool, Ohio burn plant. Robert Schildgen also graciously reviewed my ideas on national environmental strategies.

I especially want to thank Joe Brooks of the San Francisco Foundation for having the confidence to underwrite my ideas about organizing the poor. Joe is a career activist who has successfully brought social-change activism to the foundation world.

I am extremely grateful to Katharine Ball for her enthusiasm and encouragement about my proceeding with this project. Katharine provided valuable assistance in every aspect of this work, from story research through editing the text.

Any author would be fortunate to have Naomi Schneider of U.C. Press as his or her editor. Naomi not only expressed continual enthusiasm for my ideas, but her gentle manner in suggesting revisions encouraged a collaborative effort and produced a better text.

I could not have written this book, while also working full-time, without family support. I have always received encouragement from my families on both coasts. My children, Anita and Ariel, were remarkably tolerant of Daddy's frequent need to work on his book rather than play games. The joy my children bring me has certainly infused my text. My late grandmother, Hylda Levin, was a New Deal Democrat and McGovern supporter who always vowed she would take me to Canada, if necessary, to avoid the draft. Although she died in 1975, her spirit lives on.

Finally, I am most indebted to Lainey Feingold, my wife and best friend of nearly two decades. Lainey helped make me an activist and provided me with critical and enthusiastic editorial assistance. This book could not have been written without her.

Introduction

In Montgomery, Alabama in December 1955, a seamstress named Rosa Parks was arrested for refusing a driver's order to move to the back of the bus. Her arrest spurred a citywide bus boycott that brought national attention to Parks and a young minister named Martin Luther King, Jr. Although it took another decade of struggle before state-imposed segregation laws were eliminated, Rosa Parks's courageous act stands as the symbolic start of the modern civil rights movement.

The civil rights movement comprised thousands of heroic acts, but the story of Rosa Parks continues to resonate long after other events of the period have been forgotten. Forty years later, when Parks held a booksigning in a small bookstore in Oakland, California, thousands of people waited in line for hours merely for the opportunity to see her up close.

Why has Rosa Parks's stature grown rather than diminished? I believe it is because people today have nostalgia for a seemingly bygone era when individuals at the grassroots level could initiate campaigns that made a difference in the world. Underlying the reverence for Parks is the common perception that today's political climate is too complex or too burdened by institutional barriers for a modern Rosa Parks or a significant campaign for social change to emerge.

In this book I flatly reject the widely held notion that current political conditions have confined social change activism to the history books. The Montgomery bus boycott and the civil rights movement were triumphs of strategy and tactics over seemingly insurmountable

1

barriers. Similarly, today's activists use strategy and tactics to triumph in their own campaigns for change. As hostile to progressive change as the U.S. political landscape appears at the close of the twentieth century, contemporary institutional and cultural obstacles do not approach the magnitude of the barriers successfully overcome by the civil rights movement.

The critical impact of strategy and tactics on the outcome of social change campaigns is often overlooked. One likely reason for this omission is that most current analyses of U.S. politics are not written by activists. People who participate in social change activism recognize that the chosen tactics or strategies often spell the difference between victory and defeat; outside commentators, however, evaluate actions by what *did* happen, not by what alternative strategy or tactic might have brought a better result. Moreover, the value of tactics and strategies is best demonstrated at the local level, but most accounts of institutional barriers to political change focus exclusively on Washington, D.C.

In the pages to come I detail the strategies and tactics that activists in diverse fields have found necessary for success. I focus on winning campaigns and show how losing efforts might have been victorious had the proper tactics and strategies been used. I also analyze why a particular tactic was successful and why it was preferable to other approaches. By discussing the strategic and tactical choices faced by activists, I take the reader inside the thought processes of experienced activists in the midst of their struggles.

Central to all social change activism is the need to engage in proactive strategic and tactical planning. Activists must develop an agenda and then focus their resources on realizing it. Unfortunately, many activists have failed to establish and implement their own agendas and instead have focused on issues framed by their opponents. Although the contemporary political environment frequently requires activists to respond to threats or defend past gains, these defensive battles cannot be waged at the expense of proactive campaigns for change. Social change activists can avoid fighting battles on their opponents' terms by establishing a broad, realizable program for fulfilling their goals. The means of carrying out the program will often be the subject of lengthy meetings and internal debate. Once they have agreed upon an agenda and endorsed tactics and strategies, activists should expend their energy primarily on implementation, responding to the opposition's campaign solely within the framework of furthering their own programs. This proactive approach ensures that the social change organization will set the public debate, forcing the opposition to respond to the unceasing drive for progressive reform.

Against the backdrop of proactive agenda setting, particular tactics and strategies have consistently maximized the potential for achieving social change. These tactics include creating what prominent Texas community organizer Ernesto Cortes, Jr., has described as a "fear and loathing" relationship toward elected officials to ensure political accountability; forging coalitions with diverse and even traditional opposition groups; harnessing the mainstream and alternative media to the social change agenda; and effectively using sit-ins, "die-ins," and other forms of direct action.

Through a discussion of current political issues and events, I will analyze the impact of particular strategies and tactics on the outcome of campaigns around homelessness, crime, tenants' rights, the environment, AIDS policies and programs, disability rights, neighborhood preservation, and school reform. These issues serve to illustrate the diverse avenues activists use to achieve social change: state and local ballot initiatives, electoral politics, grassroots lobbying and advocacy, direct action, media events, litigation, and local and national forums and conventions. Participants in these struggles range from the Hasidic Jews of Brooklyn to the Latino parents of Milwaukee, from the urban poor of San Francisco to the rural environmentalists of the Pacific Northwest. These diverse constituencies have not always complied with the popular chant that activists are involved in the "same struggle, same fight," but they have used similar tactics and strategies to achieve their goals.

Though my analysis covers local, state, and national battles, I place greater emphasis on local battles for two reasons. First, most progressive activists are involved in struggles in the geographic area in which they live; second, local grassroots groups increasingly represent the greatest prospect for achieving significant progressive change at the national level. One way local activists can influence federal policy is by becoming part of a national coordinated strategy—witness such examples as direct action by local chapters of ACT UP (a national grouping of organizations fighting the AIDS epidemic) and disabled activists' occupation of a federal office building. In other cases, such as the Montgomery bus boycott and the fight to stop a hazardous waste incinerator in East Liverpool, Ohio, a well-fought battle with local significance can come to have great national significance. Activists do, in fact, think globally and act locally; this book reflects that adage.

Bookstores and libraries typically contain dozens upon dozens of business-oriented "how to" books. There exists a virtual industry of works designed to assist people's skills in management, negotiation, sales, communications, networking, and media relations. These volumes emphasize the tactics necessary to defeat in-house competitors, overseas competitors, and any other competitor who stands in the way of business success. People in the business of seeking social change, however, have few such resources to turn to for guidance. This book is meant to provide such guidance, particularly to a younger generation that has exhibited strong interest in fights for social and economic justice. Although the media often depict today's young people either as "slackers" or as being less interested in political activism that in acquiring a high-paying job, these individuals actually have a tremendous desire to work for progressive social change. For example, participants in the struggles of ACT UP in the late 1980s were overwhelmingly in their twenties, and they exposed themselves to risks of arrest and violence that marked earlier generations as heroic. Young people want to address poverty, environmental racism, and other forms of social and economic injustice but often lack the vehicle and the tactical skills necessary. This lack is partly attributable to the elimination in the early 1980s of federal programs such as VISTA, in which committed young people worked as organizers and activists in low-income neighborhoods. These positions provided an instant connection to community organizations fighting for social change and acted as an "alternative" career path for recent college graduates. The defunding of grassroots activists' jobs in the 1980s has left today's young people with a dearth of mentors among their generational elders.

The Republican Party's current strategy of channeling the public anxiety about the future into attacks on immigrants, racial minorities, welfare mothers, feminists, and gays and lesbians is ominous but can be overcome. Rather than simply oppose the right-wing agenda, activists must advance and frame issues that unify people around objection to social and economic unfairness rather than hostility toward others. This essential resurgence of social activism necessarily requires the significant participation of young people. From the Freedom Rides of the civil rights movement to the "no business as usual" actions of ACT UP, social activism has relied upon the energy, idealism, and broad participation of young people. To paraphrase Mark Twain, reports of the demise of progressive social change have been greatly exaggerated. A generation of activists that understands the tactics and strategies essential for success can create a new political environment for a new century.

1

Don't Respond, Strategize

In a previous era, social change activists were guided by the immortal words of Mary "Mother" Jones: "Don't mourn, organize." These words, spoken following the murder of a union activist, emphasized the value of proactive responses to critical events. Although American activists today face less risk of being killed, they still must heed Mother Jones's command. A political environment hostile to progressive change has succeeded in putting many social change activists on the defensive, and the need for proactive planning—what I like to call "tactical activism"—has never been clearer.

Unfortunately, proactive strategies and tactics for change all too frequently are sacrificed in the rush to respond to the opposition's agenda. Of course, activists must organize and rally to defeat specific attacks directed against their constituencies; if a proposed freeway will level your neighborhood, preventing the freeway's construction is the sole possible strategy. I am speaking, however, of the far more common scenarios where the opposition pushes a particular proposal or project that will impact a constituency without threatening its existence. In these cases, it is critical that a defensive response also lay the groundwork for achievement of the long-term goal.

The best way to understand tactical activism is to view it in practice. The Tenderloin neighborhood of San Francisco, where I work, is a virtual laboratory in which both the benefits of tactical activism and the consequences of its absence are clear. The Tenderloin has experienced the problems of luxury development, homelessness, and crime that have plagued urban areas throughout our nation, and it offers an excellent reflection of the challenges activists face today.

THE TENDERLOIN: TACTICAL ACTIVISM AT WORK

The Tenderloin lies between City Hall and the posh downtown shopping and theater district of Union Square. Once a center of the city's underground gay scene and home to thousands of merchant seamen and blue-collar workers living in the neighborhood's nearly 100 residential hotels, the Tenderloin has been described by the media as San Francisco's "seedy" district—a not entirely inaccurate depiction. For at least the past twenty years, the Tenderloin has had more than its share of prostitution, public drunkenness, and crime. Until the mid-1980s, it was notorious for its abundance of peep shows, porno movie houses, and nude-dancing venues; the high profile of these businesses and their flashing lights and lurid signs fostered the neighborhood's reputation.

The Tenderloin's location in the heart of a major U.S. city distinguishes it from other economically depressed neighborhoods. Many people who spend their entire lives in Los Angeles or New York City never have cause to go to Skid Row or the South Bronx; the high-crime area of East Oakland is easily avoided by Bay Area residents. However, average San Franciscans are likely to pass through the Tenderloin at some point—to visit one of the city's major theaters, to see a friend staying at the Hilton Hotel (located in the Tenderloin), to conduct business at City Hall, or to reach any number of other destinations. San Franciscans have firsthand experience with the Tenderloin that is highly unusual for low-income neighborhoods.

The thirty-five blocks at the core of the neighborhood constitute one of the most heterogeneous areas in the United States, if not the world. The Tenderloin's 20,000 residents include large numbers of senior citizens, who are primarily Caucasian; immigrant families from Vietnam, Cambodia, and Laos; a significant but less visible number of Latino families; perhaps San Francisco's largest concentration of single African-American men, and a smaller number of African-American families; one of the largest populations of gays outside the city's Castro district; and a significant number of East Indian families, who own or manage most of the neighborhood's residential hotels. The Tenderloins's broad ethnic, religious, and lifestyle diversity contrasts sharply with the virtual unanimity of its economic class: almost every resident is poor.

With government offices and cultural facilities in the Civic Center to the west, the city's leading transit hub on Market Street to the south, the American Conservatory and Curran theaters to the north, and Union Square (one of the most profitable shopping districts in the United States) to the east, in the late 1970s the neighborhood's economic revival was said to be just around the corner. This widespread belief in the imminent gentrification of the Tenderloin profoundly shaped its future. During that time, Tenderloin land values rose to levels more appropriate to the posh lower Nob Hill area than to a community beset with unemployment, crime, and a decrepit housing stock. Real estate speculators began buying up Tenderloin apartment buildings and developers began unveiling plans for new luxury tourist hotels and condominium towers.

Further impetus for the belief in imminent gentrification came from the arrival in the late 1970s of thousands of refugees, first from Vietnam, then from Cambodia and Laos. The Tenderloin was chosen for refugee resettlement because its high apartment-vacancy rate made it the only area of the city that could accommodate thousands of newly arrived families. The refugees' arrival fostered optimism about the Tenderloin's future in three significant ways. First, the refugees filled longstanding apartment vacancies and thus raised neighborhood property values and brought instant profits to Tenderloin landowners. Second, many in the first wave of refugees left Vietnam with capital, which they proceeded to invest in new, Asian-oriented businesses in the Tenderloin. These businesses, primarily street-level markets and restaurants, gave the neighborhood a new sense of vitality and drove up the value of ground-floor commercial space. Third, and perhaps most significant, those eager for gentrification expected Southeast Asian immigrant families to replace the Tenderloin's long-standing population of seniors, merchant seamen, other low-income working people, and disabled persons. The families, it was thought, would transform the neighborhood into a Southeast Asian version of San Francisco's popular Chinatown.

My introduction to the Tenderloin came through Hastings Law School, another significant player in the Tenderloin development scene. In 1979, when I was twenty-three, I enrolled as a student at Hastings, a public institution connected to but not controlled by the University of California. During the 1970s, Hastings, then housed in one multistory building, expanded its "campus" by vacating tenants from some adjacent residential hotels. Its relationship to the low-income residents of the Tenderloin is based on the perspective of territorial imperative, one shared by urban academic institutions such as Columbia and the University of Chicago. Hastings has been aptly described as the law school that "ate the Tenderloin."

Because of the school's location in a distressed neighborhood, many of its students try to help local residents. I became involved soon after starting at Hastings. My personal concern was tenants' rights, an interest developed during rent-control battles in Berkeley, where I had lived while attending the University of California. On February 1, 1980, I joined fellow law students in opening a center to help Tenderloin tenants prevent evictions and assert their rights. Our center, called the Tenderloin Housing Clinic, started with a budget of $50, and our all-volunteer staff was housed in a small room at Glide Memorial Church, in the heart of the neighborhood.

When we opened the clinic, the Tenderloin did not appear to be on the verge of an economic boom. Some thriving Asian markets had opened, and nonprofit housing corporations had begun to acquire and rehabilitate some buildings, but the dominant impression was of an economically depressed community whose residents desperately needed various forms of help. The inhabitants of the Tenderloin, unaware of the agenda of those predicting upscale development, would have laughed at anyone proclaiming that neighborhood prosperity was just around the corner. How quickly everyone's perspective would change in the months ahead.

Almost immediately, I found myself plunged into what remains my best experience of how tactical activism can transform a defensive battle into a springboard toward accomplishing a significant goal. In June 1980 I was invited to a meeting at the offices of the North of Market Planning Coalition (NOMPC). NOMPC initially comprised agencies serving the Tenderloin population. In 1979, however, it obtained enough staff through the federal VISTA program to transform itself into a true citizen-based organization. The VISTA organizers were like me: recent college graduates from middle-class backgrounds excited about trying to help Tenderloin residents.[1] The convener of the June 1980 meeting, Richard Livingston, had secured the VISTA money for NOMPC with the vision of getting neighborhood residents involved in planning the community's future. Livingston revealed that plans to build three luxury tourist hotels in the neighborhood had been launched by three of the most powerful hospitality chains in the world—Holiday Inn, Ramada, and Hilton. The three towers would have thirty-two, twenty-seven, and twenty-five stories, respectively, containing more than 2,200 new tourist rooms. The news outraged us; the encroachment of these big-money corporations would surely drive up property values, leading to further development and gentrification and, ultimately, the obliteration of the neighborhood. Fighting construction of the hotels, however, presented mammoth difficulties. None of the hotels would directly displace current residents, so the projects could not be attacked on this ground, and zoning laws allowed for the development of the proposed luxury highrise towers, which removed a potential legal barrier.

The situation seemed hopeless. The Tenderloin's residents were entirely unorganized, NOMPC's newly hired VISTA organizers were energetic but inexperienced, and our opponents were multinational hotel corporations in a city where the tourist industry set all the rules. How could we succeed in preserving and enhancing the Tenderloin as an affordable residential community for the elderly, poor, and disabled in the face of this three-pronged attack? The answer lay in tactical activism.

Prior to the threat of the hotels, NOMPC's central goal was for the Tenderloin to win acceptance as an actual neighborhood worthy of assistance from the city. The lack of participation by Tenderloin residents and agency staff in the city's political life had led to a consensus, accepted even by progressive activists, that a viable neighborhood entity north of Market Street did not exist.[2] The hotel fight gave NOMPC the opportunity to educate the rest of the city about the state of affairs in the Tenderloin. In organizing residents to fight the hotels, the overall strategy became clear: first, to establish that the Tenderloin was a residential neighborhood; and second, to insist that, as such, it was entitled to the same zoning protections for its residents as other San Francisco neighborhoods. If NOMPC could force City Hall and the hotel developers to accept the first premise, the second premise—and NOMPC's strategic goal—would follow.

The attempt to rezone the neighborhood in response to the hotel development threat was certainly not inevitable; it was the result of carefully considered tactical activism. Instead of using the hotel fight as a springboard for change, the organization could have made the usual anti-development protests, then sat back and awaited the next development project in the neighborhood. The organizational identity could have been that of a fighter of David-and-Goliath battles pitting powerless citizens against greedy developers. Livingston, NOMPC organizer Sara Colm, and other Tenderloin organizers understood, however, that development projects are rarely stopped and are at best mitigated. This is particularly true where development opponents are primarily low-income people and where the local political leadership—and this is true for most cities, large and small—is beholden to developers and real estate interests. The organizers foresaw that a succession of fights against specific development projects would destroy the residential character of the neighborhood they wished to strengthen. A rezoning of the community, however, would prevent all future development projects without directly attacking the financial interests of any particular developer. A proactive battle for neighborhood rezoning was thus both the most effective and the most politically practical strategy. "No hotels" was not a solution to the neighborhood's problem—rezoning was.

NOMPC, in concert with the local chapter of the Gray Panthers, which had members living in the Tenderloin, unified residents by forming the Luxury Hotel Task Force. The Task Force became the vehicle of resident opposition to the hotels, but it had a greater and more strategic importance as a visible manifestation that the Tenderloin was a true residential neighborhood. Although most Task Force members had lived in the Tenderloin for years, they were invisible to the city's political forces. Suddenly, hotel developers and their attorneys, elected officials, and San Francisco Planning Department staff were confronted with a group of residents from a neighborhood whose existence they had never before recognized. The Tenderloin residents' unified expression of concern over the hotels' possible impact on their lives permanently changed the political calculus of the neighborhood. Once the developers' representatives and city officials encountered the Task Force, NOMPC's strategic goal of establishing the Tenderloin as a recognizable residential neighborhood was achieved.

The battle against the hotels was short and intense. After learning of the proposal in June, we held two large community meetings in July. More than 250 people attended the meetings, a turnout unprecedented in Tenderloin history. The formal approval process for the hotels began with a Planning Commission hearing on November 6, at which more than 100 residents testified against the project. Final commission approval came on January 29, 1981, in a hearing that began in the afternoon and ended early the next morning.

The projects clearly had been placed on the fast track for approval; the city was in the midst of "Manhattanization," a building boom during which virtually no high-rise development project was disapproved. This made the accomplishments of the Luxury Hotel Task Force that much more astounding. As a result of residents' complaints that the hotels would have a "significant adverse environmental impact" on rents, air quality, and traffic in the Tenderloin, the commission imposed several conditions to mitigate these effects. The hotels had to contribute an amount equal to fifty cents per hotel room for twenty years for low-cost housing development (about $320,000 per hotel per year). Additionally, each hotel had to pay $200,000 for community service projects, sponsor a $4 million grant for the acquisition and renovation of four low-cost residential hotels (474 units total), and act in good faith to give priority in employment to Tenderloin residents.

Such "mitigation measures" are now commonplace conditions of development approval in U.S. cities, but they were unprecedented in January 1981. The ability of a group of elderly, disabled, and low-income residents to win historic concessions from three major international hotel chains in a pro-development political climate was considered an ominous precedent by local media and business leaders. *San Francisco Chronicle* columnist Abe Mellinkoff weighed in strongly against "the squeeze" in two consecutive columns following the Planning Commission vote.[3] Referring to the mitigations as a "shakedown" undertaken by "bank robbers," Mellinkoff urged the business establishment to publicly protest this "rip-off of fellow capitalists." As Mellinkoff saw it, Luxury Hotel Task Force members were "crusaders" and "eager soldiers" whom City Hall had allowed to prevail in "a war against corporations." Clearly, NOMPC's strategy had worked. The hotel fight had made the Tenderloin a neighborhood to be reckoned with.

The decision to use this defensive battle to achieve a critical goal resulted entirely from continual discussions of strategy and tactics among the thirty to forty residents who regularly attended Luxury Hotel Task Force meetings. A good example of the group's extensive tactical debates arose when the Hilton Hotel offered to provide lunch at a meeting to discuss its project. Gray Panther organizer Jim Shoch, whose tactical insights were critical to the Task Force's success, made sure that every facet of the Hilton's offer was analyzed for its implications. Some Task Force members felt that lunch should be refused so the Hilton couldn't "buy us off." The majority wanted to take advantage of a high-quality lunch, recognizing it as a vast improvement over their normal fare. Ultimately, the group went to the lunch but gave no quarter to the Hilton in the meeting that followed.

These time-consuming and often frustrating internal discussions enabled residents to understand that they did not have to accomplish the impossible (i.e., prevent approval of the towers) to score a victory. Without this understanding, the city's ultimate approval of the hotels could have been psychologically and emotionally devastating. Instead, the

Planning Commission's approval did not diminish residents' feelings that they had achieved a great triumph in their own lives and in the history of the neighborhood.

With city officials having recognized the Tenderloin as a viable neighborhood, the Task Force turned to the second half of NOMPC's agenda: establishing the Tenderloin's right to residential rezoning. In 1981, San Francisco residents could initiate the rezoning process by circulating petitions in the neighborhood in question. NOMPC began its rezoning campaign immediately after the city's approval of the luxury hotels. The rezoning proposal affected sixty-seven square blocks overall, with the strictest downzoning proposed for the thirty-five-square-block heart of the Tenderloin. In this central area, the new zoning prohibited new tourist hotels, prevented commercial use above the second floor, and imposed eight- to thirteen-story height restrictions. The strategy succeeded largely because of its timing: On the heels of the Planning Commission's approval of the hotel towers, even the pro-growth local political leadership felt the neighborhood should not be required to accept additional commercial high-rise development. But the city's sense of obligation to residents of a low-income community might quickly evaporate in the face of a new high-rise development proposal; quick action was necessary to prevent new projects from emerging as threats.

The wisdom of the strategy was confirmed in 1983, prior to the city's approval of the rezoning. A one-million-square-foot development that included hotels, restaurants, and shops was proposed for the heart of the Tenderloin. The project, "Union Square West," effectively would have destroyed the affordable residential character of a major portion of the neighborhood. Clearly, Union Square West conflicted with the fundamental premise of the rezoning proposal; the project included three towers ranging between seventeen and thirty stories, a 450-room tourist hotel, and 370 condominium units. Would the pro-growth Planning Commission turn its back on the neighborhood and support the project? In the absence of the rezoning campaign, and despite the "obligation" incurred to the community after approval of the luxury hotels, San Francisco's Planning Commission undoubtedly would have authorized the project. The tactical activism of NOMPC, however, preempted the mammoth proposal. When Union Square West went for approval on June 9, 1983, the ardently pro-growth Planning Commission chairman strongly chastised the developer. The rezoning process had gone too far for the city to change its mind. A project that would otherwise have been approved was soundly defeated.

The Tenderloin rezoning proposal was signed into law on March 28, 1985. Its passage culminated nearly five years of strategic planning that had involved hundreds of low-income people in ongoing tactical discussions. Unfortunately, as I will discuss later, the Tenderloin's reliance on strategizing and tactics declined following the achievement of neighborhood rezoning. But the North of Market Planning Coalition's transformation of a major threat into a springboard for achieving long-sought goals stands as a shining example of what can be accomplished through tactical activism.

Proactive tactical activism has succeeded in a number of other fields. In San Francisco, children's advocates found that elected officials' rhetoric about helping kids did not translate into money for youth programs. Efforts to win funds through the normal budget process consistently failed, as constituencies that could provide more campaign contributions and votes prevailed over children's advocates. Undeterred, these advocates gathered signatures to place on the November 1991 ballot a city charter amendment mandating that a specific percentage of the city budget be spent on children's services. The measure passed easily, bringing millions of dollars in additional funds for youth programs.

Similarly, San Francisco's anti-development activists recognized by the late 1970s that they could not block individual projects and began promoting an overarching growth-limitation measure. After losing narrowly at the ballot box in 1979 and 1983, slow-growth advocates gained passage of a growth-limitation measure in 1986. By requiring changes in the city's master plan, the measure imposed restrictions on housing conversions and development projects that advocates could not have achieved by fighting on a project-by-project basis.

Proactive tactical activism also has succeeded on the state level. Bill Honig, former California superintendent of public instruction, initiated the strategy subsequently used by San Francisco's children's advocates. In 1988 he placed on the state ballot, and the voters passed, a measure mandating consistent levels of state funding for education. Honig and his allies understood that school quality would not improve through annual fights with the legislature to avoid cuts. Honig's Proposition 98 spared schools from draconian cuts that would otherwise have been made during California's steep recession in the early 1990s.

The advantages of a proactive strategy are evident even when tactical activists fall short of their goal. Anger over the clear-cutting of redwood forests led environmentalists to place a "Forests Forever" initiative on California's November 1990 ballot. Although a deluge of money from opponents led to the narrow defeat of the measure, timber interests reduced forest destruction from the time the initiative qualified for the ballot to election day[4] several months later. A strategy placing timber companies on the defensive thus spared hundreds of thousands of trees, at least temporarily. The ability of proactive strategies to win significant results, even when those results fall short of the ultimate goal, illustrates the benefits of tactical activism.

HOMELESSNESS: THE CONSEQUENCES OF RESPONDING WITHOUT STRATEGY

Just as the Tenderloin's tactical activism led to a major triumph, the lack of strategic planning and adherence to a proactive agenda can lead to significant defeats. Tactical errors have led social change activists to suffer significant losses around the issues of homelessness and crime. National, state, and local governments, as well as the media, have succeeded in framing the issues of homelessness and crime in a way that has reduced public support for progressive, systemic solutions. Ironically, misdirected grassroots activists have unwittingly contributed to this situation. Activists' defensive response to the reframing of both issues has helped result in the punitive, anti-homeless agenda given full rein today.

In the public mind today, homelessness is associated with panhandling, public urination, "bums" sleeping on park benches—conduct lumped together as "problem street behavior." A decade ago, homelessness was identified not with such "quality of life" issues but with a shortage of affordable housing. An important and overlooked factor allowing this shift in perception to occur was homeless activists' lack of proactive tactical and strategic planning.

Two fundamental problems confront social change activists addressing homelessness. First, the persistence of widespread homelessness has increased public skepticism about the potential for its resolution. Neither local, state, nor national administrations have ever devoted the funding necessary to reduce homelessness substantially, a fact that gets brushed aside as time goes on. People may recognize that reducing homelessness costs money, but when the problem continues year after year without improving, the public seems to forget that the money has not been spent. The media fanfare that surrounds the awarding of any new funds to combat homelessness, particularly when accompanied by statements from elected officials vowing to solve the problem, contributes to a false sense that the necessary programs and funding are in place. An understandably misinformed public has become less sympathetic toward demands for more homeless funding because it wrongly assumes that sufficient efforts have been made and simply have failed. A common explanation for this decline in public sympathy for the homeless is "compassion fatigue." This description, however, may underestimate the extent to which people who have retained their compassion nevertheless have concluded that additional government funding would not significantly reduce homelessness.

The second fundamental problem arose from this shift in public attitudes about homelessness. As frequently occurs when a social problem is left unaddressed, anger over homelessness led the public to blame homeless people and their advocates for perpetuating the problem. Instead of responding to this public shift by pursuing proactive agendas that could regain public support, advocates accepted the conservatives' redefinition of homelessness and fought the battle on their opponents' terms. This substitution of a defensive response for a plan of proactive measures resulted in part from the lack of a broad-based constituency vehicle, which is necessary to achieve progressive social change. The experience of San Francisco, which has consistently foreshadowed national trends on homelessness, reflects how activists' failure to strategize hindered efforts to gain public support for progressive responses to homelessness.

In San Francisco, there have been only two brief periods over the past fourteen years when there existed even a rudimentary vehicle for strategic discussion, proactive agenda setting, and tactical activism around homelessness. In 1982, the emergence of widespread homelessness led Sara Colm of NOMPC to set up a "Homeless Caucus" modeled on the Luxury Hotel Task Force. Meetings were attended by a large number of homeless persons, representatives of religious groups, and social service workers. The Caucus held weekly steering committee and general meetings, which spawned spirited strategic and tactical discussions. The Caucus focused on the absence of emergency shelter space, particularly for families. Leon Zecha, who emerged as the Caucus's leader, became homeless when the van he was living in was stolen. Zecha and other Caucus members faced the difficult task of convincing City Hall to spend money on a problem—homelessness—that nobody had discussed since the Great Depression and that most people believed was only "temporary."

The Caucus zealously urged the city to create an emergency shelter system for the homeless. Through strategic alliances with social service and religious groups and the development of a coherent set of specific demands, the Caucus became the recognized leader of the opposition to City Hall inaction. The Caucus had no qualms about meeting Mayor Dianne Feinstein in her office one day and the next day holding a demonstration and "feast" in front of her luxurious Pacific Heights home to dramatize the problem of homelessness. As a result, Feinstein agreed to the Caucus's fundamental goal and in 1983 provided the funding to create what became an ever-expanding emergency shelter program.

Unfortunately, the Caucus could not sustain its success, and by 1984 the group was in decline. A key factor in the group's demise, one that has emerged elsewhere, was the rise of an alternative coalition composed of staff from mainstream religious and social service agencies. The social service coalition, known as the Central City Shelter Network, succeeded in marginalizing the Caucus as too radical and impractical an organization. Because the Network's members were now receiving city funds to operate shelters, they were loath to criticize the mayor for not doing enough. The Network became the great defender of the mayor in response to Caucus attacks, and Network members' status as mainstream charitable organizations made them appear more credible than actual homeless persons.

The emergence of alternative, "moderate" opposition groups is not unusual, and staffer Colm and Caucus president Zecha probably could have kept the Caucus going despite the rise of the Network. Like many early homeless activists, however, Zecha had the understandable desire to get on with his own life. Even the indefatigable Colm could not sustain the level of energy needed to maintain the Caucus's democratic style. The Caucus had used proactive tactics and strategies to accomplish much more than anyone had thought possible under a mayor unsympathetic to the poor. Despite its eventual demise, the Caucus had forced Feinstein to spend millions to establish a basic shelter system, testifying to the benefits of tactical activism.

The second period when a vehicle existed for tactical activism around homelessness began in 1988 after the election of Art Agnos, Feinstein's successor as mayor. In the month prior to Agnos's formally taking office, I joined social service workers and former homeless persons in a series of meetings to create a homeless policy blueprint for the new mayor. Most of us had been publicly critical of the city's homeless policy for many years and had forged working relationships with each other. We included a broad spectrum of interests and called ourselves the Coalition on Homelessness. The Coalition delivered a "consensus proposal" to Agnos during his first week in office. Our plan included proposals for specific changes in homeless policy, some that could be accomplished immediately, others within ninety days, and still others in the longer term. The proposals included the elimination of the city's scandal-plagued "Hotline Hotel" program, through which millions of taxpayer dollars were spent to house single homeless adults for one-night stays in rundown hotels. Homeless people often refused to stay in the sometimes filthy and vermin-infested rooms; nevertheless, the hotel keepers would collect payment from the city. Under the Coalition's blueprint, the hotline would be replaced by a modified rent-payment program that would enable welfare recipients who couldn't afford housing to obtain permanent rooms in residential hotels at below-market rents. We proposed that, in the longer term, homeless people be housed in hotels owned and operated by nonprofit housing corporations. Mayor Feinstein had rejected nonprofit acquisition of hotels for the homeless, asserting that homelessness was only a temporary problem. Other proposals included an end to the use of hotels for long-term housing of homeless families, the immediate repair of hundreds of vacant public housing units, and a series of reforms in the city's General Assistance program (welfare for single adults) designed to reduce the number of persons who became homeless through costly and unfair bureaucratic policies.

The Coalition's recommendations had immediate credibility because of the track records of many of those involved and the fact that many of the proposals had long been supported by every key constituency; the primary opponent to most elements of the Coalition plan had been Mayor Feinstein. However, the chief advantage of the Coalition's proposals was that they offered a concrete and specific program to an incoming mayor who had vowed during his campaign to change the city's homeless policy. This proactive approach put Agnos in the position of having either to adopt a "ready to go" program or explain why it was inadequate. The Coalition's tactical activism ensured that its consensus proposal would be the starting point for all future discussions about homeless policy.

Ultimately, the city adopted almost every component of the consensus proposal. Whereas homeless activists in most cities were still fighting for more emergency shelters in 1988, the central thrust of the Coalition's agenda was to divert funds from such stopgap measures toward transitional and permanent housing programs. The Coalition's analysis was adopted in San Francisco's nationally acclaimed 1989 homeless plan, "Beyond Shelter," written by Robert Prentice (one of the formulators of the consensus proposal), who was hired by Mayor Agnos to serve as the city's homeless coordinator. President Bill Clinton's homeless plan, as set forth in 1994 by Housing and Urban Development (HUD) undersecretary Andrew Cuomo, was essentially a redrafting of "Beyond Shelter."

The Coalition's proactive approach proved so successful an example of tactical activism that many of the plan's authors, including me, became its implementers. I met with Agnos's new social services chief, Julia Lopez, to advocate the adoption of a modified payment program that would enable General Assistance recipients to obtain permanent housing at below-market rates. Based on discussions with hotel operators, I believed they would agree to lower rents and allow welfare recipients to become permanent tenants if the risk of eviction for nonpayment of rent could be reduced. The modified payment plan lowered this risk by having tenants voluntarily agree to have their rent deducted from their welfare checks. Lopez told me such a program sounded great but that her department lacked the expertise in dealing with tenants to operate it. Because the program was my idea, she said, the Tenderloin Housing Clinic should run it. As legal advocates for low-income tenants, Clinic staff had never sought to operate homeless programs. However, the Clinic had consistently fought the practice of transforming hotels that should serve as permanent housing for poor people into temporary lodging for the same population; we wanted to restore residential hotels to their historic status as homes for elderly, disabled, and low-income people, whether working or unemployed. Not wanting to lose the opportunity to implement part of our agenda, we became participants in the homeless business. In order to become eligible for our guaranteed rent-payment program, landlords lowered rents. We were so successful that rents became significantly lower than they had been more than ten years earlier.

As the Coalition's consensus proposal gradually became city policy, attendance at Coalition meetings began to decline, for various reasons. Many of the leading architects of the proposal could no longer afford the time necessary to keep the Coalition thriving; unlike the Luxury Hotel Task Force, the Coalition never had a full-time paid organizer. Further, whereas the Feinstein regime had ignored the "outsider" advocates who established the Coalition, social service chief Lopez encouraged their input. People who once spent time at Coalition meetings were now regularly meeting with social services staff and the new mayor's homeless coordinator, himself selected by the Coalition. Finally, Coalition participation may simply have declined because we had achieved more success in one year than in the previous several years; attending Coalition meetings seemed less important.

By mid-1989, the Coalition on Homelessness had evolved from a vehicle of strategic and tactical advocacy to an independent, foundation-funded nonprofit corporation. The Coalition's staff tried to hold regular meetings to discuss issues as in the past, but most of the leading participants in the original Coalition ceased attending. We soon felt the loss of a broad-based group that could create a proactive agenda on homelessness. On May 29, 1989, the *San Francisco Examiner* ran a front-page story in which business leaders denounced Mayor Agnos for allowing camping in the park outside City Hall. In what many believe was the greatest political error of his term, Agnos had decided to allow camping outside City Hall until his programs creating alternative sources of housing were in place. As public anger over "Camp Agnos" grew, the mayor decided in July 1990 to cut his losses and sweep the park of campers. The purge became a national media story, as reporters found interest in a self-described "progressive" mayor's cracking down on the homeless. Because many of the campers had sought the Coalition on Homelessness's assistance to prevent the sweep, Coalition staff workers entered the national debate in opposition to Agnos's action, arguing that the mayor had caved in to political pressure and swept the park before his programs had become operational. The Coalition was correct about Agnos but failed to appreciate that his tolerance of camping had caused him serious political harm. The public never understood the rationale for allowing camping, and continuing the policy had become politically untenable. In their anger over Agnos's betrayal, the activists rushed to defend the campers without appreciating the risk that their fight for more low-cost housing and mental health services would be reduced to a dispute over the right to camp in a public park.

The Coalition's full-fledged attack on Agnos's action was an entirely defensive response on behalf of people whom the public saw as voluntarily homeless. The residents of Camp Agnos typically wore backpacks and had chosen to sleep outdoors rather than pay rent in residential hotels. The Clinic's outreach staff surveyed most of the campers and found the majority received enough public assistance to pay rent if they so chose. In the public mind, people should only be homeless if they could not afford housing. Now, the city's leading homeless advocacy group was arguing that people who could afford housing had the right to forgo this option and instead live under the stars outside City Hall until temporary shelter or permanent housing was available to everyone. The public and media rejected, even ridiculed, this notion; accustomed to viewing homeless people as victims of hard luck, they could not accept the idea that anyone should reject shelter. Thus, the prevailing view was that Agnos could fulfill his responsibility to the campers by ensuring that each received a shelter bed or hotel room. The Coalition countered by urging sympathizers to "storm the park" so there would be more park dwellers than Agnos could immediately shelter. This strategy, a sudden, defensive response, understandably backfired. The media, long sympathetic to homeless activists, interpreted this move as a blatant attempt to inflate the number of homeless denizens of Camp Agnos. Homeless activists were even seen as interfering with the government's effort to put a roof over people's heads.

We all make strategic mistakes. The great advantage of pursuing progressive social change through proactive agendas is that the process requires activists to see the connection between various steps. Activists often can avoid tactical mistakes if, before launching a campaign, they discuss how a chosen tactic, perhaps striking in and of itself, might create a fallout that jeopardizes the ultimate goal. In their haste to protest Agnos's sweep, the Coalition's members failed to discuss the possibility that homeless advocacy might become equated in the public mind with defending the right to camp in a public park. A key reason for this failure was the lack of a vehicle through which this discussion might occur. In the absence of a viable membership organization or representative body of homeless persons and homeless-serving agency staff, the Coalition defined its role as providing services to those who sought its assistance. When the soon-to-be-displaced park dwellers came to the Coalition for help, protecting their specific interests became the Coalition's mission. The Coalition's membership organization never met to discuss how advocacy of camping rights fit into the broader homeless agenda; long-term strategic implications were bypassed in the mad rush to storm the park and discredit Agnos.

Agnos's park sweep brought national attention unprecedented for a city homeless policy. From the *New York Times* to the *MacNeil-Lehrer News Hour,* national observers were fascinated by this action, taken by someone viewed as one of the nation's most progressive mayors. The publicity completely shifted San Francisco's public debate about homelessness and led to an entirely new model that has since emerged in cities across the United States. The model, honed by ambitious politicians and their corporate and media allies, creates a symmetry between repressive political agendas and homeless advocacy groups. A mayor—for example, Agnos's successor, Frank Jordan—calls for a crackdown on "aggressive panhandling" and public camping. Homeless advocates object on constitutional and civil-liberties grounds. The public debate shifts from society's failure to provide sufficient low-income housing to whether camping in parks should be permitted. Media coverage on the homeless suddenly shifts from stories on recently unemployed middle-aged men to sound-bites of long-haired, able-bodied young people confessing that they lie about being veterans so they can make more money panhandling. Panhandlers are no longer people trying to compensate for cuts in welfare checks; they are now drug addicts and alcoholics who use public charity to feed their habits. Public concern over homelessness has been eclipsed by other issues, particularly crime; conservatives' success at portraying the visible homeless as threats to public safety no doubt contributed to this shift. Having allowed the issue to become a fight over panhandling and camping, homeless activists must wage a battle on terms clearly beneficial to their opponents.

Homeless advocates' defensive struggle has had even more far-reaching effects. By identifying those asserting a right not to be housed as central to homeless advocacy, activists have allowed their opponents both to redefine who "the homeless" are and to frame the policy debate around this newly conceived group. Conservative critics, fearful that rising homelessness would lead to more public spending on low-income housing, jobs, and alleviation of inner-city poverty, seized on the image of the most visible homeless people to reverse the tide. The 1990s thus began with an onslaught of published material arguing that homeless advocates had misrepresented or even lied about who the homeless were and how they should be helped. Though some may contend that such a backlash accompanies every political movement, it is significant that such attacks against homeless advocates did not become "mainstream" until almost a decade of the crisis had passed. The public clearly did not have sympathy with camping or panhandling, and conservatives used homeless advocates' identification with these activities to attack their core analysis of the problem. For example, in the highly publicized *A Nation in Denial: The Truth About Homelessness,* Alice Baum and Donald Burnes claimed that neither "poverty, nor major social, economic and political forces are at the root of today's homelessness." The real "truth," around which we were all "in denial," was that "65 to 85 percent of the homeless population suffer from serious chronic alcoholism, addiction to drugs, severe chronic psychiatric disorders, or some combination of the three." Homeless advocates' "crusade" to define homelessness as the "absence of housing" was described as an "invidious" strategy to "deny the extent of substance abuse and mental illness among the homeless."[5]

A Nation in Denial was rife with unsupported allegations, false premises, and erroneous conclusions. The book's thesis necessarily assumed that drug addiction, alcoholism, and mental health problems did not beset low-income people until the 1980s and that these problems, not the inability to afford housing, caused widespread homelessness. I was particularly amused by the book's claim that "analysts have never established a definite causal linkage between the increased demand for housing, along with the rise in costs, and the rise in homelessness during the 1980s."[6] In a study for the Tenderloin Housing Clinic in 1988, I inventoried every residential hotel in San Francisco. The study found that hotel rents in the 1980s outstripped welfare grants to the extent that the vast majority of welfare recipients, who at the time constituted much of the city's homeless population, could not obtain permanent housing in single-room-occupancy hotels (SROs). The study was well publicized but apparently did not meet Burnes and Baum's subjective standard of a "definitive linkage" between rising rents and homelessness. Their book also makes the clearly erroneous claim that "recreating facilities similar to the SROs has done little to help the homeless."[7] My purpose is not to detail all the errors in this "objective" work. What is most significant about A Nation in Denial is its attempt to portray homeless advocates as opposing the "real" solutions to homelessness: alcohol, drug, and mental health treatment.[8] The identification of homeless advocacy with people who did not want available housing and who exhibited alcohol, drug, and mental health problems added weight to the argument that advocates were in denial regarding the truth about homelessness. In Chapter 5, I discuss how a television news show won a Peabody Award for a series relying entirely on this "denial of the truth" theme. Homeless advocates' defense of the right of people to camp rather than pay rent also became linked to the idea that advocates supported the spending of public assistance checks on alcohol or drugs rather than housing. The terrible irony, of course, was that groups like the Coalition on Homelessness had always put mental health and substance abuse treatment at the forefront of their agendas. The people most prominently involved in defending campers' rights also were the city's leading advocates for substance abuse and mental health services for homeless persons. Their defense of camping, however, allowed critics to argue successfully that homeless advocates either were "blind" to substance abuse or condoned such activities. Once homeless advocacy became identified with defending unpopular individual behavior rather than working to ensure housing and treatment for all homeless persons who sought these services, public support for progressive approaches to homelessness declined further.

The strategic and tactical errors made by homeless activists flowed from their willingness, even eagerness, to fight a battle on their more powerful opponents' terms. Some social change activists seem to seek out these David-and-Goliath struggles, apparently believing that defeat will be tinged with nobility. Others believe that government attacks on the most vulnerable demand strong opposition, even if victory is doubtful. I understand these sentiments, but such approaches do not generally improve circumstances for vulnerable constituencies. In the example of homelessness, long waiting lists for affordable, well-maintained housing owned by nonprofit housing development corporations demonstrate that most people want a permanent home in which to live. Activists should not have frittered away public support for this majority group by defending the "right" of people to choose to live in a park. Such people do not generally represent the most vulnerable among the homeless; to the contrary, they are often among the most self-sufficient. Like it or not, people do make value judgments about those seeking their support. In 1993, the entire San Francisco Bay Area, including Republican officials and conservative editorial boards, denounced Mayor Jordan's confiscation of shopping carts from homeless people. These "industrious" homeless people, who carefully maintained their possessions, recycled bottles and cans, and kept to themselves, were viewed in an entirely different light than the camp dwellers, whose "vulnerability" did not receive much public credence.

Homeless advocates who opposed their colleagues' decision to emphasize the right to camp and panhandle share responsibility for this strategic mistake. By remaining silent, they tacitly endorsed an approach that weakened public support for progressive solutions to homelessness. Because activists do not want to publicly criticize their allies to the potential benefit of their adversaries, effective homeless advocacy requires a broad-based vehicle for internal dissent and strategic planning. Had such a vehicle for homeless activists existed in San Francisco in 1990, a proactive and strategic, rather than purely defensive, approach could have resulted. Even those most supportive of camping rights could have appreciated a forum for internal debate.

To be fair, some activists would argue that responding to government suppression of "street behavior" is central to homeless advocacy. They reason that attacks on panhandling, public food giveaways, camping in parks, and stepped-up prosecution of "nuisance" crimes are attempts to criminalize poverty. These activists argue that the lack of housing, jobs, and mental health services has forced people to engage in "problem street behavior" and that their rights must be zealously defended.

Although strong opposition to crackdowns is important, this does not mean that panhandling and camping are homeless issues. People who panhandle, eat at food giveaways, or commit nuisance crimes are not necessarily, perhaps not even primarily, homeless, nor are campers who prefer living outside part of the "homeless" problem. The central element of any homeless advocacy campaign should be a program of specific proposals that strive to ensure housing and sufficient income to people who want a permanent place to live. A good program will put policymakers (instead of advocates) on the defensive by forcing them to respond to the agenda set forth by the social change organization. The right to pitch a tent and sleep in a public park or on a sidewalk was not included in the Coalition on Homelessness's original consensus proposal, nor was it on the agenda of the Homeless Caucus. The existence of broad-based homeless advocacy organizations that engaged in extensive tactical and strategic analysis could have kept the public debate focused on the need for affordable and special-needs housing. Instead, the absence of a specific, implementable program has given conservative politicians free rein to redefine homelessness in terms of crime, sexual harassment, and detraction from the "quality of life" for those who are not homeless.

The political popularity of "law-and-order" politicians consistently rises when they are seen as shouting down hecklers from an outcast group. A bully needs an opponent to stir the emotions of a crowd; some suspect that Richard Nixon and Spiro Agnew placed long-haired hecklers at campaign stops just to ensure the candidates an opportunity to "stand up for American values." By entering into major fights over panhandling and camping, homeless advocates have become the perfect foil for ambitious politicians; they have put significant resources into fighting against measures most of the public supports. In San Francisco, this approach not only has diverted activists' energies from developing proactive solutions but also has allowed politicians of every stripe to avoid substantive discussion of the homeless problem. When the homeless debate is framed as one of civil liberties, elected officials who claim they care about homeless people can get away with doing nothing for them. Politicians can be identified as sympathetic to homeless people simply by opposing crackdowns on panhandling or nuisance crimes. They can avoid having to commit to raise taxes on big business to increase funding for affordable housing, mental health programs, or higher welfare grants.

Even worse, homeless advocates' emphasis on civil liberties does not offer a solution to a public tired of being harassed by panhandlers and having parks taken over by "bums." Advocates do not lack such solutions; they simply do not make themselves heard over the din created by the fight over panhandlers' rights. In November 1992 Mayor Jordan placed a measure on the San Francisco ballot to forbid "aggressive panhandling" and prosecute beggars. Homeless advocates decried it as political grandstanding and a phony solution to homelessness—which it was. Voters, however, were sick of being panhandled, and even though polls showed they were skeptical of the measure's benefits, it passed. Voters were given a choice between a bad solution and no solution; a common response to the measure was, "It's better than nothing." San Franciscans subsequently passed ballot measures prohibiting panhandling near automatic teller machines and requiring fingerprinting of welfare recipients. In the general election of November 1994, voters in Berkeley, California made a left-wing mayoral candidate the top vote-getter (although he eventually lost in a runoff election) and installed a pro-tenant rent board, yet they also strongly approved anti-panhandling and anti-loitering measures. In the absence of realizable, progressive programs, the public is left with punitive measures. Demands for affordable housing, jobs, and mental health care are reduced to campaign rhetoric when not linked to a specific, viable program that advocates are actively striving to implement.

Homeless advocates can avoid becoming the equivalent of Nixon's heckler not just by developing their own proposals but also by ignoring attacks on their constituency. When advocates forgo a response, their adversaries may lose the spark necessary to ignite media attention. The benefits of forbearance can be seen in homeless issues, where critics typically use public attacks on the homeless solely as a strategy for solidifying their political base. Because advocates' defensive responses often fail either to stem anti-homeless rhetoric or expand public support for the homeless, a nonresponse may be the best tactic. Tactical activists should continue to direct their energies into a proactive agenda, leaving religious groups and legal organizations not involved in direct political advocacy to respond to attacks. Real gains come only when activists move beyond trying to preserve an untenable status quo.

Fortunately, the public may have tired of transparently political responses to homelessness. Although voters continue to pass anti-panhandling, anti-loitering, anti-camping, and related statutes, such measures increasingly are recognized as serving politicians' agendas rather than reducing homelessness. As such measures prove to have little impact, attention can refocus on progressive, systemic solutions. The failure of punitive approaches to homelessness will minimize the political benefits of homeless-bashing. Many homeless advocates were surprised by the sudden media shift against them in the early 1990s and now realize that extensive strategic discussions and a proactive approach are necessary. Federal funding for homeless programs has always been inadequate, and prospects for significant new money are grim. Because the presence of homeless persons on city streets has persisted for more than a decade, the public may simply come to accept widespread homelessness as a disturbing but unalterable fact of life. It is therefore more imperative than ever that homeless activists regain the offensive and act aggressively to broaden public support for their constituency.

CRIME FIGHTING: DEFENSIVENESS AT ITS WORST

No issue better exemplifies the disastrous consequences of progressives' approaching issues defensively than crime. Unlike homeless activists, whose strategic errors never involved abandonment of principles, many self-identified "progressives" have zealously embraced law-and-order solutions to crime out of calculation and expedience. Conservative politicians have used crime to shift the public debate away from issues such as health care reform, homelessness, environmental hazards, and economic unfairness toward an issue on which they are most likely to receive voter support. Progressive elected officials and their political allies accepted the conservatives' "more police, more prisons, longer sentences" approach to crime and actually tried to outgun their law-and-order opponents on the latter's chosen battleground. Because voters almost always prefer seasoned gunslingers to neophyte crime fighters, the Republican Party rode the crime issue to gain control of both houses of Congress in the November 1994 election. The issue also helped politicians such as California's governor, Pete Wilson, who overcame a 20 percent deficit in the polls in early 1994 to win reelection in a landslide. All of the key issues that propelled the Clinton-Gore ticket in the 1992 election were subsumed to the bipartisan focus on crime only two years later, with terrible political consequences for progressive constituencies.

How did crime become the dominant issue of 1994, amid statistics showing stagnant and even declining crime levels throughout the United States? An obvious place to start is the mainstream media, which helped crime leap to the forefront of the national agenda just as a new presidential administration, professing to be more receptive than its two predecessors to progressive social change, took office. According to the Washington Center for Media and Public Affairs, the number of crime stories on the evening newscasts of ABC, NBC, and CBS doubled from 1992 to 1993. Government records, however, found no substantial increase in crime or violent crime during the Clinton administration's first year.[9] Further, the *Tyndall Report,* a weekly fact sheet that monitors television news coverage, found that the three networks' evening news shows averaged 67 minutes per month on crime stories from January 1989 to 1992 but more than 157 minutes per month from October 1993 to January 1994.[10] Not surprisingly, media saturation on crime increased public concern about the issue. In June 1993, 5 percent of respondents in a *Washington Post*/ABC poll named crime the country's top problem; this total had increased to 31 percent by February 1994, a percentage far above all other issues.[11] Notwithstanding this sudden explosion of media crime coverage, the Department of Justice's National Crime Victimization Survey found the violent crime rate to be essentially flat from 1973 to 1992. Although the study showed that violent crime increased by 5 percent in 1993, such small annual fluctuations are typical; the 1993 increase was followed by significant declines in serious crime in twenty of the country's twenty-two largest cities for the first six months of 1994. A sharp *drop* in violent crime thus preceded an election cycle in which crime was the leading issue.[12] Media claims of escalating crime numbers, a wave of violence, and a society under siege put law-and-order issues on top of the political agenda despite the utter lack of statistical or factual evidence that crime was worsening.

But the media and conservative politicians were not solely responsible for creating a phantom "crime wave" that has helped sabotage progressive change. Neighborhood crime-fighting efforts by low-income people, often organized by progressive activists, have profoundly impacted the ongoing deterioration of inner-city communities. People in desperate need of employment programs, increased school funding, and better health care have channeled their frustration into simplistic and counterproductive demands for more police, more jails, and longer sentences, and their political representatives have heeded their call. These politicians are so eager to appear tough on crime that they pursue expensive, Band-Aid law-and-order policies funded through the elimination of programs serving less vocal members of low-income communities. When community groups hold neighborhood forums in which the speakers demand law-and-order solutions, progressive politicians naturally jump on the "more police, more prisons" bandwagon. Elected officials will not risk telling residents of low-income communities that funds for more police will come at the expense of critical "safety net" programs and may in fact cause an increase in crime. Even for progressive politicians, the label "soft on crime" is the contemporary equivalent of the "soft on communism" charge that doomed many a progressive political career in the post–World War II decades.

In fact, progressives' response to crime closely resembles their response to communism, the bogeyman crime replaced. Conservatives have framed the crime issue as solvable only through expanding the criminal justice system, and progressives have swallowed this analysis hook, line, and sinker rather than demonstrate that the "more police, more prisons" approach is a proven failure.[13] Even many grassroots activists accept the conservative framing of the crime debate. All too few are willing to define the issue by emphasizing a proactive, progressive agenda targeting economic assistance to crime-ridden areas, job programs, a higher minimum wage, and other proposals that address the preconditions leading to crime. Progressive politicians are caught in a self-defeating strategy of trying to "outgun" their law-and-order opposition rather than offer nonpunitive approaches to crime fighting.

For example, consider a statewide election mailer sent on behalf of Democratic candidates in California's June 1994 primary election. The front of the mailer pictured a body covered with a sheet, a pool of blood seeping from beneath the covering. Emblazoned over the photo was a red-inked inscription, "VIOLENT CRIME," and the message: "Random violence, car-jackings and drive-by shootings. It's time to elect leaders who will Fight Back!" Inside, the mailer set forth a "10-Point Attack on Violent Crime." The list did not include anything that came close to addressing the underlying causes of crime. This material was designed for a Democratic Party primary, not a Republican primary or a general election in which law-and-order appeals might sway independent, middle-of-the-road voters.[14] When Democratic candidates address Democratic voters by ignoring crime-prevention strategies and the relationship between crime, poverty, and race, the law-and-order agenda—like anti-communism in the 1950s—is clearly bipartisan. This bipartisanship has been aided and abetted by pressure from grassroots organizations supposedly working on behalf of low-income and working people. These neighborhood-based crime-fighting efforts have weakened social change activism, disempowered low-income residents, and hindered the implementation of national, state, and local programs necessary to improve conditions in economically depressed communities.

I became aware of the inherent strategic shortcomings of progressive-led anti-crime efforts from my own experience in San Francisco's Tenderloin district. The Tenderloin has long been considered a high-crime neighborhood. After the rezoning battles of the early 1980s, the focus shifted toward crime. Although most of the neighborhood's crime involves property break-ins and disputes between drug dealers, enough seniors had been mugged or rolled to motivate people to organize an anti-crime campaign.

I became involved in the development of neighborhood anti-crime efforts because of these resident concerns. The Clinic's street-level office had relocated to a high-crime corner, so I needed only look out our window to see why residents felt threatened. The primarily elderly residents of the Cadillac Hotel, located right across the street from our office, were particularly upset about drug dealing close to their building; some had been robbed right outside the gates. The hotel's nonprofit owner, Reality House West, was headed by Leroy Looper, a charismatic leader and savvy tactician who had risen from a life on the streets and in prison to transform the Cadillac from an eyesore into a neighborhood jewel. Looper responded to his tenants' complaints about crime by forming the Tenderloin Crime Abatement Committee (CAC). The CAC met monthly at the Cadillac Hotel. When Looper asked me to participate, I readily agreed. At the time, I was almost alone among progressive social change activists in getting involved in anti-crime efforts. Gradually, however, Looper brought in representatives of religious groups, refugee organizations, and other social service agencies.

In addition to my admiration for Looper and desire to support residents' concerns, the high percentage of African-Americans participating in the CAC attracted me to the anti-crime campaign. The Tenderloin's African-American residents had participated little in the long-running land-use battles, and I thought their involvement in anti-crime efforts might encourage community participation in other issues. The fact that Looper and key Cadillac Hotel management staff members were African-

American contributed largely to the high level of ethnic diversity typifying the CAC.

During 1984 and 1985, I regularly attended CAC meetings and ended up presiding over many of the meetings, which were festive occasions. A Cadillac Hotel resident would prepare a buffet lunch. Everyone in the audience had the opportunity to comment on the issues, and the district police captain and beat officers would provide updates on crime statistics and respond to concerns raised at the meeting. The CAC reflected the type of ethnically diverse, broad-based community empowerment effort that social change activists in all fields aspire to create. The CAC stressed the need for employment, training, and substance abuse programs and emphasized other strategies that addressed the underlying causes of crime. There was a consensus, however, that a stronger police presence was necessary until such systemic programs were in place. Many of us believed, foolish as it now seems, that the Tenderloin residents' opposition to crime in their community would bring increased government funding for programs to ameliorate the preconditions causing high levels of crime. Looper, the community's most revered leader, always saw economic development and increased local employment as the key requirements for reducing neighborhood crime. The CAC was not demanding more police simply as a tactic for obtaining economic development assistance; rather, we believed that expressing serious concern about crime would stimulate a broader influx of resources into the Tenderloin.

The CAC decided to publicize the community's resolve with a "March Against Crime." Marches are now commonplace in low-income neighborhoods, but such events were somewhat rare in 1985, and we expected—and received—tremendous media coverage. One goal of the march was to demonstrate that the Tenderloin was a residential neighborhood whose residents and businesses deserved the same level of police services received by the inhabitants of other communities. We also sought to show that the Tenderloin housed victims of crime, not simply perpetrators. As long as the public believed that Tenderloin residents were themselves to blame for crime, and thus tolerated thefts, drug deals, and muggings, there would be less support for anti-crime measures and other programs designed to help the neighborhood. The march was the perfect tactic for a community trying to reverse long-held but erroneous public attitudes about it.

CAC activists were thrilled by the success of the event. We felt the march not only had accomplished its goals but also had galvanized community activism around fighting crime. Attendance at CAC meetings increased steadily, and it seemed as if police visibility rose in the area. Crime appeared to represent the new issue necessary to maintain resident activism after the historic rezoning victory. The North of Market Planning Coalition began increasing its emphasis on crime, which soon became its chief focus and organizing vehicle. A Safe Streets Committee was formed. Although it was unclear whether the neighborhood's anti-crime efforts were actually reducing crime, many residents felt empowered because top police brass appeared to take their concerns seriously.

By 1987 we still had not received the hoped-for assistance to attack crime's economic underpinnings, but most of us attributed this lack to the pro-downtown policies of the reigning Feinstein administration. We felt a new, progressive mayor would deliver neighborhood-oriented economic assistance to the Tenderloin, and when Art Agnos succeeded Feinstein in January 1988, we all thought the Tenderloin was poised for a major turnaround. I shifted away from the crime issue after 1986 and returned to focusing on housing and homelessness, but I continued to support the neighborhood's campaign against crime and won a formal commendation in 1986 from the San Francisco Board of Supervisors for my crime-fighting efforts.

Not long into Agnos's term, I came to realize that the CAC's demand for more police and more arrests was a major strategic error. I first sensed a problem when resident participation in anti-crime efforts dropped off significantly. A committed group of residents and social service staff continued to attend CAC meetings, but the effort was more a going-through-the-motions than a part of a vibrant campaign to make a difference in people's lives. Participation in the NOMPC's Safe Streets Committee also declined, as did overall resident activism in the organization. I increasingly heard from residents who saw no point in attending crime meetings because no visible change in the neighborhood's fortunes ever resulted. A sense of hopelessness and a negative attitude toward community activism began to spread. Two factors masked this decline in community participation. First, a small but fervent group of residents with a strong law-and-order approach provided a constant public face, demonstrating residents' continued interest in crime. Second, Mayor Agnos had created a Tenderloin Task Force to develop a strategy for addressing crime and other neighborhood concerns, giving the impression that concrete action to address the long- and short-term causes of Tenderloin crime soon would occur. The community leaders' active involvement in the Task Force concealed residents' declining participation.

My concern over the Tenderloin's spending more than four years focused on crime without obtaining visible results was heightened when Mayor Agnos announced on March 1, 1990, that a police station would open in the Tenderloin. I was initially excited by the announcement, as the community had finally received something tangible after years of anti-crime advocacy. It was widely believed that Agnos had been motivated less by resident demands than by entertainment mogul Carole Shorenstein's threat to close her nearby Golden Gate Theater unless crime was reduced, but I did not care. I saw the police station as a building block that would be followed by additional government efforts to improve the neighborhood's social and economic climate. I soon learned that, to the contrary, the police station was all the Tenderloin would ever get.

There were two key reasons why aid to the Tenderloin ended with the new police station. First, the Agnos administration did not get beyond the portion of the agenda demanding more police. This failure has implications for progressive anti-crime activism in every city, as I will discuss later; in the Tenderloin example, it became clear that the other anti-crime strategies on the table—such as employment, training, and economic development assistance—were essentially viewed as throw-ins garnishing the primary demand for a more visible police presence. Our failure to develop an achievable action plan for attaining goals other than "more police" allowed outsiders to think such goals were not central to our overall agenda. I know from talking to Agnos soon after the station opened that he truly believed he had given the Tenderloin what it wanted most. He seemed surprised to learn that we had never claimed the crime problem could be solved solely or even largely by police and that the community considered the rest of the anti-crime agenda even more important. He did not have to tell me that for elected officials striving to make an immediate, visible anti-crime impact, providing additional police officers or a police station is a comparatively inexpensive strategy that will always take precedence over more systemic, nonpunitive anti-crime initiatives. Responding to the demand for more police frees politicians from committing the resources necessary for a more effective anti-crime program.

The second drawback of Agnos's provision of the police station was that the media and the public viewed it as a major coup for the Tenderloin. This perception meant the Tenderloin would receive few of the other resources it had demanded. Every San Francisco neighborhood wanted a police station, and the promised Tenderloin facility was seen as evidence of the neighborhood's strong political ties to the mayor. Residents in other parts of town claimed that the Tenderloin was now getting more than its fair share of city resources; this belief was aggravated by fears that the criminals chased out of the Tenderloin would move to nearby neighborhoods. In light of these sentiments, Agnos saw the police station as fully satisfying his Tenderloin commitments.

The announcement of the new police station marked the high (or low) point of Tenderloin anti-crime efforts. After five years of intense community involvement and organizing around crime, all the Tenderloin had to show for its efforts were more police officers and what ultimately became a small-scale, quasi–police station. The nonpunitive elements of the community's anti-crime agenda remain unfulfilled to this day. Leroy Looper, as shrewd a tactical activist as ever walked the streets of a major city, saw his own expectations for a government-assisted economic revival of the Tenderloin fall victim to the "more police, more arrests" approach. Looper's Reality House West had opened a Sizzler restaurant in the Cadillac Hotel's commercial space in the mid-1980s in an attempt to jump-start the Tenderloin's economic revitalization. Looper always assumed that city government would appreciate this investment in the neighborhood and would assist similar businesses seeking to succeed in the economically depressed community. This government assistance never materialized, leaving the Sizzler on its own to survive in a difficult business environment. Looper's vision of new employment opportunities and job training for Tenderloin residents was central to his crime-prevention strategy, and the Sizzler was a model for both. Unfortunately, Looper and the rest of us learned that even self-identified progressive politicians have come to address crime solely in punitive terms. The Sizzler closed down around the same time the neighborhood police station opened, a sad but fitting parallel that perfectly captures how even the best-intentioned progressive-led anti-crime campaigns inevitably fall prey to officials' preference for law-and-order solutions.

Whereas the Sizzler provided jobs, disposable income, and a sense of pride to Tenderloin residents, the police station caused no discernible impact upon the neighborhood. The area adjacent to the station became free of drug dealing, but the trafficking simply moved a few blocks away. I have yet to speak to a resident who feels the station has enhanced safety for the community as a whole. In fact, most people believe neighborhood crime has actually worsened since 1985, when the community's focus on crime began. The perception that neighborhood crime has worsened prevails despite the increase in the number of arrests made in the Tenderloin during this period. Even worse, because the battle against crime has yet to be "won"—and never can be won—it has proved extremely difficult to implement an action plan for the Tenderloin that centers on noncrime issues. A common refrain of "safe streets" activists, echoed happily by City Hall, is that "nothing can be done to improve the Tenderloin until we deal with the crime issue." Because crime continues regardless of the extent of law-enforcement resources, the "safe streets" emphasis has indeed ensured that the government *will* do nothing for the Tenderloin.

Where did we go wrong? The answer lies in our failure to follow the fundamental tenet of tactical activism: we simply responded to the crime problem without ensuring that crime reduction remained part of a larger campaign for neighborhood revitalization. There is a critical difference between adopting an agenda that goes beyond punitive crime prevention, on the one hand, and developing a strategy that keeps punitive demands from overshadowing everything else, on the other. By putting an economic development and social action agenda under the rubric of crime prevention without making specific demands for these positive goals, we allowed law-and-order residents, law-enforcement personnel, and politicians with repressive agendas to narrow our demands to "more police, more arrests." Such an agenda is untenable for a community desperately needing economic justice and government-aided revitalization.

Simply put, the Tenderloin's grassroots anti-crime campaign failed to frame the crime problem in a way that would lead to specific improvements in the lives of residents. Although the number of arrests and police officers both rose in the Tenderloin, there was no focused advocacy to force government to address the *preconditions causing crime*. When I speak of "preconditions," I am not simply referring to pervasive inner-city problems such as poverty, unemployment, and racial discrimination, which progressives frequently stress as the underlying causes of crime. I mean preconditions that realistically could have been addressed to increase neighborhood safety. For example, the city could have installed more street lighting, passed laws mandating outside lights on all buildings, and reduced vacant storefronts by subsidizing commercial rents to encourage businesses to move to the Tenderloin. The community could have strongly pushed for funding to expand neighborhood cultural facilities, because the presence of legitimate nighttime activities increases safety after dark. We also could have focused on the fact that a federally subsidized housing facility for seniors and disabled people was renting commercial space to a liquor store that sold fortified wines on a key corner in the Tenderloin. Had we made a national issue out of fact that the Department of Housing and Urban Development—in a Republican administration—was subsidizing a liquor store, the lease would not have been renewed, and a major problem corner in the neighborhood could have been transformed. We could have pursued criminal prosecution and small claims court "nuisance" actions against landlords who knowingly rented to drug dealers and prostitutes, the rigorous enforcement of zoning laws restricting transient hotel occupancy, the elimination of enclosed bus shelters and telephone booths used by drug dealers,[15] and the funding of an economic development entity to attract customers and new businesses into the area.

Sad as it is to admit, most, if not all, of these changes could have been achieved during the late 1980s. Our failure to achieve them resulted from tactical and strategic errors, not political weakness. Neighborhood plans consistently included many of these ideas, yet the focus of actual resident involvement rarely transcended the push for more police. Even more distressing, San Francisco's Tenderloin district is not the only community where progressive-initiated anti-crime efforts have led only to reactionary law-and-order policies. Such efforts have sprung up throughout the country and unquestionably have broadened the political base for local, state, and national anti-crime measures. However, there seems to be little recognition that organizing around demands for more police and other punitive, Band-Aid measures subverts the broader progressive agenda.

In 1994 I attended an inspiring conference on building stronger networks between nonprofit organizations and interfaith religious groups. All the main speakers decried society's squandering of resources on guns rather than butter. One speaker described budget decisions as a product of values; a progressive-oriented approach to policymaking would direct funding to the underlying problems of poverty, unemployment, and unequal education rather than more prisons and more police. The other speakers echoed this point. None had anything positive to say about society's increasing focus on crime and its neglect of society's long-unmet human needs. In fact, the purpose of creating alliances between secular and interfaith social change groups was precisely to increase the power of constituencies desperately in need of additional government support.

As I left the event, I picked up literature distributed by many of the participating organizations. I was particularly struck by material from the Pacific Institute for Community Organization (PICO), which serves a national network of congregation-based community organizations. Its mission is to improve the quality of life of families and neighborhoods by helping people help themselves. PICO's three key principles are respect for human dignity, creation of a just society, and development of the whole person. PICO has projects in eight states and forty-five cities. Its more than 325 congregations include approximately 275,000 families, of which 60 percent are Latino or African-American and 50 percent are low-income or working class. PICO's demographic and class base would seem to make it the perfect vehicle for fulfilling the conference's goal of reordering society's priorities, and the group's social analysis is also impressive. In an article titled, "What Should President Clinton Do?" published in the April 1993 *Jesuit News,* PICO's top strategists argued that a "new civil war born of despair" is taking root in our cities. This war between society's "haves and have-nots" is manifested in "violence, drug abuse, family disintegration and gang activity." The authors urge President Clinton to address the interests of low- and moderate-income families by creating a "domestic Marshall Plan to rebuild our cities out of the ashes of violence, neglect and hopelessness."

The literature included a list of PICO's accomplishments in San Francisco and accompanying press clippings. *In virtually every congregation, encompassing more than a dozen neighborhoods, the primary emphasis was on demands for more police.* In June 1993 congregations turned out 400 people for a meeting with San Francisco Mayor Frank Jordan, an ex-police chief best known nationally for arresting homeless people and distributors of free food. The congregants attacked Jordan for having issued layoff notices to eighty-five police officers. They argued that "cutting any of the police force is unacceptable," even though stopping the layoffs might force the financially strapped city to eliminate health programs for low-income people and families. PICO had never joined a broad coalition in San Francisco to push for a progressive budget alternative; the group simply wanted more police. Most of those attending the meeting were from one of the city's least crime-ridden neighborhoods, making the contrast between the rhetoric of a "domestic Marshall Plan" for the underclass and a single-issue demand for more police even more striking.

Nearly one year later, in May 1994, the network of PICO congregations held another large meeting with Mayor Jordan. According to press accounts, the meeting again centered on crime. This time the network demanded that Jordan greatly increase the number of police officers, a gesture akin to "demanding" that Ronald Reagan cut taxes on the rich. Although the organization acknowledged that statistics showed crime rates declining in the city, PICO attributed the decrease to people's "despairing" of calling the police. As in the previous year's event, the congregants felt no obligation to discuss how additional police could be provided without eliminating vital services for the have-nots, whose fate is of such concern in PICO's literature. Nor was there apparently any discussion of how adding police would address the inner city's "civil war of despair." Of the entire laundry list of demands made by the local PICO network that night, only one—implementation of a comprehensive job-training program for young people—even remotely addressed the underlying causes of crime. Not surprisingly, Mayor Jordan eagerly embraced almost all of the group's program, claiming it would contribute to the "progress we will make in addressing the needs of your neighborhoods."[16]

PICO's actual work program in San Francisco is consistent with the now mainstream, bipartisan view that police represent the basic need that local, state, and national governments must satisfy. The primary effect of PICO's activism has been to perpetuate the "permanent underclass" the organization's literature claims represents a "clear and present danger to society." Yet the people involved in PICO's San Francisco network, though not as politically progressive as those active in the Tenderloin's anti-crime efforts, are primarily registered Democrats, and their organizations' mission statements reflect ideals of social and economic justice.

Activists have two strategies for responding to PICO and the ever-growing number of self-identified social change groups pursuing a law-and-order political agenda. One strategy is to write off these constituencies as selfish hypocrites blind to their own complicity in the social injustices they decry. This course of action is tempting, but we already know its reactionary consequences: elected officials will use such organizations' support on law-and-order issues to attack vulnerable groups such as the homeless, welfare families, and undocumented immigrants. As states spend ever-higher percentages of their limited budgets on prison construction and operation while cutting expenditures in critical areas such as education, the consequences of allowing grassroots anti-crime activists to continue to diminish the possibilities for social and economic justice are becoming all too clear.

Congregation-based and other grassroots anti-crime groups must therefore be confronted about their self-contradictory approach. As much as I enjoyed the interfaith conference where I picked up PICO's literature, the event would have been far more valuable had we discussed crime prevention more fully. The unanimous applause for attacks on "Three Strikes, You're Out" and shared concern over the ever-increasing incarceration rate among African-Americans masked deep disagreement about how crime fighting relates to the broader social and moral agenda. This disagreement must be brought into the open. Leaders of congregation-based organizations must examine whether their activities are increasing rather than decreasing the chances of a "class war." The same is true for all grassroots anti-crime activists whose demands for more police, more arrests, and more prisons devastate African-American communities and actually diminish the possibilities for progressive change. I strongly suspect that organizations confronted publicly with their contradictory approach toward social justice will reassess their positions.[17]

Conservative politicians recognize that by focusing the public debate on crime, they can win support from voters who oppose them on most other issues. California Governor Pete Wilson recognized that he could not win reelection on his handling of the state's economy, environment, or education system; voters' hopes for the future were sagging. Wilson addressed low-income working people who suffered under his administration's policies by emphasizing that "crime victims are Democrats, Republicans and independents. They are of every ethnic group. They are in every neighborhood in this state."[18] His Democratic opponent, Kathleen Brown, spent most of her campaign trying to prove she was even tougher than Wilson on crime; however, not only did her opposition to the death penalty make her stance politically untenable, but no California Democrat, and particularly no female Democrat, could beat Wilson on crime. Crime became the main issue in the 1994 general election races in California, even though the previous year violent crime had fallen off statewide for the first time in ten years.[19] Running on the issues of crime and illegal immigration, Wilson won in a landslide, and his success led to significant Republican gains in other California state races—this in a state that Clinton and two Democratic senators won easily in 1992.

Crime also became a major issue in the governor's races in two of the country's other populous states, Texas and Florida. Although crime was not the only issue that helped George W. Bush defeat incumbent Democratic governor Ann Richards in Texas, Richards observed during the campaign that she could never prove her success in fighting crime as long as news programs inevitably began with murder reports.[20] In Florida, challenger Jeb Bush labeled incumbent Democratic governor Lawton Chiles "soft on crime," using a commercial featuring the mother of a murder victim to drive home the charge. Chiles took an unusual step for a modern Democrat, arguing that improved health care and education were critical to preventing crime. Chiles prevailed, leaving Florida as the most populous state with a Democratic governor. The Republican landslide of November 1994, coupled with the earlier election of law-and-order mayors in San Francisco, Los Angeles, and New York City, testifies to the way in which the bipartisan acceptance of "more police, more prisons, longer sentences" has significantly reduced the prospects for fulfilling a progressive political agenda.

Social change activists who support anti-crime organizing among disenfranchised groups often argue that it is not the organizer's job to tell poor people what their priorities should be. They claim social change advocates should work for the goals and agendas of their constituency base, not inject their own values. According to these activists, if people perceive crime as the number one problem in the community, an organization claiming to represent the neighborhood has no choice but to focus its resources on fighting crime; otherwise, residents will no longer view the organization as a vehicle for channeling their concerns.

These arguments are persuasive and have carried the day in the Tenderloin and other low-income communities. Unfortunately, they rest upon incomplete reasoning. First, tactical activism requires organizers to help disenfranchised people successfully respond to critical problems in their lives. I have never had to tell a poor person that his or her housing is substandard or that most politicians do not care about his or her plight; this is understood instinctively. I have, however, spent hours in meetings with people who feel besieged by diverse social problems, including crime, and have a difficult time assessing how to solve them. In such situations, the organizer should ask residents how demands for more police connect to the larger agenda. If, as is often the case, this agenda centers on improving the neighborhood's overall quality of life, then the organizer and residents must work through the available strategies for accomplishing this goal. If the number one problem is public drug dealing, a winning strategy will eliminate the preconditions, not simply call for more arrests. As discussed in Elliott Currie's *Reckoning: Drugs, the Cities and the American Future*,[21] several studies show that the results of major police offensives against drug dealers are necessarily short-lived. Without other changes, street dealing reappears as soon as the police presence abates. A crackdown in response to pressure from one community simply transfers the illegal activity to other neighborhoods; they in turn organize and six months later create pressure for a crackdown in *their* area, returning the dealers to their initial community. The result is a lot like a tennis game, with neighborhood anti-crime groups volleying drug dealers back and forth. Even if the local police force were doubled, the additional officers would be outnumbered by the endless stream of dealers. I have seen this phenomenon firsthand in the Tenderloin. The police drive up and arrest some people, and everyone scatters. Ten minutes after the police leave, the dealers return. As I noted, the increased police presence in the Tenderloin failed to enhance people's feelings of safety and failed to change the neighborhood's image as a haven for illegal drug activity.

I am convinced that many community organizations endorse more police and more jails approach because this is the easiest way to claim immediate success. PICO's literature cited the organization's power in extracting commitments from the mayor for more police; had the congregants made their chief demand the development of employment programs to be financed by progressive taxes on downtown corporations or real estate interests, Mayor Jordan would have told them to take a hike. This response would have thrown a wrench into the group's carefully staged "accountability" session, and people would have left the meeting without a quick victory. Easy gains such as a beefed-up police force, however, are won at the expense of progress on broader, more significant issues. Organizations that have the potential to achieve success on "big picture" issues disempower themselves when they instead focus on agendas—such as more police—that politicians are eager to accommodate. Grassroots neighborhood groups have the power to redirect the public debate over crime toward nonpunitive, preventive solutions; organizers endorsing such solutions are best serving their constituency's concerns about crime.

Focusing on crime also reduces resident involvement in many social change organizations. Members of the Tenderloin's North of Market Planning Coalition, after years of attending meetings on safe streets, felt the organization had failed when crime continued to rise, and meeting attendance fell off. Because there was no common understanding about the limits of the anti-crime strategy, the sense of victory so crucial to continued volunteer involvement never was achieved. An organization built on the success of proactive tactical activism steadily declined in influence and member participation by focusing on unwinnable anti-crime campaigns. Organizers who understand that focusing on law-and-order approaches to crime might hurt the organization's effectiveness must raise this issue. This is not "telling people what's important to them"; rather, it is a process of ensuring that people know all the implications linked to pursuing certain goals.[22]

Another reason organizers critical of anti-crime strategies should not remain silent is that activists committed to progressive social change are wasting their time if they are not willing to inject their personal values into the communities in which they work. If your organizational base tries to adopt positions with which you disagree, you accomplish nothing by remaining silent. The legendary Saul Alinsky never hesitated to denounce the insurgent racism of the blue-collar Chicagoans he had organized and empowered. Requiring your organization to analyze the broader agenda underlying law-and-order rhetoric is equally essential.

Finally, the issue is not whether residents' concerns over crime should be ignored; rather, it is how to develop a specific agenda to address the local preconditions creating the criminal landscape. Once crime is placed in the broader context of an overall action plan for the neighborhood, activism can move toward winning specific and demonstrable improvements in residents' lives. Tactical activism requires that low-income communities stop following the false idols of more arrests, more police, more jails, and longer prison terms and start demanding tangible improvements of unsafe streets.

COMMUNITY POLICING: "THE BEAT COP IS BACK"

The emergence of "community policing" has strengthened support for law-and-order solutions to crime in low-income neighborhoods. Community policing shifts officers from patrol cars to walking beats and emphasizes daily police contact with area merchants and residents. The program is summed up in the 1990 slogan with which New York City launched its "Safe Streets, Safe City" community policing campaign: "The beat cop is back." The premise of the program is that the community must assume responsibility for working with the police to reduce crime. The program's focus on cooperation, personal responsibility, and neighborhood empowerment has made community policing the centerpiece of anti-crime platforms of liberal mayors in cities ranging from New York to Berkeley.

Programs that emphasize community input into and control of law enforcement certainly should be encouraged. Unfortunately, the chief goal of community policing is apparently to prevent political heat from merchants and homeowners in particular areas rather than to emphasize public control of police departments.[23] Instead of addressing the preexisting conditions causing crime in low-income neighborhoods, community policing can worsen the chances that such conditions will be removed or ameliorated.

My own experience with community policing began in 1990 with the start of the Community Police on Patrol (CPOP) program in the Tenderloin and the adjacent Sixth Street neighborhood in San Francisco. Because street crime was hurting tenants in Sixth Street's many residential hotels, the Tenderloin Housing Clinic decided to invite the police captain and sergeant in charge of CPOP to a tenant meeting. The officers explained how CPOP would help the tenants and made commitments to undertake specific actions that would improve hotel security. Although the officers implied more than once that area residents were themselves to blame for high crime rates, the tenants left the meeting feeling that the police cared about their concerns. However, as time passed and the commitments remained unfulfilled, the sergeant was contacted for a status report. Indignant that the tenants doubted his commitment to their concerns, he promised strong action "in the near future."

A key demand of the residents was for the CPOP officers to pass through hotel hallways during the evening hours, when trouble most often occurred. The tenants noticed that the officers failed to keep their commitment to patrol hallways but spent lengthy periods each day talking in the pawn shop located in the hotel's commercial space. In fact, tenants all along Sixth Street observed that officers who had no time to focus on crime affecting residents had plenty of time to visit regularly with merchants. Although most of the businesses on Sixth Street are pawn shops and liquor or gun stores, the merchants—unlike residents— were not implicitly blamed by the police for crime in the area. For example, the police never told merchants selling fortified wines that they were hardly in a position to complain about public intoxication and urination on Sixth Street.

The failure of the CPOP program to fulfill its commitments led the Clinic and hotel residents to meet with the Sixth Street anti-crime group. The group, led by merchants, strongly supported CPOP and cautioned the residents not to jeopardize the program. The merchants' position was understandable: they wanted the police to come when they called, and they were already receiving the level of police service sought by residents. In the end, the residents benefited little from CPOP; the real test of the success of community policing appears to be whether merchants are happy with it. To this day, Sixth Street merchants are regularly quoted in the media praising the police's impact on the neighborhood, thus providing perfect cover for city neglect of the residents' concerns. Here we glimpse a key flaw in focusing community organizing work around police issues: police tend to work more closely with merchants than residents, and in low-income communities merchants' concerns rarely transcend their need for a safe business environment. Residents' problems go far beyond "safe streets." They do need police (but need them most after businesses close). Unlike merchants, residents also need a wide variety of other city services, including quality housing, job training, and health care. Programs such as CPOP rarely become part of a cohesive strategy to improve a neighborhood.

Many residents of low-income communities like to know police officers on a first-name basis and support the "more police, more arrests" approach to crime. Community policing provides grassroots organizers with support for such residents in the form of beat cops and regular meetings between residents and police. Government support for such law-and-order organizing dramatically exceeds the level of public funding allocated for organizing the poor for better housing, jobs, or health care. One can only marvel at the naiveté of liberal mayors who initiate community policing; they are spending funds on a program that bolsters the political base of their law-and-order opponents. Rather than help liberal politicians on the crime issue, CPOP helps make crime the central issue in low-income communities. As former mayors of New York City and San Francisco have learned, a career politician is not going to defeat an ex-police chief or ex-prosecutor when the central issue is crime. With its focus of resources on merchants, community policing mirrors, rather than challenges, cities' historically unfair distribution of resources in low-income neighborhoods.

Community policing not only directs people away from social change activism and toward law-and-order advocacy but also provides a fraudulent model of community empowerment. Although marketed as a way for low-income residents to take "personal responsibility" for fighting crime, the process actually gives residents no meaningful role. The police make all decisions about personnel, staffing, priorities, resource allocation, tactics, and strategies. District captains and beat officers who develop relationships with residents can be transferred to other neighborhoods without any advance notice or discussion with their presumed "partners" in fighting crime. Residents can make suggestions at meetings; subsequent adoption of such ideas by the police presumably constitutes resident empowerment.

Beat officers will be the first to admit that community policing should not replace resident participation in other neighborhood organizations.

Practically speaking, however, CPOP's organizing resources and ability to control the local debate about crime have increasingly focused low-income residents' attention on the law-and-order agenda. Tactical activists must redirect this energy by openly discussing the need for residents to develop and implement a proactive agenda on crime. Inner-city residents are desperate for neighborhood improvement, and in the absence of organizational alternatives will understandably turn to well-marketed but inherently flawed programs like CPOP.

Although anti-crime efforts cross racial lines, African-American leaders, whose inner-city communities have been torn asunder by drug trafficking, property crime, and violence, have been least willing to jump on the "more police, more prisons, longer sentences" bandwagon. The Reverend Jesse Jackson held a three-day conference on crime in Washington, D.C., in January 1994. Participants included representatives of the National Rainbow Coalition and National Black Caucus of Elected Officials, as well as ministers, businesspersons, and activists. The conference rejected government's continued reliance on prisons and penalties and called instead for the Clinton administration to develop an urban policy and jobs programs that would reduce crime and violence. The delegates also noted the racism that frequently underlies the crime issue, an issue often ignored by grassroots anti-crime activists. Jackson's demand for crime-prevention programs no doubt had an impact on the 1994 crime bill; 25 percent of its $30 billion price tag includes funding for social and economic programs to prevent crime. The chief funding infusion to alleviate inner-city poverty during the period when Democrats controlled the White House and Congress had to be labeled a "crime bill" in order to achieve passage; there is no stronger testimony to the strategic error of progressives' acceptance of law-and-order measures as the chief urban priority.

Elected Officials

INSPIRING FEAR AND LOATHING

Ernesto Cortes, Jr., organizer of the Industrial Areas Foundation network in Texas and the San Antonio–based Communities Organized for Public Service (COPS), has plainly described activists' necessary relationship to elected officials: "It's unfortunate that fear is the only way to get some politicians to respect your power. They refuse to give you respect. They don't recognize your dignity. So we have to act in ways to get their attention. In some areas, what we have going is the amount of fear we can generate. We got where we are because people fear and loathe us."[1]

This assessment by one of the United States's premier community activists and tacticians is harsh but accurate. Today's activists confront a political landscape in which too many ostensibly progressive politicians require strong prodding before they will support their own constituency's agenda. Without such pressure, self-identified "progressive" elected officials all too often betray the interests of those responsible for their election.

The typical characteristics of the contemporary "progressive" officeholder explain much of the problem. The career path for such individuals no longer begins with years of service fighting for change at the grassroots level; instead one becomes an aide to a legislator, a job that provides access to funders and puts the aspirant in the position to be tapped for electoral openings. The modern "progressive" official, with rare exception, is not a product of a grassroots or democratic nominating process and views politics as a career vehicle rather than a means for redressing social and economic injustice. He or she is not ideologically driven, takes pride in "pragmatic" problem solving, values personal loyalty over ideological consistency, and views social change activists as enemies because they place their constituency's interests ahead of the official's political needs.

In the rare cases when a candidate from a neighborhood or other grassroots base does get elected, he or she tends gradually to become like other politicians once in office. The ambition to assure reelection or attain higher office requires new or stronger connections with a whole range of financial interests. Even grassroots candidates require significant funding for organizers, literature, and overhead expenses if they are to prevail in any race beyond a small-sized local one. The ever-growing power of money in politics has led most politicians to put their funders' interests above those of their volunteer constituency base. The importance of campaign dollars means that even the best-intentioned, most progressive candidate has to spend considerable time courting and meeting with potential funders, who often do not share the values of the candidate's core supporters.

Grassroots politicians are typically independent of traditional campaign funders and can't get elected without a strong volunteer base. Once in office, grassroots politicians are contacted by representatives of financial interests who opposed their candidacy. These representatives soon ingratiate themselves by offering to help retire the inevitable campaign debt. Many elected officials at the local level receive low salaries, making them receptive to the often luxurious fundraising events that are a regular part of political business. Like most other people, elected officials are awed by power and wealth. They don't go home and report, "I met with some poor people from the Tenderloin, and it was exciting"; they boast, "I met with the president of Bank of America!" They're easily excited by the trappings of power and the social component of their new status. The election-night celebration is often the last opportunity for meaningful personal contact between the candidate and the volunteers who sacrificed their personal lives to walk precincts, staff phone banks, and get out the vote.

Although progressive-identified officeholders have helped facilitate social change, many of these officials, considered allies, end up suppressing activists' agendas as effectively as clearly labeled enemies do. Having helped elect these officials, progressive constituencies feel loyalty toward them, show reluctance to hold them accountable for their campaign commitments, and hesitate to attack them for acts the constituencies would strongly oppose if undertaken by conservative politicians. Concerns over maintaining access, appearing "reasonable," and fulfilling the personal ambitions of organizational leaders contribute to this pattern of nonaccountability. Progressive constituencies' failure to demand accountability of the officials their votes and volunteer labor put into office has become a major obstacle to achieving social change. Activists must understand that people feel betrayed when politicians fail to deliver on their campaign promises to support progressive change, and they respond with cynicism to subsequent social change efforts. They also join the ranks of nonvoters, thus impairing the election prospects of authentic progressive candidates. Without political accountability, working to elect candidates to office becomes a fool's errand.

Adopting a "fear and loathing" approach toward elected officials, particularly self-identified progressives, is essential for achieving social change. Activists must focus on results, not promises; they must pursue their agenda, not the politician's. They also must learn to deal with problems that arise within their own organizations when individual members develop allegiances to politicians, ties that may subtly (or not so subtly) affect how the group deals with constituent issues. To preserve harmony, organizations tend to bypass potentially divisive discussions about the credibility of elected officials considered allies. Failure to address such internal disagreements openly, however, all too often results in failure to achieve the organization's goals. Even when an organization is unified in its approach to a supposedly friendly politician, the politician can use many tactics to delay, damage, or deny fulfillment of the organization's agenda. Politicians employ highly paid consultants to develop strategies for achieving their goals; social change activists must understand and adopt their own strategies for using politicians to bring about progressive change.

"WE'RE WITH YOU WHEN YOU'RE WITH US, AND AGAINST YOU WHEN YOU'RE NOT"

After Jerry Brown's reelection in 1978 as California's governor, an unusual alliance developed between Brown and antiwar activists Tom Hayden and Jane Fonda. Hayden had formed a statewide citizens organization in the mid-1970s called the Campaign for Economic Democracy (CED) and ran a high-profile, though unsuccessful, challenge to

California's incumbent Democratic senator, John Tunney, in the 1976 primary.

When Hayden was challenged over his organization's apparent alliance with the then very fiscally conservative Brown, he claimed that CED would support the governor when he supported the group's issues and oppose him when he opposed its issues. Because many on the political left distrusted Hayden, his assessment of the ideal relationship between social activist organizations and elected officials was perceived as simple window-dressing for his ambition to attain political power. However, regardless of Hayden's motives for adopting his formulation or whether CED pursued it in practice, this ideal is the best model for tactical activists in dealing with elected officials.

The advantages of remaining independent of elected officials are well known to longtime activists. As I will discuss, groups that become too closely aligned with elected officials invariably see their agendas subsumed to those of the politicians, with potentially disastrous consequences for both sides. Conversely, a group that remains outside the electoral process forgoes the opportunity to help elect candidates who might advance the group's agenda. The success of the right-wing agenda since 1980 largely has rendered moot progressives' "pure" stance of ignoring electoral politics.

The ideal of supporting candidates only when they support your issues may seem obvious; the difficulty lies in the implementation. Elected officials value personal loyalty above all else; because tactical activists must place their constituency's agenda over the politician's, the potential for conflict always exists. The strains of this tension are most severe when a self-styled neighborhood activist or progressive is elected to office. These officials feel entitled to the unwavering loyalty of neighborhood and progressive organizations and argue that any criticism from the political left lends comfort to their conservative enemies. Adopting a "tough-love" stance toward such officials thus makes many activists feel disloyal or, even worse in the current political world, "unreasonable" or "too idealistic." Nevertheless, for tactical activists striving to accomplish social change, an independent stance brings both power and respect; to succeed, they must accept the credo that, in regard to elected officials, it is better to be feared than loved.

Let us recall the statement of Texas organizer Ernesto Cortes, Jr.: "We got where we are because [politicians] fear and loathe us." Cortes did not arrive at this conclusion after years of battling exclusively with conservatives who refused to deal fairly with his Latino constituency. Rather, he reached this frank assessment after dealing with his many political allies. Among COPS's closest allies was then San Antonio's mayor Henry Cisneros, later Clinton's secretary of housing and urban development. Rather than revel in Cisneros's historic victory as the city's first Latino mayor and then sit meekly as promises were broken and commitments left unfulfilled, COPS demanded performance. When Cisneros failed to perform, COPS publicly attacked him for ignoring his constituency's concerns. Unlike far too many progressive groups, Cortes says, COPS does not endeavor to be liked by politicians: "When we start worrying whether or not politicians like us . . . then we'll be just like everybody else."[2]

I wish I could say that Cortes is wrong and that fear need not be used to motivate elected officials. It would be so much easier if progressive constituencies were treated with the same respect as large financial donors. It would also be great if activists could relate on some basis other than intimidation to politicians they have supported. Cortes's comments, however, mirror exactly my own experiences with "progressive" officials. With rare exception, these politicians serve low-income constituencies out of fear of losing their progressive public image and hence support from progressive voters. Activists who put their constituencies' needs ahead of the politician's agenda must be willing to sacrifice friendship with the official in order to achieve their goals.

Tactical activists also must let officials know when they are right and when they are wrong. Politicians deserve public credit when they fight hard for fairness and social justice. The favorable publicity they receive will prompt similar conduct in the future. But there is virtually never an excuse for silently allowing a supposed ally to act against your constituency. Particular members of an organization or constituency may have personal reasons not to protest, publicly or privately, a wayward vote, but tactical activism requires that some element of the constituency take such action. Organizations that engage in the necessary strategic and tactical discussions in formulating a proactive agenda will have determined in advance when and how to respond to betrayal by a supposed political friend.

FOCUS ON RESULTS, NOT PROMISES

Focusing on results rather than promises would seem an obvious approach. In our workplaces, our investments, and our consumer choices, we evaluate performance by actual results, not promises. In my experience with social change activists, however, I have been routinely astonished at how often elected officials are viewed as allies without having done anything to earn the moniker. Politicians need only agree to take certain positions in the future to earn the support of many progressive organizations. This makes strategic sense for politicians but not for advocates of social change. Given the ease with which they can achieve progressive credentials, politicians have no incentive actually to *do* anything to serve progressive constituencies. As a result, few officials feel it politically necessary to wage a major fight against the status quo on behalf of progressive reform. As a former leader of San Antonio's COPS puts it, "When politicians deliver, we applaud them. Not until then.... Politicians' work is to do your work. When you've got somebody working for you, you don't bow and scrape."[3]

I witnessed firsthand the damaging consequences of going easy on progressive officials during Art Agnos's tenure as mayor of San Francisco. Agnos ran for mayor in 1987 as a self-identified progressive. His eagerness to wear this label, coupled with his excellent record as a state legislator, brought him broad support among social change constituencies. Activists saw the race as their big chance to win City Hall after enduring nearly ten years under Dianne Feinstein, a centrist who had failed to identify herself with any of the powerful movements—gay liberation, anti-development/neighborhood preservation, and rent control—sweeping San Francisco during the 1980s. There was a general feeling that the city had undergone great changes but that the person in charge hadn't grown with it. By 1987 the gay community had built its own political organization and wanted a mayor who would support "domestic partners" legislation and appoint more gays and lesbians to city commissions. Anti-development forces, who had won a critical battle to restrict highrise development through a 1986 ballot measure, wanted a mayor who would appoint a Planning Commission favoring the preservation and development of affordable housing. Rent-control activists particularly felt the need for a new mayor. The key issue on their agenda—the imposition of rent control on vacant units—had twice passed the Board of Supervisors, only to be vetoed by Mayor Feinstein. Rent-control activists felt it essential to elect a mayor committed to signing a vacancy-control law; Agnos's promise to do just that gave him the nearly unanimous support of tenant groups.

Agnos and his campaign tacticians created a grassroots campaign organization unprecedented in the city's history. The campaign included more than 500 precinct leaders, many of them motivated primarily by the candidate's support for stronger rent control. I was extremely enthusiastic about Agnos; my wife and I spent most of our nonworking time contacting voters for the campaign. My own interest centered on Agnos's commitment to enact a new homeless policy, his personal interest in improving the Tenderloin, and his support of various measures to preserve and expand low-cost housing. I never had great expectations that Agnos would back strong vacancy-control legislation, but I believed political factors would force him to sign whatever measure his tenant supporters passed through the Board of Supervisors.

Agnos was elected with a staggering 70 percent of the vote. Rent-control activists should have had no problem quickly cashing in. However, they violated the fundamental rule of dealing with elected officials: demand results.

Soon after taking office, Agnos met with rent-control activists to discuss a strategy for enacting vacancy control. After establishing a clear tone of friendship, Agnos explained that he had promised real estate industry representatives that he would at least "sit down with them" prior to moving forward with vacancy control. He requested that tenants meet with landlords in his presence to see if a "win-win" compromise on vacancy control could be reached. Agnos emphasized his continued support for vacancy control but felt he must first attempt to mediate a settlement.

Rent-control activists expressed virtually no protest of Agnos's plan. A few pointed out that dialogue with landlords on the issue had already been tried and failed, and others argued against wasting time on such a charade. Nobody asked Agnos why he never expressed his desire to mediate between landlords and tenants during a campaign in which he consistently identified tenants as his allies. Neither did anyone question his sudden concern for a constituency that had actively worked against his election and funded his chief opponent.

Why did rent-control activists meekly accept Agnos's waffling on the chief issue on their political agenda? Because Agnos's carefully crafted campaign identity as a friend of tenant interests overshadowed post election reality. They, like other activists who later had problems with Agnos, were willing to accept as good-faith action a clear betrayal of their constituency. Agnos had not actually done anything as mayor to demonstrate his pro-tenant stance; he merely had created personal relationships with leading rent-control activists during the campaign, which became "proof" of his support for tenant interests. The consensus among rent-control activists was that Agnos was "our" mayor, whom "we" had elected. Denying Agnos the political space he claimed to need, it was argued, would be the height of arrogance and eventually could turn him against tenants. Having felt left out for more than a decade, rent-control activists did not want to jeopardize their new access to power by fighting over what seemed nothing more than a procedural delay. A course was thus established whereby Agnos had no reason to fear the tenant constituency. As a result, he afforded tenants and their chief agenda item no respect for the balance of his term.

Agnos's "procedural delay" was only the first of many clever strategies he used to brush aside vacancy control while steadfastly proclaiming his commitment to it. After several months were spent in pointless meetings with landlords, Agnos was forced to admit the failure of the "mediation process." He then announced a new justification for his failure to enact vacancy control: lack of votes on the Board of Supervisors. This excuse had superficial validity during Agnos's first year in office, but by 1989 the newly elected Board of Supervisors could have passed vacancy control if Agnos had made it a priority. However, it had become clear to the board's most progressive members (but not to rent-control activists) that Agnos did not care whether vacancy control was enacted in 1989.

Agnos further demonstrated his lack of commitment to the constituency, in a tacit way, by showing the kind of fight he could put up for a goal he really wanted. This demonstration came with his all-out effort to pass a November 1989 ballot initiative for a new stadium for the San Francisco Giants baseball team. In order to achieve a goal that he had never supported in his mayoral campaign and that his core neighborhood supporters opposed, Agnos used every political chit at his disposal. He had gay and lesbian leaders announce that the stadium would increase funding for AIDS services; he got the Sierra Club to support the proposed stadium as good for the environment; and he made political deals with various supervisors in exchange for their backing. Despite all this, the stadium initiative failed.

Meanwhile, Agnos still had not lifted a finger to help the passage of vacancy control. I was not alone among tenant activists in recognizing the discrepancy between Agnos's vigorous attempt to pass the stadium initiative, on the one hand, and his lack of effort on vacancy control, on the other. Despite their recognition of Agnos's inaction, however, leading rent-control activists continued to view him as committed to their cause. Had these activists evaluated the mayor's actual accomplishments the same way they would evaluate the performance of any consumer product, they would have concluded that Agnos was never going to produce on vacancy control. Nevertheless, as long as Agnos remained publicly committed to the proposal, rent-control leaders continued to identify him as the tenants' friend.

The November 1990 election posed a great opportunity for vacancy-control advocates. With a governor's race, high-profile statewide environmental and consumer initiatives, and strong local candidates from the gay and lesbian community, the election promised to generate an unusually high progressive voter turnout. But Agnos, and hence rent-control advocates, ignored this special opportunity to submit vacancy control to the voters, instead working to elect a clear pro-vacancy-control majority on the Board of Supervisors. When this majority was achieved, vacancy control was finally enacted in 1991 (with Agnos's approval). Almost immediately, however, the measure became subject—as advocates had always known it would—to a landlord-sponsored referendum on the November 1991 ballot. After the landlords succeeded in qualifying the referendum, Agnos held a meeting with rent-control activists. He observed that, fortunately, the referendum would appear on the same ballot on which he sought reelection; therefore, his campaign could also fund the pro-vacancy-control effort. I was not alone in recognizing the true import of the mayor's statement: he had intentionally delayed vacancy control so as to assure a high tenant turnout for his reelection bid.

Ironically, Agnos's secret strategy resulted in both his and vacancy control's defeat. The real estate interests Agnos had tried so hard to placate in 1988 poured more than $1 million into defeating vacancy control. When mayoral candidates who also supported vacancy control unexpectedly entered the race, Agnos compounded his betrayal of tenants by playing down the issue and failing to provide the funding he had promised. The result: lacking both money and any grassroots campaign, vacancy control lost in a landslide. The man Agnos finished second to in November, former police chief Frank Jordan, drew strong support from elderly tenants who, having reaped no benefit from Agnos on rent-control issues, went instead with the law-and-order candidate.

Jordan failed to muster a majority, however, necessitating a December runoff between him and Agnos. That election crystallized the deep hostility rent-control activists felt toward the mayor. Agnos and tenant activists met soon after the runoff campaign began, and, for the first time since Agnos took office, tenants spoke bitterly of his betrayal of their interests. I began the meeting by confronting the mayor with my belief—shared by many others—that he had sabotaged vacancy control by waiting until November 1991 and then breaking his promise to fund the campaign. Agnos agreed he had broken his promise, claiming his "political survival" was at stake. The meeting continued in this vein, with tenant activists torn between their anger at Agnos and their fear of aiding Jordan.

Agnos lost in the runoff, glaring proof of his personal unpopularity. I had ignored his campaign in the general election but felt his reelection was preferable to four years under his anti-poor, pro-landlord opponent. I contacted dozens of tenant activists about working for Agnos in the runoff but made no effort to change their minds when they declined to participate. Rent-control activists had good reason to shun Agnos, and I was not about to jeopardize my credibility by defending him. Some very savvy political activists refused to endorse Agnos in the runoff, and although I took a different approach, their position was understandable.

Rent-control activists made a major tactical error in establishing a relationship with Agnos based on friendship rather than fear and hence allowing him to substitute promises for action. When Agnos sought to act as a mediator between landlords and tenants right after taking office, rent-control activists should have refused. Tactical activism required tenants to make it clear at the outset that, having helped elect Agnos, they now were entitled to results. Silence in the face of a politician's initial betrayal sends a clear message that your constituency feels itself too weak, too confused, or too afraid to merit respect.

Suppose Agnos had employed the tactics of most politicians and expressed hurt and dismay at rent-control activists' refusal to meet with landlords. Suppose he claimed also that the activists were being "unreasonable," were only "shooting themselves in the foot." What should have been the response? Tactical activism would have had the rent-control activists give the mayor an ultimatum: either be our ally or be widely publicized as our betrayer. The activists should have emphasized that the campaign was over and that the time had come for results, not promises. By demonstrating their willingness to stand up for their agenda, rent-control activists would have conveyed a sense that they believed in the power of their constituency and were not afraid to take on the mayor. Had they done so, one of three possible results would have followed. First, and most likely, Agnos would have backed down. He was not seeking a political fight with tenants, merely trying to manipulate them in furtherance of his own agenda. Second, Agnos could have sought to divide the activists by offering to meet with whoever was willing to attend. This strategy probably would have failed, because rent-control activists unified enough to give the new mayor an ultimatum would not be so easily divided. Third, Agnos could have announced his refusal to work further with rent-control activists. This would have been the most unlikely scenario of all, because a new mayor hardly wants to break with a main campaign constituency early in his term.

Had rent-control activists carefully analyzed the tactical and strategic avenues available both to them and to the mayor, they would have recognized that they would gain more credibility with the mayor by refusing his delaying tactic than by agreeing to it. Because they caved in at the outset, Agnos came to count on their subservience to his political agenda in the years ahead. The result four years later was a landslide defeat on rent-control activists' chief issue, the temporary decline of San Francisco's once-powerful tenant movement, and the election of a new mayor openly beholden to real estate interests. The bright hope of the Agnos years ended in tragedy for progressive interests.

The model of the relationship between rent-control activists and Art Agnos has been repeated many times with other constituencies and other elected officials throughout the country. San Francisco's rent-control activists are certainly not alone in erroneously identifying an elected official with his or her promises rather than actual performance. Today's self-styled progressive politicians are uniquely adept at using their power and winning public personalities to distract social change activists from their agendas. These politicians are experts at the psychology of "win-win"—they know how to make their campaign supporters feel bad for demanding action instead of promises. Moreover, their patronage power enables them to make strategic allies of social change leaders. By appointing such leaders to prestigious boards, commissions, or task forces, the politician can display his loyalty to social change constituencies without having to act in behalf of their agenda. These leaders can also be used to suppress dissatisfaction with official policies at the grassroots level and to provide press quotes disputing charges that the officeholder has betrayed the social change constituency. Neighborhood activists who have toiled for years in obscurity are understandably flattered at being invited to meet with the mayor, the governor, or a legislator. It is not easy to attend such a meeting and then strongly oppose the official's reasonable-sounding plans.

It is precisely because the new generation of political leaders has such an array of tactics to divert social change that tactical activists must also demand results and the fulfillment of campaign promises. Once activists understand and accept this fundamental relationship between social change groups and elected officials, they will avoid the principal pitfalls preventing change. Elected officials spend millions of dollars on campaign consultants in developing tactics and strategies to woo voters; social change activists must engage in their own less costly but equally productive tactical sessions to create the relationships with politicians necessary to achieve progressive aims.

PURSUE YOUR AGENDA, NOT THE OFFICIAL'S

Self-styled "grassroots" officials are also effective at subsuming activists' agendas to their own. If a politician is willing to be guided entirely by the tactics, strategies, and agenda of a social change organization, great. I have no problem even with a politician's loudly claiming credit for the accomplishment of the activists' goal, because officials willing to act at their constituency's request should be applauded. However, politicians and activist groups frequently start out on the same page but then find their agendas diverging. For example, a politician often commits to an issue but subsequently recognizes that certain other constituency groups oppose it. The politician does not want to engage in a big political fight with the opposition group, nor does he or she want to be seen as having betrayed the social change organization. The solution? Reframe and repackage the activists' agenda so that the politician can claim "victory" and convince the activists of the same. This political tactic is commonly used: grassroots activists bring a problem to public attention, prompting a politician to hold a press conference and vow action, with the result being a task force to study the problem. The creation of a task force to study a problem and propose solutions has become the leading strategy by which new-style "win-win" politicians subsume activists' agendas into their own. They subtly switch the agenda from "We demand action now" to "We created a task force to address this critical problem." As the politician gives victory pats on the back, the activists' goal of getting something concrete done disappears.

Although grassroots-grown task forces, such as the Tenderloin's Luxury Hotel Task Force, can serve to focus activist energies, task forces sponsored by government officials are usually boondoggles. Approach them with caution. Elected officials who seek to avoid real change often use them as appeasement measures. How many times have you seen the announcement, amid great fanfare, of a new task force, which is to take twelve months to produce a report on an "urgent" problem? Task forces are excellent weapons for slowing activist momentum. They can divert activists from their real goal and nearly always eat up a lot of time that could be better spent. Yet serving on a task force can be an attractive proposition for a grassroots organizer, who may get no other sign of recognition from the powers-that-be. However, such official flattery can undermine activist goals. Similarly, serving on a task force may be attractive to politically ambitious activists, whose real agenda is personal advancement. Those personal goals often end up conflicting with the goals of social change. Activist organizations should determine the function of any member assigned to serve on a government task force and hold him or her rigorously accountable for promoting the organization's views.

Progressive social activists who enthusiastically participate on task forces usually argue, "If we don't participate on a task force, they will come out with horrible recommendations." I say, so what? If that happens, discredit the recommendations. Discrediting task force reports is a fairly simple exercise. One can point to the biased composition of the task force, question individual members' agendas, point to the heavy political pressures placed on the task force, or note its failure to consider vital information. In any case, after an initial splash, most reports from task forces, commissions, and the like are widely ignored. For example, consider "Beyond Rhetoric: A New American Agenda for Children and Families," a 500-plus-page report brought forth with great hoopla in 1991 by the illustrious National Commission on Children. Despite major media coverage on the day of its release and the presence on the commission of notables such as then Arkansas governor Bill Clinton, the report sank from view before a week was out. It has yet to resurface.

The task force tactic has become so transparent by this point that it is a wonder that anybody outside the official's staff accepts the legitimacy of such a panel. In addressing homelessness, the first "action" of virtually every mayor or governor in this nation is to form a task force to study the problem and propose solutions. The fact that every report produced by these task forces is ignored has apparently not deterred right-minded people from continuing to serve on and give credibility to such bodies.[4]

The creation of task forces is only one way for politicians to supplant activist groups' agendas with their own. The same purpose may be served by holding a public hearing to address an activist organization's concerns. Public hearings may even be more effective than task forces in funneling activist energy into the politician's agenda. Typically, the social change organization seeks a government response to a problem. A politician, seeking to play the white knight, announces a hearing to investigate the issue. Social change groups agree to the hearing because it gives them a chance to mobilize their members and is expected to produce some tangible results. The organizers pack the hearing room, and the crowd cheers as speaker after speaker rails against the injustice in question. The official who called the hearing plays to the crowd and shows that he or she is squarely in the its corner. The media are out in force, and excitement is in the air.

There is only one problem: all too often, such hearings are held by officials with no legal authority to address the targeted problem. Or they occur prior to the drafting of legislation on the subject. The politician accomplishes his or her goal through the hearing itself, gaining the audience's loyalty and the general public's approval for promptly responding to an injustice. A social change organization, however, rarely achieves its goal through a public hearing. The real work for accomplishing change—through either legislation or public pressure campaigns—occurs after the hearing. By that time, the politician has moved on to other issues, leaving the activist organization on its own. Tactical activists can avoid this pitfall by making their agenda clear at the outset to the politician seeking involvement. If a politician is not committed to fighting beyond the hearing, do not allow said official to reap the publicity benefits of the event.

Hearings can energize a constituency base, but this benefit will backfire if people see that nothing concrete has come from their trip to City Hall. Tactical activism requires that groups only work with officials committed to fulfilling the social change agenda. The smart politician understands that working for the group's agenda is also the best strategy for achieving his or her own political aims.

FEAR AND LOATHING ON THE ENVIRONMENTAL TRAIL

In his best-selling lamentation on the state of American political life, *Who Will Tell the People: The Betrayal of American Democracy,* William Greider assesses the prospects for progressive social change in a tone of great despair. Greider views the concentration of wealth, the decline in voting among the middle and lower economic classes, and the control of government by "elite" decisionmakers as but a few of several factors that have left most Americans with little or no influence upon the civic life of the nation. Central to Greider's widely accepted thesis is his portrayal of the difficulties faced by environmental activists and organizations. Their principal problems are twofold. First, environmentalists are victims of "random lawlessness" when the government refuses to enforce its own environmental regulations. Describing the Environmental Protection Agency's failure to obtain compliance with 80 percent of its hazardous waste enforcement orders, Greider concludes that federal laws so easily manipulated by political or corporate intervention "cannot truly be called laws at all." Greider's second argument is that many environmental laws are enacted with the intention that they remain "hollow." A former congressional committee staff aide who spent six years drafting environmental laws asserts that "the worst situation is not the absence of laws, but the presence of law in name only. Right now, we have lots of laws in name only." Greider notes that such hollow laws are invariably passed with "great fanfare, self-congratulation, and grandiloquence," even though it is only the public that is fooled.[5]

Who or what is responsible for the nonenforcement of environmental laws and the enactment of purely symbolic measures? Greider primarily blames industry, citing a study showing that in the 1980s approximately 92,500 people earned their living by arguing over the content of federal regulations. He also blames Republican-appointed administrators who oppose the regulations they are employed to enforce and "sophisticated" members of Congress who cynically seek voter popularity by passing environmental laws they know either will not be enforced or will not make a difference. When, inevitably, the laws are subverted, such legislators can simply blame the regulators and then go on to other business. Greider's final villains are the Washington-based mainstream national environmental groups. He observes that the "Big Ten" organizations are largely concerned with maintaining their standing in the Washington political establishment; displaying too much fervor would jeopardize their role in insider negotiations. The Big Ten's focus on appearing "reasonable" has led to widespread and justified suspicion that some big-name environmental groups are in collusion with industry against grassroots environmentalists who are less willing to compromise environmental goals.[6]

Significantly, Greider substantially accepts the national organizations' view that Washington-based environmentalists are "trapped between the grassroots demands for fundamental change and a political system that will not even consider them."[7] Greider also sympathizes with the lengthy legal and regulatory battles undertaken by the National Resource Defense Fund, the Environmental Defense Fund, the Clean Air Coalition, and other groups, though he implies that such actions typically fail to achieve meaningful results. Greider never asks leaders of these groups why they fight for laws they know will never be enforced. Nor does he ask his mainstream environmentalist sources why the confrontational tactics that have proven successful locally should not also be used toward Congress. These questions are critical, because they point to environmentalists' failure to establish a "fear and loathing" relationship with national politicians as the leading cause of the betrayal of democracy on environmental issues.

Grassroots activists frequently have criticized the failure of mainstream environmental organizations to hold political officials accountable. For example, Lois Gibbs, leader of the fight over Love Canal and now director of the grassroots Citizens Clearinghouse for Hazardous Wastes, has stated that the Big Ten groups prefer to identify where a candidate stands and then endorse that position rather than condition an electoral endorsement on support for the environmentalists' own agenda.[8] Although critical of national groups' unwillingness to "dirty their hands" dealing with grassroots constituencies,[9] Gibbs views their tactics as "not bad—that is the only way you can operate on Capitol Hill."[10] This perception of two separate environmental movements—a grassroots one operating at the local level, and a national one based in Washington, D.C.—using tactics appropriate to their respective forums is shared by mainstream environmental leaders. These leaders argue that environmentalists cannot enter the Washington debate unless they sound reasonable to Washington officials, something major environmental groups are willing to do but grassroots activists are not.[11] As a result, grassroots activists give up important access to the Washington-based policy debates and cede decisionmaking to mainstream groups that lack an active constituency base.[12]

In my view, it is neither helpful nor accurate to say there are two environmental movements, each employing a tactical style appropriate for its chosen political forum. In order to prevail at the local or national level, environmentalists must develop a "fear and loathing" relationship with elected officials, be willing to confront officials to ensure political accountability, and use the courts to enforce environmental laws. Environmentalists will fail locally and nationally when they subvert organizational agendas in order to retain access or appear reasonable to politicians who are in their political debt; seek gains through political friendship or trust rather than fear; and fail to retaliate publicly against officials who betray commitments. Local grassroots activists can and must apply their confrontational approach to federal officials who control national environmental policy; the erroneous concepts that grass-roots tactics only work locally, that local activists cannot significantly influence national environmental debates, and that winning in Washington requires playing by insider rules have contributed to the lack of grassroots influence in the national arena.

As Goes East Liverpool, So Goes the Nation   A campaign waged by Greenpeace and residents of East Liverpool, Ohio, to force the Clinton administration to keep a well-publicized campaign promise exemplifies the strategic direction that local and national environmental groups must follow if they are to prevail in the political arena. This ostensibly local struggle against the Waste Technologies Industry (WTI) hazardous waste incinerator has significant implications both for national environmental campaigns and for grassroots efforts throughout the United States. The battle against the project has been led by local groups with the strong backing of Greenpeace, one of the largest national environmental organizations to recognize that confrontational tactics successful in local efforts can similarly influence policy in Washington.

The battle over the East Liverpool facility would seem an unlikely subject for a national campaign by a prominent environmental organization. The incinerator's proximity to houses, churches, and schools and its emission of such toxics as lead, mercury, and dioxin into a low-income neighborhood in a city of which few have ever heard would appear tailor-made for local grassroots, rather than mainstream, Washington-based, activism. During the 1992 Clinton campaign bus tour, however, Democratic vice presidential candidate Al Gore described the WTI incinerator as an unbelievable idea that highlighted the concrete differences between the parties on environmental issues. Speaking of the incinerator in Weirton, West Virginia in July 1992, Gore said, "I'll tell you this, a Clinton-Gore administration is going to give you an environmental presidency to deal with these problems. We'll be on your side for a change, instead of the side of the garbage generators, the way [previous presidents] have been."[13]

Because Gore's environmental treatise, *Earth in the Balance*,[14] attacked solid waste incinerators and praised their grassroots opponents, environmentalists saw the election of Clinton-Gore as the death knell for the WTI facility. This expectation was heightened when the vice president issued a press release on December 7, 1992, stating that "serious questions concerning the safety of an East Liverpool, Ohio hazardous waste incinerator must be answered before the plant may begin operation. The new Clinton-Gore administration will not issue the plant a test burn permit until these questions are answered." Attached to Gore's release was a letter to the comptroller general raising several questions about the impact of the incinerator and how it was approved; the letter was signed by Gore and six U.S. senators. The *New York Times* interpreted Gore's statement as "sending a clear signal" that the "new administration plans an aggressive approach to enforcing environmental laws."[15] Incinerator opponents had even greater reason to cheer when the new administration appointed Carol Browner to head the Environmental Protection Agency. In the early 1980s, Browner had worked on anti-toxic issues for Clean Water Action and Citizen Action.[16]

Unfortunately, the Clinton administration broke its pledge to its environmental supporters by issuing a temporary permit in March 1993 allowing the incinerator to begin commercial operation. It did so despite the Ohio attorney general's claim that the facility violated state law and the EPA's own assessment that it could pose health risks 130 times above the agency's acceptable level.[17]

The Clinton-Gore-Browner flip-flop on the WTI facility served as a test of environmentalists' willingness to hold the new Democratic administration accountable for its commitments. It was no different from San Francisco Mayor Agnos's asking his core rent-control supporters to meet with their opponents as a condition of his fulfilling his promises to their constituency. Just as the tenants' surrender early in Agnos's term paved the way for four years of broken promises and political inaction, Clinton's betrayal on the WTI project, if left unchallenged, would set a precedent for future betrayals on other issues. Every major environmental group, along with grassroots activists, should have recognized Clinton's agenda and demanded accountability. Clinton, Gore, and Browner should have been heckled and protested at every public appearance. This confrontational approach was not the exclusive responsibility of grassroots activists or of mainstream organizations; the interests of *all* environmentalists were at stake, because the response to the WTI flip-flop would determine environmentalists' power for the balance of Clinton's term.

However, Greenpeace was the only major environmental organization that understood the far-reaching implications of Clinton's test. Grassroots activists across the country were busy working on their local issues and had no common forum in which to analyze the Clinton-Gore-Browner betrayal of East Liverpool residents and formulate a strategic response. Greenpeace, which understood the broader significance of the administration's action, took the lead in forming a coalition that used confrontational, direct-action tactics to embarrass Clinton. Greenpeace recognized that "if Clinton-Gore can break their promise on WTI—their first environmental commitment after the election, their first promise to an individual community—they can break them all." Rick Hind, legislative director of Greenpeace's toxics campaign, has learned from experience that politicians "only give you attention when you blast them, and in some cases activists must use the equivalent of a two-by-four."[18] Greenpeace and East Liverpool activists have used several tactics that prove instructive on the successful use of confrontational tactics in the national arena.

The Arkansas Chicken   Direct action against the White House began immediately after issuance of the East Liverpool incinerator's permit. In March 1993, anti-incinerator leader Terri Swearingen and seven other East Liverpool residents took the public tour of the White House. Once inside, they refused to leave until they could speak to Clinton. The eight activists were then arrested. Following this action, Swearingen and her fellow residents joined with Greenpeace for a "Put People First, Not Polluters" national bus tour. The motto perfectly captured the contradiction between Clinton's campaign bus theme of "putting people first for a change" and his sacrifice of the people of East Liverpool to benefit garbage interests. The bus tour began in April 1993 and traveled across the nation to twenty-five communities with hazardous waste incinerators. It won publicity for the East Liverpool campaign in local papers wherever it went. The tour arrived in Washington, D.C., on May 17, 1993, and more than 200 people protested in front of the White House, chanting for Al Gore to "read his book" and singing "We Shall Not Be Moved." Seventy-five people were arrested, including actor Martin Sheen and Greenpeace executive director Barbara Dudley. The *Washington Post* noted that the demonstrators seemed to be Clinton voters who never expected to march against him;[19] one East Liverpool mother of three said of Clinton, "We have got to make him more afraid of us." Terri Swearingen observed that "Clinton talks about change and about giving us an environmental presidency. And so far, where is the change? There is no difference between Clinton and Bush."[20]

The day after the protest, EPA chief Browner announced a major revision in the procedure for approving and overseeing the nation's hazardous waste incinerators. The new program halted approvals for new incinerators for eighteen months and adopted many of Swearingen's and

Greenpeace's demands. In typical Clinton administration fashion, however, the EPA exempted from the new rules the East Liverpool reactor and most of the other facilities already in the permitting process. The battle against WTI thus raged on. After Browner's announcement, the president, described by Greenpeace as the "Arkansas Chicken," consistently refused requests to visit East Liverpool. A White House rally was held on November 1, 1994 at which participants dressed like chickens and carried chickens, the better to "tell Bill Clinton that he is a chicken." Greenpeace and the residents directly affected by WTI were doing their utmost to instill political fear in the White House. Unfortunately, other national groups and grassroots activists throughout the nation have failed to mobilize around this litmus-test issue. As Greenpeace's Hind put it in April 1993, "The dirty secret is that we have been soft-pedaling this administration because we hoped that they would live up to their commitment. But it's clear that they are either totally incompetent or are on the other side."[21]

While the fight against the issuance of a permanent permit for WTI continues, the damage to the overall environmental cause is already evident. The first two years of the Clinton administration brought only one significant piece of national environmental legislation, and this measure, the California Desert Protection Act, was passed at the last minute of the 1994 congressional session solely to assist California Democratic senator Dianne Feinstein in her tough reelection battle.[22] Even worse, national environmental issues have receded to the deep background of the public agenda; public opinion polls in 1994 regularly found that fewer than 5 percent of Americans viewed such issues as among the country's most pressing problems.[23] There may not have been a single congressional race in 1994 decided on the basis of the candidates' environmental stands (which clearly contributed to the Republican landslide).

Tactical activists should be well past the point of expecting any of the national groups, with the exception of Greenpeace and at times the Sierra Club, to hold their officeholding "allies" accountable for their commitments. Nobody should be surprised by the cozy relationships between Washington, D.C.–based mainstream environmental leaders and industry lobbyists; the clamor for access compels such leaders to seek power breakfasts with Gore and Browner rather than to picket them. The real issue is why so many grassroots environmentalists have ceded control of the national environmental debate to the mainstream organizations. There is no rule requiring disputes about EPA regulations or congressional legislation to be fought within the Beltway. Members of

Congress who have failed to show leadership on environmental issues can be targeted for high-profile, direct-action media confrontations when they return to their districts. Top EPA officials such as Browner are always touring the country; inaction by the mainstream national organizations should not deter grassroots groups from picketing these officials at every stop. The greatest missed opportunity for local activists concerns Al Gore. Gore, who has rapidly become the Teflon vice president, declared in *Earth in the Balance* that "the people in a democratic society need to be prepared to hold their elected officials accountable." Gore should have been held accountable for his broken promise on the WTI facility and for his administration's entire record of environmental failure.

Presidents regularly visit the hometowns of aggressive grassroots environmental groups. Politicians like Bill Clinton who are sophisticated enough to ascend to the presidency operate under the fear-equals-respect paradigm. They only betray their friends (e.g., Lani Guinier) and only respond out of fear (e.g., Randall Robinson). They get very defensive when attacked by core support groups—witness Clinton's relations with AIDS activists, who, he believes, should support him based on promises, not results.[24] A cut-and-dried betrayal such as the Clinton administration's flip-flop on WTI should dog a president wherever he goes. When national officials break promises, grassroots environmental activists should go after them in the same way ACT UP went after the medical industry for delaying development of and access to treatments for AIDS. Politicians should not be permitted to proceed with "business as usual."

Environmentalists' reluctance to create high-profile confrontations with their ostensible officeholder allies also explains the lack of national media attention paid to environmental issues. Carl Pope, executive director of the Sierra Club, notes that media coverage of the environment has declined 50 percent in recent years. He argues that "if candidates for public office saw more environmental coverage in the media, or if they were challenged on issues at news conferences and in public forums, we would hear more about the environment in campaigns." Pope believes the media should put environmental issues back at the top of the national agenda and help to "frame the terms of the public debate."[25] But he and other environmental leaders who decry the lack of coverage fail to recognize that high-profile conflict between elected officials and protesters *creates* media coverage. The media, particularly television news programs, are far more likely to cover a colorful protest by environmentalists against a representative, senator, or federal official than a press conference about a new dioxin study. Because the arrival of top officials and officeholders almost ensures media presence in many communities, environmental activists can use public confrontations both to instill fear in politicians and to move their issue into the public arena.

Grassroots activists in East Liverpool, Brooklyn (Chapter 3), and elsewhere have shown that when environmentalists create newsworthy conflicts, the media will come. Similarly, local activists can expand national coverage of environmental issues by taking direct action against federal officeholders. As discussed in Chapter 7, local chapters of ACT UP have disrupted even presidential news conferences to demand accountability on AIDS issues; environmentalists should not hesitate to do likewise to further their goals. Confrontations at news conferences and similar tactics increase media coverage and help frame the issue as activists desire. As ACT UP founder Larry Kramer has noted, "It is controversy that helps an issue stay before the public so that more people join in the debate, in the process becoming, one hopes, politicized."[26] Environmental victories are most readily won when debates on environmental issues are framed by environmentalists, not the mainstream media.

Environmentalists can thus increase their national media coverage and political clout through confrontation on critical "local" disputes such as the East Liverpool incinerator clash. The nationalization of grassroots struggles is essential for ensuring that federal officials keep their promises to both local and national environmental groups. Environmentalists are not the only progressive constituency whose gains are deferred if not reversed by regulatory roadblocks; but other groups have overcome such obstacles by demanding accountability from their political allies. In Chapter 7 I discuss the historic fight during the 1970s to ensure that congressional legislation preventing discrimination against disabled persons would not be weakened by government regulations. This battle closely paralleled the permit fight over the East Liverpool incinerator in that it occurred in the opening months of a Democratic administration after years of conservative Republican rule. Much as environmental leaders overwhelmingly supported Bill Clinton, the leading disability rights activists had strongly supported Jimmy Carter, and some had worked on his campaign. The key difference between the two fights, however, lay in the willingness of both local and national disability rights activists to declare war on their Democratic "allies." Carter, health, education, and welfare secretary Joseph Califano, and Senate leader Alan Cranston were subjected to a level of pressure that has never been similarly directed at national Democratic leaders in battles over environmental regulatory issues. The disability rights activists won their fight, proving that the involvement of local grassroots activists in national, Washington-based campaigns not only is possible but often is essential to achieving progressive social change.

I recognize that a national environmental strategy based on local direct action against federal officials faces two chief problems. First, it has been argued that grassroots efforts to hold federal officials accountable are invariably sabotaged by national mainstream groups. A commonly cited example is the Clinton administration's backsliding on its commitment to preserve the ancient redwood forests of the Pacific Northwest. Local environmental groups, arguing for strict regulations on timber harvesting, organized an effective campaign for preservation during Clinton's "timber summit." After considering eight options for protecting the forests, however, Clinton created and selected "Option Nine," which allowed continued but reduced harvesting. Clinton's position infuriated grassroots environmentalists, but such mainstream groups as the National Wildlife Federation undermined local activists' attacks on the president by defending Option Nine as environmentally sound.

The message of Option Nine should not be that it is pointless for grassroots activists to take on the president. Rather, the willingness of national groups to cut deals with federal officials confirms the need for grassroots activists to nationalize local issues. Clinton would have had a far more difficult time prevailing on Option Nine if local environmentalists nationwide had banded together with their Oregon brethren to publicly oppose the plan. The prospect of significant grassroots opposition might have kept national groups from endorsing the flawed proposal. Local opposition groups acting alone will always face an uphill battle against the political influence of mainstream environmental organizations. Of course, grassroots activists fighting Option Nine may not have been able to use the same confrontational tactics against national officials that were employed in connection with the East Liverpool incinerator (a national awareness tour, for example). A dispute involving ancient forests in a specific locale is harder to nationalize than an incinerator controversy, as burn plants exist throughout the country.

Nevertheless, grassroots environmental groups working on issues totally unrelated to forests make a terrible mistake if they allow supposed allies to enact policies such as Option Nine without reprisal. Such inaction creates an assumption of nonaccountability that can impede the success of any local struggle. Grassroots environmental activists must make common cause with each other not simply on altruistic grounds (which is always a plus) but because it is in each organization's self-interest to impose a consistent practice of accountability on the national politicians who turn to environmentalists for support.

The prospect of a "sellout" by national environmental organizations is less of an obstacle to local pressure campaigns against national officials than is the diffuse nature of environmental politics. Environmental issues are all over the map, literally and figuratively. Such issues are so substantively and geographically diverse that there is no universal litmus test to determine who is a "pro-environmental" official. (The need for such litmus tests is addressed in the final chapter.) The process for ensuring political accountability to a multi-issue environmentalist agenda is thus unusually complex. For example, if a coastal lawmaker is a consistent opponent of offshore oil drilling, local environmentalists may be reluctant to picket him or her for voting to relax clean-air standards in Midwestern cities. Similarly, a politician who strongly supports his or her district's environmental agenda will likely be perceived as "pro-environment" regardless of votes on other environmental issues.

Applying this analysis to local activists' relationship to national political administrations, is it unrealistic, or even strategically wrong, to ask activists to jeopardize federal support on their key issue by protesting a betrayal of a remote environmental constituency? If the Clinton administration has the power to prevent construction of a dam opposed by local activists, should these activists attack Al Gore over Option Nine or the East Liverpool incinerator when he comes to town? Or should they remain silent about these issues and talk only about why Gore must stop the dam? Multi-issue organizations like the Sierra Club face this dilemma every day, which explains why they are reluctant to transform any one issue into a national crusade. As a result, unfortunately, there is no clear make-or-break environmental position—at least, none known to the electorate. This dilemma goes to the heart of environmental activists' and organizations' strategic shortcomings in dealing with elected officials. Once activists accept that politicians are motivated by fear, not friendship, it follows that the gains grassroots activists wrest from politicians should not be understood as political "favors." To use the example above, the administration is not going to decide to prevent the dam because Al Gore was treated well by local activists; on the contrary, such treatment is likely to have the opposite effect. If Gore, or any other top federal official, decides to support the environmentalists' position, he will do so because of a political calculation based largely on the fear of reprisal. A politician who fears adverse political consequences will act in accordance with environmentalists, even if they launch public attacks on issues such as Option Nine or the East Liverpool incinerator. In fact, such protests can strengthen local campaigns on an issue by forcing officials to prove that, contrary to the protesters' charges, they really are committed to the environmental cause. Local activists must apply a similar analysis before supporting a member of Congress whose "pro-environmental" stance does not extend outside the district or state. The diversity of environmental issues can therefore help local environmentalists, but only if they create a "fear and loathing" relationship with the national officials who look to them for support.

Of course, there is an alternative approach for environmentalists who feel uncomfortable engaging in public protests against their purported allies: avoid electing Democrats. Ronald Reagan's appointment of James Watt as secretary of the interior created a membership bonanza for national environmental groups that did not end until Democrat Bill Clinton's 1992 victory. Mainstream environmental groups rarely hesitated to attack Watt or Reagan, and their conflict with Republican presidential administrations put environmental issues at the forefront of national policy debates. A similar membership surge followed the November 1994 Republican sweep, and the Congressional assault on environmental legislation in 1995 brought loud protests from even the most accommodating mainstream groups. Having Republicans in power eliminates the cross-pressures that deter many environmentalists from holding Democrats accountable. Republicans may be less likely to take environmentalists for granted and in some cases will actively court their support as a strategy to erode their opponents' traditional base. Such factors partially explain why the last significant federal environmental measure, the Clean Air Act of 1990, became law under the Republican Bush administration. Electing Republicans is obviously a foolish strategy for enhancing environmental protections. Yet if grassroots environmentalists persist in letting Democratic officials betray commitments without protest, then electing Democrats is unlikely to advance the environmental agenda significantly.

Some activists have urged the creation of Green parties. This idea makes more strategic sense than aligning with Republicans, though it sidesteps the critical need for environmentalists to demand accountability of Democrats. The obvious problems with a Green Party strategy are: first, lack of money; second, a public and media consensus favoring the two national parties; and third, the poor track record of progressive third parties despite declining public confidence in the Democrats. A non-Green but avowedly pro-environment third party has achieved great success in Vermont, and a strong Green Party candidate ran unsuccessfully against a Republican and an incumbent Democrat in the 1994 New

Mexico governor's race.[27] The creation of a meaningful Green Party alternative would require the emergence of a compelling environmental issue that the two major parties refuse to address. For example, a proposed water project that would harm rivers and wetlands across an entire state could lead to a successful Green Party effort if, despite broad public opposition, the two major-party candidates endorsed the plan. Such an issue did not emerge in the 1994 New Mexico gubernatorial race, in which the Green Party platform emphasized a mix of populist proposals that emphasized but were not centered on environmental concerns.[28] The presence of ongoing Green parties could make Democrats more responsive to environmental concerns, or it could simply increase the clout of mainstream groups at the expense of local environmental activists. The Sierra Club's New Mexico chapter endorsed the incumbent Democratic governor despite his poor environmental record; few, if any, mainstream environmental groups are likely to renounce their allegiance to Democrats or liberal Republicans and support the Greens. Because the public associates such well-known groups as the Sierra Club with pro-environment positions, such organizations' unwillingness to bolt the Democrats is yet another factor hampering Green Party efforts.

The Grand Illusion   Environmental activists reluctant to attack Democratic federal officials for their betrayals must at the least blow the whistle on the passage of what Greider calls "hollow laws." Such laws allow legislators to wear a false pro-environmental mantle while creating the potentially dangerous illusion that Congress has addressed a critical problem. Hollow laws can prevent the enactment of real solutions; Congress will not quickly revisit an issue it has ostensibly resolved. Grassroots activists are in a particularly strong position to undercut such phony, politician-created environmental "victories." When the media, pursuing a local angle, ask grassroots groups how this new federal law will help their efforts, activists can reveal the hoax behind the hype. Ideally, the hollow measure can be exposed through such means prior to enactment; if it does pass, the activists' post-"victory" assessment may greatly affect public attitudes about the measure. The willingness to expose hollow laws also requires a "fear and loathing" approach toward officials, as politicians do not appreciate having a high-profile piece of legislation credibly undermined. Exposing the hollowness of the law also weakens the credibility of the mainstream environmental groups that joined the politician's charade. If a hollow bill is attacked early enough in the process, grassroots opposition can significantly improve the measure. For example, in January 1990 New York governor Mario Cuomo, still at the height of his popularity, announced he would place a multi-million-dollar environmental bond on the November ballot. At the press conference announcing the bond, Cuomo was surrounded by representatives of all but one of New York's leading environmental groups. But the mutual lovefest between Cuomo and the environmentalists was interrupted by the New York Public Interest Research Group (NYPIRG), which protested the small allocation of funds for recycling. Media coverage of the event ended up focusing on the Cuomo-NYPIRG dispute. NYPIRG's willingness to attack a Democratic governor and leading presidential aspirant got results; the amount of money included in the bond for recycling was eventually increased nearly fourfold.

Declaring an elected official an ally when you know the law he or she sponsors will not be enforced only sends a message of powerlessness and cowardice; such tactics will never achieve social change. Nor should such environmentalists receive sympathy when, predictably, their legislative "achievement" is undermined in the regulatory process. Environmental groups' legislative approach to officials recalls Charlie Brown's annual failure to anticipate that Lucy will remove the football as he approaches to kick; after enough betrayals, the groups have only themselves to blame for continuing to play by the same rules.

CONFRONTING BUREAUCRATS: TACTICAL ACTIVISM IN SCHOOLS

When tactical activists target elected officials over issues within the officials' control, the strategic ground rules are clear. Parents seeking to improve their children's schools, however, face a more complex challenge. The vast majority of school districts (New York City is the rare exception) are officially governed by elected school boards. Board members, typically professional educators or parents of school-age children, put in long hours of unpaid labor on behalf of the schools and set district policy. However, an unelected superintendent is the primary shaper and implementer of the scholastic program. The superintendent heads a bureaucracy of managers, administrators, consultants, accountants, and other staff who are not directly accountable to the elected board. The superintendent and his or her staff usually create policy options on a particular issue and then present the board with a systematic analysis of the costs and benefits of each alternative. The elected board cannot run the district on a day-to-day basis, so it must rely on the superintendent to carry out its decisions. The board must also rely on school administrators' objectivity in gathering facts and framing policy choices.

Other critical factors heighten the power of school superintendents and top administrators over elected officials. Unlike mayors or governors, school superintendents presumably are chosen for their professional skills rather than their popularity with voters. Although superintendents' decisions inherently reflect their political and philosophical outlook, their status as professional educators gives their viewpoints a patina of scientific objectivity. They are supposed to be above the political fray, giving them an advantage over the elected school boards for whom they work. After all, there are no special educational requirements for school board nominees; in most cases a candidate must simply be a registered voter. School superintendents commonly have doctorates in education and extensive professional education experience. This disparity in qualifications for making judgments about school policy facilitates board deference to superintendent decisions.

Although elected school board members are the only people in the district directly accountable to the public, boards are often negatively viewed as political bodies. Board members who challenge a superintendent's policy on behalf of their constituency open themselves to charges of meddling in school administration or of playing politics with our schools. Unfortunately, such concerns often are justified. However, the meddling that has compromised the credibility of school boards has primarily involved personnel rather than policy issues. Many school districts employ thousands of people, and some board members act as if their election entitles them to secure jobs for friends or relatives. The public may grudgingly accept that overtly political officials will distribute patronage jobs, but the practice does not sit well with parents concerned about their own children's education. Once a pattern emerges of school board intervention in district personnel decisions, parents understandably begin demanding that the board stop interfering with the superintendent. Board meddling in personnel matters can result in the restriction of board—hence, public—control over school policy issues.

Parents seeking to improve their children's schools thus face different obstacles from those facing other social change activists. The tactic of focusing and maintaining pressure on elected officials has less value when the officials are constrained strongly from intervening in policy decisions. Unlike local, state, or federal representatives, individual school board members, no matter how committed, rarely have the authority to hold special investigative hearings on matters of particular constituent concern. Nor do they have personal staff available to evaluate and influence policy. School boards do have the power to terminate their superintendent's employment, but a board that discharges its administrative chief over every disagreement will be thrown out of office by angry voters. Although school board members have less power than other politicians, parents must still utilize their relationship with these officials to achieve their goals. Challenging entrenched school bureaucracies after a long day of work, shopping, and child care is a daunting task, but models for success exist. I have been most impressed by the tactics and strategies used by parents at the Fratney School in Milwaukee, Wisconsin. Confronted by a school superintendent unsympathetic to their plans, strong opposition from district administrators, and an elected school board unaccustomed to challenging superintendent decisions, the Neighbors for a New Fratney succeeded in establishing the school of their dreams.

La Escuela Fratney: Using School Boards to Make Bureaucracies Work The idea of the Fratney School ("La Escuela Fratney") emerged in late 1987, after the Milwaukee school district announced the closing of an antiquated school building in northeast Milwaukee.[29] The neighborhood around the school was one of the few racially integrated working-class communities in the city. Neighbors for a New Fratney, a small neighborhood group comprising minority leaders, parents, and teachers, formed soon after the closure and proposed a new type of school. The "new Fratney" would be governed by a council of parents and teachers and would use innovative and progressive teaching methods. Because the community had a large Latino population, the proposed school would also be two-way bilingual and multicultural.

The ability of the neighbors to formulate a comprehensive and ambitious school proposal on such short notice failed to excite district administrators. They had their own plan for the vacant building: creation of an "Exemplary Teaching Center," where veteran instructors would coach teachers having performance difficulties. The experienced teachers, or "master instructors," would supervise troubled teachers, who would work with classes for six-week training sessions. Although the district's proposal might have benefited problem teachers, parents understandably were not thrilled about having their children taught by a steady flow of the district's worst instructors. The parents also saw no reason to install the training center in a neighborhood whose demographics favored the creation of a bilingual school.

The Milwaukee school board scheduled a public hearing to obtain community input on the proposal. The board generally backed the actions of its superintendent, an African-American with support in Milwaukee's large black community. To get the board to question the superintendent's plan, the neighbors needed a large turnout at the public hearing. Fortunately, and this is not always the case in school-reform efforts, the Fratney community included people with experience in community organizing. Residents circulated flyers announcing the meeting, resulting in a large turnout. The school board, seeing the parents' commitment, ordered the superintendent to meet with the Fratney group to work out a mutually acceptable compromise. The school board's willingness to address the parents' concerns was an important victory; the board rarely questioned the superintendent's decision on curriculum issues. Moreover, the school board's action sent a message to the community that mobilizing and organizing paid off; all too many elected officials prefer sending the opposite signal.

The superintendent, unaccustomed to challenges to his authority, took literally the board's directive that a mutually acceptable solution be found. He put forth a proposal that combined the teacher training center with the New Fratney proposal. The parents and teachers advocating new Fratney were mystified by the superintendent's plan. The teacher center would be run directly from the central administration office, whereas the proposed new Fratney would be controlled by a parent-teacher council. The issue of school control could not be compromised: Fratney could be run either by the district or by the council, not by both. At the meeting to work out a compromise plan, the district administrators seemed genuinely threatened by the parent-teacher coalition. Although the administrators were employed to carry out the dictates of the public through assignments from the elected school board, district officials felt their perspectives should predominate over those expressed by their constituents, the parents. Of course, the district bureaucrats did not view themselves as accountable to parents or to an electorate; their duty was to fulfill the superintendent's agenda.

The New Fratney representatives left the meeting astonished at the district's inability to recognize the obvious advantages of their proposal. They also discerned a dynamic that would prove extremely helpful in their campaign. The superintendent, who opposed the New Fratney plan, chaired the meeting, and other administrators present clearly tried to avoid saying anything that would cause them problems with their boss. This concern was manifested in their tentative speaking style and their formal deference to the superintendent. After the meeting, three district staff members secretly told the Fratney group that their proposal was sound and that compromise should be avoided. The New Fratney activists thus learned they had friends in the administration who could serve as a strategic "fifth column" in their battle against the bureaucracy.

The superintendent's failure to reach compromise with the Fratney group forced the school board to choose between the two plans. The board recently had expressed support for site-based school management and had received much criticism from African-American parents regarding the school bureaucracy's refusal to consider parent input. Despite the favorable political backdrop and a school board sensitive to parent concerns, however, the neighbors of New Fratney understood that the board's tradition of support for its superintendent did not bode well for them. They thus were surprised when the board not only voted in favor of their proposal but ordered the central office to cooperate with their efforts.

The board's action only began, rather than ended, the teacher/parent campaign for a new Fratney. Just as congressional enactment of environmental laws simply shifts the focus of the battle from elected officials to regulators, school reform requires significant bureaucratic involvement. The forces that lose in the political arena remain poised to achieve victory in the administrative forum. Would the dream of the new Fratney go the way of the never-enforced Clean Water Act, or would the neighbors apply the necessary tactics and strategies for success?

The parent-teacher coalition made all the right moves, despite being surprised by the administration's repeated attempts to sabotage their plans. Part of the coalition's success came from its boldness in confronting bureaucratic opposition. For example, in the weeks following the school board's decision, no meetings were scheduled between the Fratney group and district administrators. The administration did, however, set up its own meeting to plan the new Fratney without informing the parent-teacher coalition. When the Fratney group heard about the gathering, it sent a parent to attend. The parent's presence surprised the administrators, who assumed they had successfully kept their meeting date secret. Once their artifice was uncovered, they had no choice but to begin the process of joint meetings.

The Fratney group also succeeded because of its willingness to use grassroots mobilizing to attack bureaucratic opposition. When the community recommended the hiring of a bilingual principal for the new Fratney, the administration responded by recommending a woman who had worked only in suburban school districts and who spoke no Spanish. The candidate did speak German, however, so the administration presumably had satisfied the "bilingual" requirement. In the face of such obvious sabotage, the Fratney neighbors could have grown weary of fighting and simply accepted the district's choice. Instead, the neighbors attacked the administration's selection as an insult to the Latino community. The Neighbors for a New Fratney mobilized parents to oppose the candidate, comparing their struggle to that of students at Gallaudet College for the Deaf in Washington, D.C. who opposed the hiring of a non-hearing-impaired president. Meanwhile, the Milwaukee schools had hired a new school superintendent (his predecessor had departed voluntarily for reasons unrelated to the Fratney controversy). Parent attendance at school board meetings, combined with community outcry, forced the new superintendent to reverse his predecessor's decision and reject the candidate. The district then hired for Fratney an interim principal who was acceptable to the community.

The school board's hiring of a superintendent less hostile to the neighbors did not lessen opposition among anti-Fratney district administrators. Resentful over the intrusion of parents into their domain, the district's bureaucrats impeded progress toward the new Fratney at every turn. The parent-teacher group had to fight to obtain budgetary information and clerical support; the administration even refused to provide new desks to the school. Purchase requisitions went unprocessed, leaving the new Fratney with no books until two days before the opening of school. Again, the neighbors responded by playing hardball. After their requests for new desks were repeatedly denied, the neighbors told the administration they had switched their position and wanted to keep the old desks so they could show the press how the administration was refusing to support the new Fratney. Faced with this threat, the district finally ordered the furniture.

Shortly before the new Fratney was to open, the neighbors noticed a change in the administration's attitude. The new superintendent and his assistant had made it clear to district bureaucrats that the new Fratney was to be supported, not opposed. The superintendent visited the new Fratney on the first day of school and concluded it was a "model" of school reform. He also emphasized the need for significant parental involvement for such reform to succeed.

What does the success of the Neighbors for a New Fratney demonstrate about applying tactical activism to our schools? First, the essential element to their success was their development of an agenda, along with tactics and strategies for implementation. The neighbors' ability to develop quickly a comprehensive, innovative, and realistic proposal for a bilingual school for the Fratney site was all-important. Had the neighbors simply opposed the superintendent's plan without offering their own program, the school board would not have had the alternative it needed to buck its appointed leader. However, the neighbors' creation and advancement of a consensus proposal for a new Fratney is both impressive and atypical. Unlike many other progressive social change issues, schools often generate widely disparate prescriptions among activists. Although progressive parents generally support increased public school funding, less school bureaucracy, reduced class size, and a nonsexist, multicultural curriculum, there is not always agreement on how to achieve these goals.

Further, in a period of declining public school budgets nationwide, parents' primary involvement with schools often comes through fighting cuts to popular programs. Some parents organize to keep art or music; others lobby for teacher's aides or enrichment programs. Parents are so involved fighting to keep what little they have that proactive planning toward a common objective is ignored. Many parents also lack the time to engage in the type of extensive discussions and meetings that successful tactical activism requires. The Neighbors for a New Fratney were fortunate to have a core group of extremely committed parents and teachers, and participation increased as word got around that something important was actually getting done. When parents are limited to a defensive posture, a sense of momentum never emerges, and a lasting reform organization cannot grow. As long as the debate is framed around budget cuts rather than a specific, parent-initiated plan for reform, business as usual will continue in our schools.

The second lesson from New Fratney is that grassroots organizing tactics are essential to overcome bureaucratic sabotage. If the Neighbors for a New Fratney had followed the strategy used by Washington-based environmental groups against the EPA or Interior Department, the new Fratney would not exist today. The neighbors adamantly refused to play along with bureaucratic stalling and did not hesitate to contact school board members and/or the press when help was needed. True, the neighbors were not up against major corporate interests. Nor did they need to appear "reasonable" to maintain their bargaining position on other issues or to ensure insider access. However, the neighbors' campaign was distinguished by a ferocity of purpose that would likely have prevailed in any arena. The neighbors overcame the hostility and sabotage of the school district bureaucracy because they passionately believed in their cause and would not stop short of success. In response, the district bureaucrats acted like the Wizard of Oz when Toto pulled away his curtain: after all their tricks failed, they stood powerless in the face of parent-teacher unity.[30]

Unlike Washington-based environmental organizations, which confront bureaucrats with paid staff and experts, school reform groups rely almost entirely on volunteer parents and teachers who are directly affected by the outcome. Most of those who participated in and supported the Neighbors for a New Fratney were simply parents motivated by concern for their children's education. Milwaukee's school board members, like most elected officials, were particularly responsive to pressure from those actually impacted by their decisions. Every organizer understands this principle, but few social change organizations have salaried staff responsible for organizing parents to improve schools. This situation must change. With all the foundation and academic money being spent to research how to improve our schools, the need for paid parent organizers who will apply the rules of tactical activism to school reform goes unrecognized. Funding such organizers would result in the creation of ongoing parent organizations that can develop proactive agendas and strategies for improving public schools. For some reason our society believes that parents, who have less time than most people to do political work, can really influence schools without technical and organizing assistance. Tactical activists know what it takes to prevail in other arenas; why shouldn't school reform be given equivalent resources?

The answer may be that school board members, like other elected officials, do not cherish the creation of such politically independent parent organizations. Such organizations would hold board members accountable and might advocate policies that would empower parents at the board's expense. In the past decade, hundreds of school districts, including those in New York City, Chicago, and Denver, have initiated school-based management councils. The councils are designed to give parents increased responsibility for textbook selection, curriculum, and the overall running of schools. However, a 1993 study by the Parents Coalition for Education in New York City found that "parents play a minor role, at best" in the management of public schools. The group's director concluded that, despite the rhetoric to the contrary, school-based management councils do not ensure sufficient parent input.

As the Fratney experience amply demonstrates, school superintendents are even less inclined than school boards to increase parents' role in setting school policies. Neither superintendents nor school boards are likely to ask foundations and governments to fund paid parent organizers for school reform. This attitude is evidenced by the lack of training among parents seeking greater school involvement and by the fact that only Minnesota, Virginia, and Iowa require elementary school teachers to be trained in parent involvement.[31] Therefore, in the absence of a Fratney-type crisis that forces people to unify around a common goal, multi-issue social change organizations may have to redirect resources toward schools for serious reform efforts to succeed. Fortunately, this process has already begun. The Association of Community Organizations for Reform Now (ACORN), the country's largest grassroots organizing group, has recognized that schools are a leading concern of their predominantly low-income, minority constituency. ACORN worked primarily with African-American parents in Brooklyn to transform a former furniture store into a school for their kids. The parents worked collaboratively with district officials in hiring the school's nine teachers and principal. As in the New Fratney campaign, parental anger channeled into social change activism resulted in the creation of a model school.

Some progressive activists see a danger in increasing parents' role in school policy, fearing this will lead to a fundamentalist Christian or right-wing takeover of the schools. As evidence for this thesis, such activists cite the 1993 discharge of Joseph Fernandez as head of the New York City school system. Fernandez was ousted for advocating a multicultural "rainbow curriculum" designed in part to increase tolerance of lesbians and gays. The Catholic Church joined right-wing Christian fundamentalists to create the pressure leading to the school board's vote against Fernandez; the coalition also had mixed success in electing a slate of candidates to school district institutions.

Progressives should not capitulate to bureaucratic control of schools for fear that conservative attitudes will win out. Social change activists in New York City rose to the challenge and created their own successful slate of school district candidates. Upon Chancellor Fernandez's departure, he was replaced by the equally progressive Ramon Cortines. In the South and in rural school districts, the courts or state legislative or administrative bodies can rein in fundamentalist attacks on schools. Opposing increased parental participation in school issues is like opposing democracy because the process enables Jesse Helms to get elected to the U.S. Senate. Fundamentalist parents have been proactive on the school front, and progressives can and must do likewise if we are to ensure a better future for our children.

Coalition Activism

ROUNDING UP THE UNUSUAL SUSPECTS

I am a great believer in coalition politics. The sight of social change organizations accomplishing goals by working with other organizations and constituencies is wonderful to behold. Unfortunately, building and maintaining activist coalitions in the 1990s has become harder than ever. The absence of effective coalition building has deprived social change activists of what often represents *the* strategic key to success. It is therefore critical for tactical activists to understand how, when, and why coalitions should be used and to draw important lessons from successful activist coalitions forged among even the most disparate constituencies.

Although the term *coalition* can be used in many different ways, activist coalitions typically combine two or more organizations in pursuit of at least one mutual objective. Some coalitions involve organizations whose members are actively involved in an issue; others constitute a paper list of groups whose participation may not extend beyond the endorsement of a particular cause. Historically, progressive activists have identified strongly with coalition building. From the worldwide coalition of anti-Fascist activists fighting for a free Spain in the 1930s to the broad antiwar coalitions of the 1960s and 1970s, social change organizations have allied in common struggles. The signature chant—"The people, united, will never be defeated"—reflects the left's almost spiritual faith in coalition politics.

The question thus emerges: if activists preach and practice unity, why are progressive causes so often defeated? Are "the people" not united, or are they not united with the right combination of other people to prevail? The simple answer to both questions is yes. Progressive social change activists often fail to unify; more important, when they do unify, they often fail to create a broad or powerful enough coalition to obtain success.

THE PROBLEM OF UNITY

Many social change organizations do not believe in working in coalitions. Perhaps the most prominent example is the highly regarded Industrial Areas Foundation-Texas. IAF Texas is a spinoff of Saul Alinsky's original Chicago-based Industrial Areas Foundation. Like Alinsky's "back of the yards" organization in Chicago, IAF Texas was largely created through parish-based organizing efforts. The hundreds of families who comprise IAF Texas are overwhelmingly Latino, Catholic, and working class. The organization's success at empowering and mobilizing its members has improved the quality of life for its constituency and brought national acclaim.

In his laudatory discussion of the group in *Who Will Tell the People: The Betrayal of American Democracy,* William Greider makes a point about coalitions that I have heard repeated time and time again: "IAF leaders see . . . hollowness in many [coalitions]: Real people are absent from the ranks. The IAF leaders are also wary of using their people as fodder in someone else's crusade."[1] These comments reflect legitimate and very common concerns about coalitions felt by organizers of membership-based social change organizations. These concerns raise four important issues. First, participation in coalitions may enable those without a political base to use yours to pursue their own agenda. Second, coalitions may allow other organizations to claim credit for your work. Third, coalitions may hamper organization building. Groups seeking foundation support need to show a track record of accomplishments; press clippings crediting a coalition rather than specific groups could impair fundraising efforts and ultimately an organization's survival. Finally, coalitions require individual groups to cede control of strategy and tactics. The need to compromise on tactics, as well as on style and substance, makes some groups wary of joining coalitions.

When leaders of groups such as IAF express such doubts about coalitions, it becomes easy to understand why many organizations view unity suspiciously. However, IAF Texas members also acknowledge that forming coalitions with non-Latino working people in Texas is essential for the accomplishment of significant political, economic, and social goals. Greider, citing IAF Texas leader Ernesto Cortes, Jr., writes, "Cortes does not think the IAF Texas network will achieve full status as a major power in the state until it succeeds at creating a presence among the white blue-collar workers in Eastern Texas and elsewhere—people who have common economic interests but are in social conflict with blacks and Hispanics."[2]

The lesson from IAF and similar groups regarding coalitions is clear. Social change organizations that can fulfill their agendas on their own do not need coalitions. When the agenda broadens, however, success requires expansion of the political base through coalition building.

With Whom Should "The People" Unite?   After social change organizations recognize that their agenda is best fulfilled by working in coalition with other groups, the question arises: With whom should they unify? Claude Rains's line in *Casablanca* about "rounding up the usual suspects" often seems to apply—the usual suspects (i.e., national progressive organizations) are regularly rounded up into coalitions for or against a particular cause. In many cases, the coalition's existence does not extend beyond the listing of organizations in a *New York Times* advertisement on the issue. Many of the groups frequently included on these lists lack a viable political base, which may explain why they are so eager to join coalitions whereas groups such as IAF Texas, which have such a base, are wary of such involvements. A similar "smoke and mirrors" approach occurs at the state and local levels, as coalitions rapidly come and go without regard to the ideological uniformity (or lack thereof) among the diverse organizations and individuals named.

There is nothing wrong with creating a coalition of groups identified with the political left. Such an amalgam can effectively pressure elected officials and organizations who are sensitive to progressive constituencies. Unfortunately, in the United States of the 1990s, all too few politicians, government bodies, or corporations exhibit such sensitivity. A coalition of groups with similar constituencies often does not bring greater results than likely would be achieved through the actions of a single group, which further explains why tactically sophisticated organizations like IAF Texas disdain such involvements.

The great value of coalitions lies in their ability to propel to success groups who could not prevail on their own. To gain this advantage, an activist often must find a basis for partnership with organizations whose culture, politics, and overall agenda differ greatly from his or her own but whose interests on a particular issue coincide. Forming coalitions with groups you may oppose on other issues requires the highest level of tactical expertise. The process involves defining the essential point of mutual interest and creating a structure for decisionmaking and accountability. An astonishing example of tactical coalition building at the grassroots level took place when Hasidic Jews and Catholic families joined forces to fight construction of a waste incinerator plant in the Brooklyn Navy Yard. The ability of these two constituencies, long at each other's throats over distribution of public resources, to unify for a common goal shows what can be accomplished through coalition politics.

An Alliance for the Ages The Williamsburg neighborhood of Brooklyn, New York, is primarily inhabited by two ethnic groups: the Satmar sect of Hasidic Jews, a deeply religious group whose customs, practices, and appearance hearken back to earlier centuries; and Latinos, primarily Puerto Rican and Dominican Catholics.[3] The fittingly named Division Avenue separates largely Hasidic northern Williamsburg from the primarily Latino south side. These disparate groups share one of the most environmentally dangerous neighborhoods in all of New York. Williamsburg is part of the city's "lead belt," and the Latino section is home to the Radiac Corporation, a multimillion-dollar business that serves as a storage and transfer facility for toxic, flammable, and radioactive waste. Radiac sits adjacent to homes and businesses, less than a block away from a public school serving more than 1,000 local children. The facility could not meet current minimum buffer-zone requirements, and its federal permit has long expired. No environmental impact study has ever been done for Radiac.

The Brooklyn Navy Yard incinerator project was conceived in 1979 after state environmental officials started pressuring New York City to stop using the world's largest landfill, Fresh Kills on Staten Island, as its exclusive repository for trash. The unlined and unlicensed Fresh Kills had become a threat to local waterways, and Mayor Ed Koch had proposed building at least five massive incinerators, one in each borough, to replace it. Koch's response to landfill problems reflected a national trend. Incinerators seemed like an easy way to get rid of trash and create energy at the same time. The Brooklyn Navy Yard incinerator was supposed to generate 465 million kilowatt hours of electricity a year.[4] The flaw in the logic of incinerators, however, is that almost everything that is safe to burn is better off recycled. Burning toxic and nonrecyclable materials reduces them to an ash that endangers people's health. Moreover, incinerators emit hazardous chemicals into the atmosphere, including lead, mercury, and dioxin.

Although the incinerator issue had been fought throughout the 1980s, widespread opposition to the project did not galvanize until Mayor David Dinkins announced in September 1991 that the city was going forward with its plan to build a fifty-five-story incinerator at the Brooklyn Navy Yard. The incinerator would burn 3,000 tons of trash daily, emit half a ton of lead each year, and be Brooklyn's largest stationary source of nitrogen oxide (a component of smog), according to a NYPIRG analysis. The Environmental Protection Agency has determined that lead is a "probable human carcinogen." The particular impact of lead poisoning on children is well recognized, and the U.S. Public Health Service estimates that one out of six children nationwide is at risk because of lead exposure. With studies of the Williamsburg lead belt already having found high concentrations, the proposed new source of lead sent alarm throughout the community.

In addition to sharing environmental problems, the Hasidim and Latinos of Williamsburg are competitors for what scarce public resources flow to the community. These resources fund various services, including schools, police, and, most important, housing. Historically, community activists from each group have felt that the other got more than its proportionate share of subsidized housing units in the neighborhood. In an area with high housing costs and limited incomes, access to government housing subsidies is highly desired. Both groups have rapidly growing populations. Because they do not use cars or public transit on the Sabbath, the Hasidim must live within walking distance of their synagogues. Latinos' resentment toward the Hasidim over the housing issue has led to violence between members of the two groups and would seem to make partnership on any issue unimaginable.

Concern about children, however, has a way of making anything possible. The culture and traditions of both groups are children- and family-focused, and both groups have a long-term commitment to the community. Because the proposed waste incinerator would add another environmental risk to children in a community already beset with such problems, the Hasidic community strongly opposed the project. The Latinos also recognized the environmental risks in their community. A Latino organization called "El Puente" (The Bridge) runs a community development center that includes a clinic, a high school, and various programs, many for youth. As part of its program to improve community health and inspire youth service and leadership, El Puente started a "Toxic Avengers" project designed to close down or limit the scope of activity at Radiac. The Toxic Avengers had discovered that, in the event of a fire at Radiac, a poisonous cloud of smoke and gas could travel as far as four miles in only thirty minutes. The deadly fumes could do severe harm to eyes and skin, inflict neurological damage, and cause birth defects in the children of victims.

In 1991, the Toxic Avengers obtained a state hearing on Radiac. In planning outreach for the event, the group decided to ask the Hasidim to participate. Rabbi David Niederman, who had recently become executive director of United Jewish Organizations (UJO) of Williamsburg, agreed to come to a planning meeting after receiving assurances that he would be safe. Thus, in May 1991 Niederman walked through a Roman Catholic church into the offices of El Puente and offered to help lead a march through Latino streets to publicize the Radiac hearing. The young people from the Toxic Avengers wanted to work with the Hasidim on environmental issues and were deeply impressed by the rabbi's offer. So astounding was Niederman's gesture that El Puente founder Luis Garden Acosta compared Niederman's visit to Nixon's first trip to China; thus was the necessary contact made for the two often-warring groups to work in coalition against the incinerator plant.[5]

Niederman's UJO represents the secular arm of the Hasidic community. To outsiders, the Hasidim seem internally homogeneous; in truth, the Hasidic community is no different from other religious groups, whose outward unity often masks internal differences and debate. There are two main Hasidic sects in Brooklyn: the Satmars, who make up about 40 percent of the population of Williamsburg; and the better-known Lubavitchers, who live chiefly in another area of Brooklyn at a distance from the incinerator. The Satmars eschew television, radio, and all secular newspapers. Their community offers no organized coeducational activities for children after kindergarten, and their strong religious doctrine prevents them from socializing with the non-Orthodox even in their own community. The Satmars are known for their vehement opposition to Zionism and to the state of Israel itself. They believe it was a sin to create a Jewish state prior to the coming of the Messiah. The Satmars' position directly conflicts with that of their rival, pro-Zionist Hasidic sect, the Lubavitchers.

Upon becoming UJO's director, Niederman tried a new approach for addressing Hasidic-Latino relations in Williamsburg. Niederman had been primarily involved in international Jewish refugee work for most of his career and only recently had become significantly involved in local community affairs. His background of negotiating with often hostile world leaders to achieve freedom for Jews in areas such as the Middle East gave him a perspective on international and ethnic cooperation that helped him in his work at the UJO.

In 1985 the Satmars turned out 15,000 people for a march across the Brooklyn Bridge in an attempt to prevent the city from signing a contract for the incinerator. Their effort had failed to kill the project, however, and it seemed clear they would need additional political allies to prevail. Nearly ten years into the fight, Niederman and his Hasidic constituency sought to broaden the anti-incinerator campaign from primarily the Satmars and NYPIRG to include Williamsburg's dominant population group, the Latinos.

Luis Garden Acosta, the founder and leader of El Puente, spearheaded Latino efforts to build a coalition with the Hasidim. Garden Acosta, a health administrator, had helped develop the idea of "environmental racism," which emphasizes the government's policy of disproportionately imposing environmental hazards on minority communities. He frequently expressed the view that the Williamsburg Latinos' culture included an appreciation for nature and a connection to the land. Moreover, El Puente had led community struggles against the Hasidim over education and police, giving the group the credibility necessary to work on the incinerator issue with a constituency many Latinos distrusted. Like Rabbi Niederman, Garden Acosta brought a worldview to his local activities. His perspective on global unity led him to reach out to the Polish, Italians, and other white ethnics of Williamsburg so as to make the anti-incinerator coalition as inclusive as possible. El Puente's creation of the Toxic Avengers to fight for environmental justice brought the group widespread publicity even before Garden Acosta entered into a coalition with Niederman and the UJO. Despite Garden Acosta's awareness of environmental issues, however, NYPIRG and the UJO had limited contact with the Latino community around the waste incincrator proposal prior to 1991. Niederman clearly recognized that in a community whose majority Latino population resented the Hasidim's allocation of resources, the UJO would have to make the initial public overture to begin the coalition process.

In opposing the incinerator, Williamsburg's low-income residents found themselves up against powerful moneyed interests. Wall Street was eager for the business it would get when the city issued the bonds necessary to pay for construction of the incinerator. Among Wall Street investment firms with a stake in the incinerator was Lazzard Freres, whose Felix Rohatyn was New York City's most powerful and influential investment banker. Rohatyn's power over municipal credit and city budgets made ambitious elected officials extremely reluctant to oppose him. Wall Street firms were major sources of campaign funding for local and state politicians, who could then support projects like the incinerator without having received funds from the project sponsor. Business groups strongly supported the incinerator, as did unions eager to benefit from the project's construction jobs. The *New York Times* took a vehemently pro-incinerator editorial stance, joining various other power brokers in the city. The law firm retained by Wheelabrator, the company hoping to build the incinerator, made major contributions to local and state legislative campaigns, including $45,000 for Rudolph Giuliani's 1993 mayoral race.

The politically savvy Satmars, however, had the other kind of capital politicians can't live without: votes. They had delivered a large vote for David Dinkins in a close mayoral race in 1989 because of his stated opposition to the incinerator. Candidate Dinkins had promised to delay a decision on the incinerator project until 1993 and had won strong support among Brooklyn voters for his stand. His reversal on the issue in the fall of 1991 brought Mayor Dinkins public condemnation from the Satmars, Latinos, and other incinerator opponents. Niederman told the *New York Times* on September 8, 1991, that "this plan repudiates everything that had been told to us by mayoral candidate Dinkins and suggests that cynical politics as usual is the engine driving this decision." Environmental groups expressed similar feelings of betrayal and were alarmed that the mayor's new pro-incinerator stance appeared to be coupled with abandonment of the city's commitment to step up recycling. In November 1990 the Dinkins administration had frozen citywide recycling efforts, and now it appeared that trash incineration had replaced recycling as the centerpiece of the city's solid waste management program. Further fueling suspicion over the decision was the fact that Dinkins's top deputy mayor, Norman Steisel, was widely viewed as Wall Street's representative in the administration. Steisel had been Koch's city sanitation commissioner when the incinerator project was first proposed.

In a show of political arrogance and foolishness, Dinkins did not inform the Williamsburg activists about his decision in advance. Instead, the UJO, NYPIRG, and El Puente learned of the city's action through a front-page story in the *New York Times*.[6] The Dinkins bombshell was announced only two weeks prior to a New York state legislative joint hearing regarding environmental impacts on racial minority and low-income communities. The Brooklyn Navy Yard trash incinerator fit perfectly into the proceedings. When the Koch administration and its corporate allies had sought an incinerator site in the 1970s, the Brooklyn Navy Yard had seemed ideal. The city owned the land, and the site was not slated for gentrification or office development. Finally, and perhaps most important, the Navy Yard was located in the type of economically depressed minority community regularly subjected to environmental hazards.[7]

In response to Dinkins's announcement, Garden Acosta and Niederman held a joint press conference attacking the city's attempt to impose an environmental hazard on yet another minority, low-income community. Ludovic Blain III, chairman of the board of NYPIRG, placed the incinerator proposal in the context of the 1967 Kerner Commission report detailing our nation's movement toward a society of separate and unequal racial groups. The three groups' joint participation in a high-profile event solidified their unity in opposing the incinerator.

The press conference spurred a rush of grassroots activity against the project. In January 1992 a standing-room-only crowd of more than 500 residents from the nearby Clinton Hill and Fort Greene neighborhoods attended a rally to support recycling and oppose the Navy Yard incinerator. Brooklyn borough president Howard Golden and Manhattan borough president Ruth Messinger joined in denouncing "the environmentally hazardous approach" of trash incineration. The officials' comments followed a report issued by city comptroller Elizabeth Holtzman demonstrating the hazards associated with the incinerator. The report concluded that this level of emission would increase the exposure of children to lead poisoning.[8] Arthur Kell, a toxics expert with NYPIRG, added that in addition to lead the incinerator would emit mercury, dioxin, and hazardous ash.

Over the next several months, similar meetings were held around the city, including one in the heart of the predominantly African-American Farragut housing projects, across the Navy Yard from Williamsburg. Religious leaders turned out in force, including an impassioned Reverend Mark Taylor of the Church of the Open Door. Taylor didn't mince his words: "These are issues of death. The issue cannot be separated from the gunshots in Farragut and Fort Greene Houses. It's like the issue of Rodney King's beating, and the issue of wanton violence . . . I, too, am of the mind that if you elect someone who looks like you and talks like you, but doesn't vote like you—you need to think twice."[9] His and many others' dedication to the issue would parallel and combine with the Williamsburg activists' efforts.

As anti-incinerator pressure mounted from elected officials, environmental groups, community organizations, and residents of neighborhoods adjacent to the Brooklyn Navy Yard, city officials claimed they would take no position on the project until the city's comprehensive solid waste management plan was presented. To ensure that the plan would exclude all proposed burn plants, the anti-incinerator coalition successfully pushed for legislation requiring prior approval of the solid waste management plan by the city council. Such an approval process not only would transfer some decisionmaking authority away from the now pro-incinerator Dinkins administration but also would create an opportunity to kill the project at last through city council rejection.

On March 23, 1992, a day prior to the city council's scheduled vote on the incinerator, Emily Lloyd, the mayor's sanitation commissioner, pledged to delay construction of the facility until 1996. Because the city previously had planned to begin building in 1994, Dinkins's decision to "cool it" on trash burning, as a headline in the *New York Daily News* put it,[10] appeared to mark the beginning of the end of the incinerator proposal. The press focused on the political value of Dinkins's decision, noting that the mayor had removed an "explosive issue" from his 1993 reelection campaign.[11]

The anti-incinerator coalition did not stop the pressure, however. An April 1992 meeting brought more than 1,000 residents to a neighborhood school to show unified opposition to the incinerator. Attendance was drawn equally from the Satmar and Latino communities. The particular school that hosted the event, PS 16, had been the subject of a bitter fight between El Puente and the Satmars in 1986. In that dispute, which focused on a wall erected to create an exclusive entrance for Hasidic girls in an overwhelmingly minority school, El Puente led a nearly month-long school boycott and protested in front of the home of the Satmars' chief rabbi (not Niederman). The anti-incinerator event, as Garden Acosta noted, transformed PS 16 from a "symbol of segregation into a symbol of unity."[12] An effort to bring the incinerator fight to national attention fell short when Jerry Brown, campaigning in the New York presidential primary against Bill Clinton, failed to make a scheduled speech at the event. Nevertheless, the willingness of two completely distinct groups who distrusted each other and fought over many issues to join forces against the incinerator sent a powerful message throughout the state.

Unfortunately, Dinkins failed to accept the prevailing assessment that killing the Brooklyn incinerator was to his political advantage. Instead, as part of a citywide deal to obtain the necessary city council approval of his solid waste plan, Dinkins agreed to close down two smaller incinerators in other communities, upgrade a third, and increase citywide recycling in exchange for votes to include the Williamsburg project in the plan.

The anti-incinerator coalition blasted the mayor's decision. On the eve of the city council vote on the waste management plan, activists brought nearly 800 children—Hasidic, Latino, and African-American—to City Hall to urge the council to reject the mayor's plan. Rabbi Niederman told the crowd that "just because we are poor does not mean our children must breathe air made poisonous by garbage-burning incinerators." Luis Garden Acosta of El Puente focused on the pathbreaking coalition that had been formed between the often-warring groups, noting that "in our common air we have found our common ground. Emboldened by this special unity, we urge the council to reject the solid waste plan." The UJO, El Puente, and other groups had joined NYPIRG to create a "no burn" and "recycle first" alternative to the mayor's plan. Despite the coalition's effort, in August the council approved a solid waste plan that included the incinerator project. The battle then shifted to the New York State Department of Environmental Conservation (DEC), long criticized by environmentalists for simply rubber-stamping incinerator permit applications.

The Williamsburg coalition redirected its energies toward convincing Governor Cuomo's administration to deny the necessary permits. At a September 1992 strategy session, NYPIRG advanced the idea of holding a march from Brooklyn to Manhattan. Niederman and Garden Acosta supported the idea, but several Latino housing activists present at the meeting had several reservations about staging another joint event with the Hasidim. First, only a few months earlier new strife had emerged between the Hasidim and Latinos over who would get apartments in three housing projects. In 1991 a court-issued consent decree had put 190 black and Latino families at the top of waiting lists for those projects. The settlement seemed to diminish longtime black and Latino anger over the Hasidim's occupying 68 percent of these apartments despite constituting only about 40 percent of the area's population. In May 1992, however, the Latino community learned that the UJO had applied for $810,000 in federal funds to study the feasibility of turning 1,102 apartments in two of the projects into tenant-owned co-ops. Latino leaders condemned the application as an attempt to circumvent the consent decree. The extent of their anger was evident on May 13, 1992, when more than 1,000 Latinos held a protest against the Hasidim's funding application.

Niederman claimed the UJO's motives were misunderstood and emphasized his opposition to further division between the Hasidim and the rest of the community. He insisted it was in the community's interest to have more stable housing. Niederman sent letters to Latino leaders offering to resubmit the HUD application as a joint effort, but this offer was rejected as untimely. Latino leaders also claimed that the application would bar minority families who could not afford to purchase an apartment from living in the complexes. Significantly, Luis Garden Acosta had publicly joined in Latino criticism of the UJO proposal. Though referring to Rabbi Niederman as a "valued friend,"[13] Garden Acosta told the press that Hasidic leaders still failed to grasp that deep wounds were festering in the Latino community over the Hasidic community's housing strategy. Garden Acosta noted that the government's "preferential treatment for the Hasidic community" underscored the Hasidim's inability to create a common vision for housing in Williamsburg.

Although Garden Acosta was able to put aside community disputes while working with the UJO against the incinerator, it is understandable that activists primarily engaged in housing issues would not want to work with the Hasidim. Many Latinos simply felt, as one city councilman put it, that the Hasidim would "work with us when they want to be with us and work around us on other things."[14]

Housing activists objecting to the march on Manhattan also felt the Latino community had not received due credit for its turnout at the April 1992 mass meeting, and they expressed concern that the Hasidim would produce more marchers, making Latinos look weak. These activists perceived that whoever received credit for the eventual defeat of the incinerator would have an advantage over future use of the Navy Yard, and they wanted to make sure Latinos would get their fair share of whatever housing, jobs, or other services were created on the site. If the Hasidim were publicly perceived as primarily responsible for defeating the incinerator proposal, they would obtain the bulk of the spoils.

Latino community opposition put Garden Acosta in a tough position. He acknowledged the strategic value of the march. However, agreeing to a tactic opposed by leaders in his own community would undermine his standing. Garden Acosta understood that Latino unity was essential for the coalition to succeed. Ultimately, he joined other leaders in concluding that the long-term goal of maintaining a strong coalition outweighed any strategic benefit that might come from the march. The plan for the march was thus deferred, and NYPIRG began working with the disgruntled housing activists to reduce their suspicions toward the Hasidim. Brooklyn Legal Services, which had a track record of representing Latinos on housing issues, was brought in to help build trust. The housing activists eventually overcame their reservations, and the march to Manhattan was held to commemorate Martin Luther King Day the following January.

Meanwhile, the coalition focused on new tactics and strategies. Of central concern was the need to delay state issuance of the building permit until after November 15, 1992. This date was critical because the 1990 amendments to the federal Clean Air Act applied to projects whose permits were issued after this deadline. The amendments prohibited new pollution in smog-plagued cities until pollution from other sources was reduced. New York City did not want construction of the Navy Yard incinerator conditioned on reduction of pollution elsewhere and was pressuring the Cuomo administration to act promptly to exempt the project from the amended Clean Air Act.

The anti-incinerator campaign thus needed to marshal all of its resources to defeat what *New York Newsday* aptly described as the city's "Race to Pollute."[15] The UJO, NYPIRG, and El Puente sought to increase their strength by creating a formal coalition called the Community Alliance for the Environment (CAFE). CAFE also included representatives of the nearby African-American community of Fort Greene, among them the charismatic Reverend Taylor of the Church of the Open Door and Mildred Trudy of the community organization Crispus Attucks. Also joining were local environmental groups such as the Fort Greene/Clinton Hill Coalition for Clean Air and the WWW (Williamsburg, Waterfront, the World); several religious leaders affiliated with the Catholic Church; and individual activists unaffiliated with the Latino or Hasidic communities.

On October 2, 1992, CAFE learned that the state was planning to skip its normal bureaucratic procedures to ensure a ruling on the Williamsburg incinerator prior to November 15. The Department of Environmental Conservation made no secret of its plans, stating in a letter that it was concerned about meeting the Clean Air Act deadline. A DEC spokesperson further tipped the agency's hand, telling *Newsday* that "this thing has been going on for a long time. It's time to bring it to an end."[16] The anti-incinerator coalition immediately seized on the agency's willingness to sidestep standard procedures for the benefit of the toxin-spewing project. Larry Shapiro of NYPIRG set the tone, calling the state's plan an "outrageous abuse of power." Rabbi Niederman described the state's fast-track timetable as "a conspiracy between the state and the city to rush a health hazard into the community."[17]

As anybody who has tried to gain support of controversial projects knows, it is a terrible mistake to allow process questions to emerge. People who may feel uncomfortable opposing a project on the merits can seize on procedural irregularities to justify opposition. The DEC thus opened up an entirely new front of controversy, and CAFE exploited it to the hilt. On October 29, 1992, CAFE and NYPIRG filed suit in U.S. District Court in Brooklyn to enjoin the state DEC from issuing the incinerator permits before the Clean Air Act amendments took effect on November 15. The suit condemned the state's aiding and abetting the city's "mad rush" to obtain the trash incinerator permit. Although the DEC spokesperson correctly pointed out that the permitting process for the incinerator had been in progress for nearly a decade, this fact was lost amidst the clamor created by the agency's effort to sneak in under the old Clean Air Act. Opponents described the fast-track process as a "railroad job," and the lawsuit specifically denounced DEC Commissioner Thomas Jorling for "devastating the administrative review process for the purpose of adding more pollution to the environment."

The Latino, Hasidic, and NYPIRG alliance thus succeeded in using a procedural irregularity to turn the history of the incinerator project on its head. A project commenced in the 1970s, whose permit process began in 1985 and whose original timetable called for completion by 1986, was understood in 1992 to have been "railroaded" through the process. Opponents hammered the state's chief environmental official for making a mockery of his own administrative procedures and circumventing state and federal law in order to turn "the lungs of New Yorkers into toxic waste dumps."[18]

The pressure on Jorling was coupled with a campaign to get Governor Cuomo to intervene. Cuomo was wary of statewide environmental leaders, but he knew how to count votes. Members of his administration also recognized that missing the November 15 deadline would not kill the incinerator project outright. In late October a DEC regional director, appropriately named Carol Ash, told the *Staten Island Advance* that the city's agreement to close two existing incinerators and reduce emissions at a third would readily satisfy the Clean Air Act requirement. The Cuomo administration could thus eliminate the stench of state procedural improprieties, keep New York City happy, and keep the Brooklyn incinerator alive by ignoring the November 15 deadline. And that is precisely what happened. On November 3, 1992, only days after the filing of CAFE's lawsuit, Jorling issued a two-sentence memo that effectively ensured that he would not issue his ruling before the more stringent federal rules went into effect. On December 23, 1992, however, the DEC's administrative law judge gave New York City what it sought by ruling that the more stringent Clean Air Act requirements did not apply to the Williamsburg incinerator.

The ruling catalyzed incinerator opposition. Continuing to implement a proactive strategy and keep incinerator supporters on the defensive, CAFE launched a new, multipronged attack. On December 26, only three days after the judge's ruling, the UJO's attorney announced that CAFE would file an administrative appeal and that one basis of the appeal would be newly discovered evidence that showed the proposed incinerator site sat atop the graves of Revolutionary War prisoners. The existence of the burial site had been documented in a Revolutionary War–era map of Brooklyn located in the New York Public Library. The map labeled the incinerator site "Prisoners Graves," the dead being fighters for independence who died in British captivity.[19]

The need to protect the burial site as a piece of history raised yet another issue for incinerator backers to overcome. Though the Williamsburg activists used other tactics and strategies, the burial site issue demonstrated their never-ending ingenuity and creativity. In May 1993 veterans and community residents led a march to the Navy Yard and held a memorial for the Revolutionary War dead to raise public awareness that the city wanted to construct an incinerator over veterans' graves. The march was sponsored by such groups as the Society of Old Brooklynites, Wallabout Landmarks Preservation Committee, and the George P. Davis American Legion Post #116. None of these groups had previously been publicly involved in anti-incinerator efforts. CAFE was also a sponsor but wisely made sure the other groups were the center of attention.[20]

Although the alleged existence of the burial site never became a major threat to the project, the issue expanded the anti-incinerator coalition. CAFE was constantly looking to include new and diverse constituencies. Though coalition politics would seem to reward ongoing openness to new allies, concerns over turf, control, and credit often forestall a coalition from broadening after its initial creation. Coalition expansion also requires an understanding of how to attract a potentially valuable new participant. Had CAFE used the discovery of the burial site as part of its own campaign, the issue would not have been more than a one-day news curiosity. By allowing control of the issue to remain with the groups most concerned about veterans and landmarks, CAFE both expanded the anti-incinerator base and made the burial site seem a serious objection to the project.

CAFE also was willing to work in concert with local and state elected officials. Although this may seem an obvious tactic in a campaign that included legislative strategies, many coalitions reject such alliances for fear of being either sold out or accused of selling out. The anti-incinerator coalition had nothing to fear on either front, because it represented what every politician respects most: a real electoral base. Officials such as Mayor Dinkins who betrayed the coalition lost future electoral support. The coalition's ability to obtain strong support from Republicans and Democrats, reformers and machine politicians, and urban and suburban legislators (even though the latter's constituents may never have visited Williamsburg) became critical to its success. The same tactical activism that led to the formation of the diverse anti-incinerator coalition created a broad legislative alliance that brought politicians of radically different styles and ideologies into the cause.

CAFE's chief strategic response to the administrative law judge's December 23 ruling was at last to hold the long march from Brooklyn to Manhattan that had been delayed by the Latino housing activists. More than 1,000 people participated in the march across the Williamsburg Bridge. The marchers included Hasidim, Latinos, and African-Americans, many of them carrying candles. Brooklyn-bound traffic on the bridge was snarled for forty minutes. The march, like the 1991 state hearing on environmental racism and the July 1992 rally prior to the city council vote on the solid waste plan, highlighted the unity among the coalition's diverse groups. CAFE used its public comments at the pre-march rally to accentuate the community's united front. Niederman of the UJO stated, "We are proud to have all of our communities together to demonstrate a health hazard in our community. We are here united and we will march united."[21] Alexei Torres, a CAFE spokesman from the Latino community, noted that the march was occurring "on the eve of Martin Luther King's birthday. We are marching for unity and in light of the racial tension that has a hold of the city, we will demonstrate, different ethnic groups together, in a show of outrage."[22] The New York Times's photo of the march was captioned "Environmental concerns unite a neighborhood."[23]

Less creative activists would have used the march to focus solely on the environmental hazard of building a fifty-five-story incinerator adjacent to a residential neighborhood, and the media coverage would have interested only those New Yorkers concerned about environmental issues. CAFE, however, used the march for a larger purpose: what was really on display was a show of racial unity. Martin Luther King's dream has not been realized in most of the United States, but it was being transformed into reality in Williamsburg. A community striving to realize King's dream, the marchers seemed to say, must not be torn asunder by a $550 million trash incinerator. CAFE's message had particular resonance in New York City, a once-famed melting pot now being unpleasantly transformed by racial segregation and ethnic warfare. All New Yorkers, even those totally disinterested in the incinerator issue, could find in the march a sense of hope, a model for the future of the city and perhaps even the nation. The coalition put Governor Cuomo, a son of poor Italian immigrants, in a difficult position: building the incinerator would mean wrecking a multiracial, multiethnic, unified community. It is no wonder that the Cuomo administration continued to take its time before making a decision.

Following CAFE's January appeal of the administrative law judge's ruling, several months passed without a final decision from DEC chief Jorling on the Navy Yard permits. CAFE used this period to press publicly for a state hearing in Williamsburg prior to the permit decision. Though the DEC judge found no need for a new hearing, Luis Garden Acosta noted that "no other community in New York state has had a permit process for a facility like this without a public hearing." The last hearing on the incinerator had been held in 1987, but it did not take place in Williamsburg. CAFE wanted Jorling to hold and attend a meeting in the affected community. This new demand had two strategic advantages. First, it brought to the forefront another process defect surrounding the incinerator: public officials and individual citizens could rightfully question why the state's top environmental officer would refuse to come to Williamsburg to hear residents' concerns firsthand. Second, if Jorling sought to eliminate this controversy by actually holding and attending a Williamsburg meeting, the event certainly would receive statewide media attention. There is nothing the media like more than footage of a state official trying to justify his or her conduct before a hostile and disbelieving local audience. Jorling would have greater difficulty ruling for the incinerator if Williamsburg's fierce opposition received great statewide publicity.[24]

In addition to targeting Jorling's refusal to hear the community's concerns, CAFE used the period prior to his ruling to press for state legislation mandating that the 1990 Clear Air Act amendments apply to the Williamsburg incinerator. The administrative law judge had ruled that the amendments did not apply because the city had submitted a completed permit application prior to the November 15 deadline. The proposed legislation would reverse this ruling and require the city to show a reduction in air pollution from other sources before the state could issue a permit. After the city lost its 1992 "race to pollute," state and city officials had downplayed the importance of the revised federal guidelines. Now that legislation threatened to require city compliance with the new regulations, the Dinkins administration barraged state legislators in an effort to kill the bill.

Once again, the anti-incinerator coalition had framed the issue so as to place itself on the high ground. As Larry Shapiro of NYPIRG put it, "It's really a sad commentary on the Dinkins administration's commitment to air quality and public health that their only air-quality goal in Albany this year is trying to make the air worse."[25] Powerful elected state officials, including the Democratic assembly speaker, favored CAFE's legislation, and the Republican Senate majority leader expressed no opposition. Their support forced Dinkins administration lobbyists to fight even more furiously for the politically unpalatable goal of dirtier air for the city.

After complex negotiations between Cuomo and the two legislative leaders, a compromise agreement was reached on July 7, 1993 that only partially exempted the Williamsburg incinerator from the new federal rules. The agreement also required the city to study the possible health effects on the neighborhoods surrounding the project. The need to determine the quantity of emission reductions available from the old incinerators meant a further delay of the state's decision on the incinerator permit. The agreement also created a basis for lawsuits challenging whether the city had in fact sufficiently reduced pollution citywide before approving the Brooklyn incinerator. One legislative official told Shapiro, "There are two lawsuits per line" in the bill.

The legislative compromise had the twin advantages of returning the focus of the debate to the coalition's resident base and of reemphasizing health and air-quality issues. The January 1993 Brooklyn to Manhattan march necessarily had been followed by an Albany-based strategy. Such legislative strategies put resident-based organizations on the sidelines while the technicians with state-level experience do their work. These scenarios carry the potential for intracoalition conflict, as people who once felt centrally involved in a struggle can begin to feel left out. Conflict also can emerge when the coalition includes individuals or groups whose desire for the limelight is the primary motive for their participation; the shifting of the fight to a different stage may further the coalition's aim but not their own interests.

In CAFE's case, the focus on the state legislature in Albany caused no problems. The relationship between the organizations was based on mutual recognition of each group's particular roles. Unlike coalitions where such conflict does emerge, CAFE had two primary member organizations (UJO and El Puente) with true constituency bases. Neither group had to fear that a period out of the limelight would turn its people away from the struggle, nor was either merely using the incinerator issue to build organizational status. NYPIRG is a statewide organization accustomed to working with state legislators on environmental issues; the UJO and El Puente recognized that it would be more effective in Albany, and both strongly supported its efforts there. It also was obvious to NYPIRG that its ability to influence votes on the incinerator was based on the legislators' knowledge of the Hasidic-Latino position on the issue. Both Niederman and Garden Acosta were considered influential among elected officials and traveled to Albany together for key meetings with legislators. Although NYPIRG's status gave it access to many legislators, Niederman and Garden Acosta greatly facilitated the process of educating state officials about the incinerator.

The legislative compromise also meant that a state decision on the permit was no longer an imminent possibility. The November 1993 mayoral election was approaching, giving CAFE a new political opening. Dinkins had drawn broad support from Williamsburg and surrounding neighborhoods in 1989 for his pledge to halt progress on the project until 1993. His 1989 opponent, Rudolph Giuliani, had strongly supported the incinerator. When asked in 1989 what he thought would happen if the project were not built, Giuliani replied, "The dirtiest city in America would become dirtier."[26] By 1993 Dinkins had already positioned himself as pro-incinerator. The UJO remained bitter over Dinkins's betrayal on the issue, and the mayor's mishandling of a conflict between African-Americans and Hasidim in Crown Heights left the Williamsburg Satmars aligned with Giuliani. The Latino and African-American residents surrounding the Navy Yard also were angered by Dinkins's incinerator switch—and they were a constituency the mayor had to have in order to win reelection. Partly in an effort to weaken the mayor's pro-incinerator stance, a Fort Greene community organization invited Dinkins to a meeting scheduled for September 21. After he agreed to attend, the mayor's staff learned that most of those likely to be present wanted to discuss the incinerator. As more than 200 people awaited the mayor's arrival, a call to his campaign office revealed that Dinkins would not be appearing. His absence angered the crowd. Dinkins thus sacrificed his political allies for the construction of a burn plant. It did not speak well for the mayor's reelection hopes that he was afraid to appear in front of his natural base.[27]

Giuliani had lost in a very close election in 1989, and a change in his stance on the incinerator could enable him to make inroads into the mayor's base. He therefore switched from ardent supporter of the incinerator to skeptic; his favorite phrase was that the city should retain incineration as a "last option"[28] in case recycling and other alternatives failed to cope adequately with the city's waste. Two weeks before the election, Giuliani moved even further toward an anti-incinerator stance, telling a Brooklyn community newspaper that as mayor he would launch "a massive recycling program so there isn't a need to build a new incinerator."[29]

Giuliani prevailed in the 1993 mayor's race by only 55,000 votes. Although Dinkins's switch on the incinerator was not central to his defeat, the Hasidim's move to Giuliani, similar defections by Latinos and even African-Americans, and a lower African-American voter turnout affected the outcome. All of these constituencies opposed Dinkins on the incinerator issue.

After taking office in January 1994, Giuliani seemed willing to reconsider the need for the entire project. He asked his sanitation department to study whether it would be more cost-effective to haul garbage to out-of-state landfills or to build the $550 million incinerator. During the long period of time CAFE had delayed the project, an unexpected glut of landfill space had developed on the East Coast. The *Wall Street Journal* reported on August 11, 1993, that municipalities that had spent billions of dollars to build big incinerators now lacked the trash to keep the plants burning full blast. Residential and commercial customers were collectively losing millions of dollars, as incinerating garbage cost twice as much as dumping it at a landfill. Seizing the opportunity to take advantage of the reduced landfill rates made fiscal, environmental, and political sense. A month after his request for a study, however, Giuliani appeared to reverse himself. He proposed major cuts in city recycling programs and asked the city council to scale back its recycling goals. Giuliani also decided to continue to seek a state permit for the Navy Yard incinerator. A mayor who began his term viewing incineration as a "last hope" and "an insurance policy" if all else failed now appeared to have adopted the agenda of his predecessor.[30]

Rosie Baerga, a leader of CAFE, accused the mayor of having pulled a "snow job"[31] to mask his pro-incinerator position. Other factors may also have been at work. *New York Newsday* reported on March 8, 1994, that Wheelabrator Environmental Systems, the incinerator developer, had assembled an all-star team of lobbyists to obtain state and city go-aheads on the project. The corporation that would financially profit from the incinerator had previously kept itself out of the public eye, preferring to let New York City and the DEC repel attacks from incinerator opponents. This reticence presumably had changed. Wheelabrator's lobbying team included a former state assembly speaker, a law firm with close ties to the Giuliani administration, and a political consultant to the top Republican on the state legislative solid waste commission. The hiring of this team represented a new, aggressive approach from incinerator proponents; to CAFE, which was as unified as ever and ready to fight, the introduction of this high-priced talent simply meant that Wheelabrator was running scared.[32] CAFE was finding it easier to win enthusiastic backing from liberals and African-Americans who had hedged on their anti-incinerator position while Dinkins was mayor. With Dinkins gone, such individuals had no reason to hold back their support of the coalition.

While Giuliani equivocated, CAFE maintained its focus on the DEC's pending decision on the permit. In early March, the DEC revealed that it was delaying, apparently indefinitely, its ruling on whether to approve the city's pollution trade-off proposal. NYPIRG jumped on the DEC by again demanding that it hold fact-finding hearings on the city's pollution reduction plan. Having repeatedly won favorable publicity by focusing on unfairness in the permit process, incinerator opponents now decried the DEC's use of faceless bureaucrats to make decisions properly in the purview of the governor's environmental chief.[33] In claiming that the delegation of a major decision to "underlings not accountable to the public" was unprecedented, NYPIRG's Shapiro created the impression that the entire permit process was a "railroad job."[34] Shapiro was no doubt correct in the claim that such procedures had not occurred in the past, but neither the DEC nor Wheelabrator's public relations team noted that the issue of pollution trade-offs itself was new. Instead, the DEC spokesperson stated that he did not know if the process had a precedent, thus appearing to confirm NYPIRG's charge.

Shortly after Shapiro's attack, a hot new issue surfaced: samples taken from the Navy Yard revealed high levels of toxic chemicals in soil and groundwater. The presence of such toxic waste had apparently gone undetected for the almost fifteen years since the planning began for the incinerator. CAFE and its allies reacted to this discovery with renewed attacks on both the permitting process and the incinerator plan itself. Although the DEC had learned in the summer of 1992 that a nearby area contained toxic hazards, the city sanitation department claimed it had not been informed. The failure of the DEC to disclose its findings while considering approval of the incinerator project led to harsh words from CAFE leaders. Luis Garden Acosta described the Navy Yard as "Williamsburg's Love Canal." He also attacked incinerator proponents as people who are unconcerned about the interests of children and families and "who are locked into a plan without the courage to say 'Enough!'" Rabbi Niederman echoed Garden Acosta, stating that "there are so many unknowns in the process and at the site that it requires us to dig in and not leave even one stone unturned." Reverend Mark Taylor led a highly effective news conference that included Niederman, Delia Montalvo of El Puente, NYPIRG delegates, and a host of other community leaders. Taylor called for an end to environmental racism at the Navy Yard, stating, "Community residents are being shut out and ignored by the process."[35]

Garden Acosta and Niederman's response to the toxic discovery illustrated coalitions' capacity to use the one-two punch. NYPIRG also responded publicly, demonstrating that three separate constituencies reflecting broad and diverse support could share a unified position. By contrast, when organizations not working in coalition are asked to comment on an event, each organization is likely to address its own discrete issues, advancing no unified strategic position. Readers of an article containing these widely varying responses could well conclude that the groups are out of sync or perhaps even in conflict. Groups not working in coalition frequently leave such an impression, because coordinating a press response requires the type of mutual discussion and analysis that typified CAFE.

The discovery of toxic waste required the state DEC to investigate whether the Navy Yard should be assigned to the Superfund program. Such a designation would delay the project for at least a decade and likely kill it. The discovery also started a debate over why the toxic chemicals had not previously been discovered, when the historic use of the Navy Yard for shipping made the presence of toxic chemicals foreseeable. In

April 1994 CAFE found out that the New York City sanitation department had learned of the toxic contamination of the incinerator site in 1988 but had failed to inform the state agency considering approval of the project. Charges of a cover-up by incinerator advocates thus emerged. Mayor Giuliani ordered an investigation to determine why the report was not forwarded to the state, and the attorney general looked at whether any laws were broken. Although the DEC now insisted that no construction permit would issue until completion of an investigation and cleanup at the site, it continued its permitting process and, amid all of these new concerns, preliminarily approved the city's pollution trade-off application. Perhaps Wheelabrator was actually getting something out of its high-priced lobbyists. However, the preliminary approval became clouded by the discovery in late April that the DEC's regional counsel had reviewed the city's application while seeking employment with the city. Questions were raised over possible bias, as the counsel knew his prospective employer desperately wanted DEC approval of the application under his authority.

As the incinerator plan enters its second decade, it now confronts a dizzying array of social, political, and economic obstacles. On June 13, 1995, CAFE, New York City Public Advocate Mark Green, and more than 100 health care professionals launched a drive to force the city to prepare a new environmental impact statement on the incinerator. Although Mayor Giuliani rejected the request, it is unlikely he will proceed on a project whose health risks were last evaluated in 1985. It may be only a matter of time before the burial ground at the Navy Yard symbolically includes the incinerator.

The coalition's ability to delay for so long, perhaps even to prevent, construction of the Navy Yard incinerator is one of the great social change success stories of the past decade. To understand the magnitude of the achievement, consider the massive gentrification and development boom that swept New York City through most of the 1980s. The Koch administration was accustomed to getting what it wanted, particularly when its opponents were predominantly low-income, minority people. Wall Street also expected to obtain what it desired (in this case, the lucrative bond contracts that were part of the incinerator project); Felix Rohatyn and his colleagues were not accustomed to being stymied by the likes of Williamsburg's Latinos and Hasidim.

In addition to surmounting Wall Street, the anti-incinerator coalition had to overcome nearly fanatical pro-incinerator editorializing from the vaunted *New York Times*. It is often remarked that *Times* editorial policy becomes more progressive the further the issue lies from the paper's New York City headquarters. Readers of its daily national edition often miss its pro–Wall Street, pro-development, anti-rent-control local editorial slant. Support for the incinerator became a litmus test for political candidates seeking the coveted *New York Times* endorsement. The perceived objectivity of the *Times*—despite its inflammatory anti-incinerator comments—gave politicians the ability to claim they supported the incinerator on the "merits" rather than because of the campaign funds donated by pro-incinerator forces.

The *Times*'s emphasis on politicians' position on the incinerator became apparent when Elizabeth Holtzman sought the Democratic nomination for U.S. Senate in 1992. Holtzman, a vocal incinerator opponent, had spent four years in Congress before serving as Brooklyn district attorney and then New York City comptroller. With her Senate bid, however, she became a victim of the *Times*'s pro-incinerator zealotry. In a September 13, 1992 editorial evaluating candidates for the Senate primary, the *Times,* after briefly noting Holtzman's expertise and proven track record, stated:

> Still, legislative effectiveness also depends on a capacity for conciliation, not a strong point for Ms. Holtzman, who sometimes seems to prize the image of a brave, lonely figure standing up for principle even when she has to sacrifice principle to make her stand. A notable example is her position on the decision to build a new incinerator in Brooklyn.
>
> There is no choice: even if the city takes all the other steps needed to manage its waste, the incinerator must be built. Every responsible observer accepts that—yet even now Ms. Holtzman opposes it with distortions that play to the exaggerated fears of New Yorkers who need facts, not demagogy.

The coalition was thus opposed by Wall Street, the Koch and Dinkins administrations, and New York's most prestigious media outlet. Governor Cuomo, himself allied with Wall Street and the *Times,* was more an opponent than a friend of the coalition. Cuomo's environmental appointees strongly supported the incinerator and kept the project alive well after its existence could be rationally justified. New York state's self-proclaimed liberal fighter for the common person could have killed the project at any time; yet his administration would have promptly approved the plan if not for the fear of political reprisals from incinerator opponents.

With the influential business, legal, government, media, and construction unions behind it, the Brooklyn Navy Yard incinerator project must have seemed a walkover. The idea of Williamsburg's Spanish-speaking Latinos allying with their neighborhood enemy, the Satmars, would have appeared unimaginable, and the project sponsors likely gave little thought to the possibility that Williamsburg's residents could defeat their plan.

Many people played critical roles in the anti-incinerator campaign, but the entire effort would not have happened without the tactical activism of the unlikely duo of Rabbi David Niederman and Luis Garden Acosta. Both men risked their standing in their respective communities by working together for a common goal. Each leader had the courage and wisdom to recognize the benefits of a coalition to his community. For the Hasidim, working on the incinerator issue with Latinos helped reduce overall tensions and even violence. Whereas high-profile riots and violent disputes have occurred recently between the Lubavitcher sect and African-Americans in Crown Heights, no such incendiary acts have occurred in Williamsburg since the inception of the coalition. On the contrary, by 1994 the once-warring communities were working on joint projects to screen children for lead poisoning and to rehabilitate a six-story building for future occupancy by both Latino and Hasidic tenants. The two groups also were collaborating on a ten-year plan for Williamsburg and jointly coordinating state grants for community development. Niederman saw the alliance with Latinos against the incinerator as the beginning of "a new era for the community."[36]

Garden Acosta saw El Puente—"The Bridge"—as a vehicle for bridge-building with the Satmars and was willing to make a leap of faith to create a new, positive relationship with his community's longtime adversaries.[37] Neither the Latinos nor the Hasidim were planning on leaving Williamsburg, and both recognized community war as a very real and mutually destructive possibility. This danger motivated leaders of both communities to improve their relations. Moreover, both communities faced the same threat in the incinerator; failure to block it would leave future generations of Hasidim and Latinos alike forever menaced by a pollution-spewing furnace. As Garden Acosta stated, "We all breathe the same air."[38] This long-term commitment to a particular piece of land made possible a partnership that otherwise likely would not have occurred.

The Williamsburg partnership illustrates how progressive groups can overcome their suspicions of coalitions, as voiced by IAF Texas and others. First, because El Puente and the UJO each had a true constituency base, neither group could be accused of using the other's base for its own ends. Second, the coalition was able to forestall each group's concerns that it would not get its fair share of credit for the coalition's success.

This was no simple task, because CAFE included many organizations and individuals in addition to the three central participants. But there was a mutual interest at work: defeat of the incinerator would redound to the individual credit of all participating organizations. Rabbi Niederman and Garden Acosta made sure that their constituencies came to view the coalition as a partnership whose members shared responsibility for every gain or loss. All participants displayed a willingness to subordinate individual glory to the broader goal.

The nature of the Williamsburg coalition rendered moot the issue of who would win credit for the successful campaign. CAFE was a temporary entity, created as a vehicle through which UJO, El Puente, NYPIRG, and other groups could oppose the incinerator. For the same reason, the success of CAFE never had the potential to impact negatively any of the organizations' funding streams. The credibility of each group was only enhanced by participation in the coalition.

If we assume that even organizations most suspicious of coalition participation would agree to the benefits of the Williamsburg alliance, we must wonder why similar efforts are so rarely pursued. The greatest factor is the tendency of social change activists and organizations to wear ideological blinders when it comes to coalition building. Organizations become so committed to working with their cultural and political allies that they fail to recognize opportunities to make common cause with groups that have conflicting agendas. In retrospect, David Niederman's overture to El Puente and Garden Acosta's positive response seem obvious tactical moves. Experienced activists in either community could readily foresee that public interest in the incinerator issue would jump dramatically through formation of such an alliance; Niederman's decision to attend the Radiac meeting was such a slam dunk that if he had not initiated the contact, it would have happened anyway . . . right?

Wrong. Before Niederman's overture to El Puente, his UJO constituency often viewed Latino neighbors as violent, anti-Semitic, and fervent in their desire to drive the Hasidim out of Williamsburg. The very idea of trusting Latinos was absurd to many Hasidim. Niederman's simplest and easiest decision would have been not even to consider working with Luis Garden Acosta and the Latino community. He could have echoed the many committed activists who view an opponent on one issue as the enemy on *all* issues. But Niederman placed his constituency's true interests over a desire for ideological conformity. He told Garden Acosta during their first meeting that he saw the incinerator fight as "a beginning, a bridge to bring the two communities together."[39] Working together on a common issue could serve to dispel distrust and improve chances for defeating the project. Though Garden Acosta felt this was a "clear act of courage," Niederman saw it simply as a necessary step for groups facing the same environmental hazards.[40] The UJO never conditioned its alliance on either group's relinquishing its demands on housing, jobs, or school issues, so Niederman understood that his overture might be only a limited proposition. It is a tribute to Niederman's tactical activism that a decision that seemed shocking at the time appears logical, obvious, and even inevitable in retrospect.

Luis Garden Acosta faced even greater risks in choosing to work with the UJO. His constituency simmered over the Hasidim's ability to use their political skills, bloc voting, and mass mobilizations to extract what the Latinos considered (with some justification) a disproportionately high share of public resources. They were not about to work in partnership with their enemy. After Garden Acosta and Rabbi Niederman shared leadership of the May 1991 march through the streets of the Latino community, many concluded that El Puente had capitulated to the Hasidim.[41] People passing Garden Acosta in the street asked him to explain his rationale for working with the Satmars. In response, a lesser leader or strategist might have sought to elevate his or her community status by publicly snubbing the UJO. Alternatively, Garden Acosta might have offered to work only with NYPIRG on the incinerator issue. Instead, he stood firm behind his belief that an alliance with the Hasidim was in the best interests of both communities. After years of feeling that his community spent too much time acting defensively, Garden Acosta saw the alliance with the Satmars as a proactive strategy to move Latinos into a more positive relationship with their longtime adversaries.[42]

COALITIONS WITH IDEOLOGICAL OPPONENTS

If two groups with valid reasons for distrusting each other can join in pursuit of a common goal, so can organizations in all fields of social change activism. For example, progressive organizations are frequently forced to battle hostile government bureaucracies. These bureaucracies are often impervious to election results—election of progressive officials does not translate into greater bureaucratic attention to progressive constituencies. Many bureaucracies are saturated with highly paid administrators whose costly salaries require eliminating the front-line staff that serves the public.

Like progressives, organizations with pro-business, anti-tax ideologies bemoan the spiraling costs of bureaucratic administration. If these two diverse constituencies could unify in an effort to redirect funding away from upper management and toward direct services, everyone would benefit. However, mutual ideological distrust ensures that these two constituencies rarely discuss common concerns. As a result, both remain frustrated by overfed bureaucracies: progressive groups are unable to improve them on their own because they are viewed as lacking credibility on management or administrative issues; the pro-business, anti-tax groups that are perceived to have expertise in these areas make no headway because their criticism of the bureaucracy is viewed simply as a strategy for eliminating government regulation of selfish corporate interests. With progressives and conservatives standing divided against the misuse of government resources, their common goal of enhanced service remains unfulfilled. The lack of a broad coalition on this issue has left Americans of all economic classes feeling angry that their lives are too much controlled by the whims of highly paid, unelected bureaucrats.

My own attempt to channel this widespread sentiment in a progressive direction came through a charter amendment on San Francisco's November 1994 ballot. The initiative sought to improve housing-code enforcement by removing this responsibility from a bureaucracy hostile to tenants and transferring it to a citizens' commission. Low-income tenant advocates supported the measure because they were angry about the city's lax approach to substandard housing, whereas landlords and builders were persuaded to join us on fiscal grounds—they had to pay fees to fund the city housing- and building-code administration. All three groups had an incentive to support a measure that would impose citizen budget oversight and were angry that fees were being spent on new, highly paid administrators while staff serving the public was cut. Landlords, the Tenderloin Housing Clinic's longtime adversaries, had no problem agreeing with our position that eliminating substandard housing should be the city's top priority; their objection was to the city's costly and misplaced focus on inspecting housing that was *not* substandard. The builders had their own list of bureaucratic grievances, but they agreed that slumlords must be the prime target of city action. The resulting coalition was widely perceived as the most unusual and unexpected in recent city history.

Some people were amazed that landlords would agree to work with me on any issue, particularly something as major as a charter amendment affecting control of a $19 million department. A few tenant activists argued that if landlords supported our measure, it must not be as progressive as we claimed; others thought there must be a pro-landlord loophole in the initiative, although they knew I was the sole author. These attitudes reflected a common misunderstanding of the strategy necessary for achieving significant social change. Activists should not pursue an agenda based on what one's adversary will oppose; the goal is to achieve what one's own constituency needs. The first approach not only is actively defensive and reactive but also prevents the accomplishment of goals that may only be obtainable through a coalition with longtime adversaries. The tenants' most active partner in the initiative campaign was a group of Irish-American residential builders. Though not direct adversaries of low-income tenant advocates, they were generally perceived as being among the city's most conservative constituencies. The Clinic was accused of making a deal with the devil; some people felt it was better for low-income children to continue to live in heatless, rodent-infested apartments than for a reputable progressive activist like me to give credibility to the builders and their controversial president, Joe O'Donoghue. It was presumed that our alliance with builders was based on political considerations other than our constituencies' mutual self-interest. Advocates for low-income tenants, the homeless, and other victims of lax code-enforcement understood the need to make strategic alliances and strongly supported our broad, coalitional approach. The charter amendment passed in the election of November 1994, ending years of hostile bureaucratic control of city housing-code enforcement. Tactical activists willing to work with traditional adversaries to achieve their constituencies' goals should expect to be criticized, regardless of the results, by some of their usual allies.

Land-use battles also offer social change activists opportunities to prevail through coalitions with ideological opponents. In November 1989, San Francisco Mayor Art Agnos sponsored a local ballot measure that would make it easier to get approval for office development in an undeveloped area of the city. On the surface, this appeared to be a classic contest between neighborhood/slow-growth activists and the pro-growth/labor-developer faction. Agnos, however, had run for mayor as a slow-growth, neighborhood supporter, and his backing of the measure led many of his allies to advocate a proposal they clearly would have opposed under a conservative mayor. The shift of key slow-growth supporters to the pro-development side should have spelled doom for opponents of the measure. However, Calvin Welch, San Francisco's preeminent progressive activist for two decades, had an idea: he contacted longtime adversary Walter Shorenstein, the city's largest owner of downtown office space. Shorenstein recognized that the initiative could facilitate expansion of office development, reducing demand for office space in his own buildings. Shorenstein then joined Welch in opposing the measure on the grounds that San Francisco needed more affordable housing rather than more offices. Shorenstein contributed sufficient campaign funds to give Welch and other affordable-housing advocates a fighting chance in the election.

Welch's side prevailed in a very close race, and there was no doubt in anyone's mind that his alliance with Shorenstein was the key to victory. After the measure's defeat, Mayor Agnos renegotiated the development agreement by adding 1,300 more affordable housing units and reducing office development in the area. Welch's brilliant approach to coalition politics forced the city to commit more than $30 million in additional funds to low-income housing. But it also gave Welch a reputation for "untrustworthiness" among some activists bitter over his refusal to subordinate housing interests to the mayor's political agenda. Rather than winning admiration for having convinced one of the nation's wealthiest commercial developers to fund a campaign for more affordable housing, Welch was vilified for "cutting a deal." The fact that this "deal" solely benefited housing advocates, who would have fought the initiative regardless of Shorenstein's position, was overlooked. Welch had fallen out with Agnos over other issues early in the administration; his opposition to the initiative ensured that he would remain an outcast for the remaining two years of Agnos's term. It is this type of experience that makes activists with less commitment and stature than Welch hesitant to form coalitions with ideological opposites, even if such alliances are essential for their constituency to prevail.

THE LIMITS OF COALITION POLITICS

Although the Williamsburg coalition represents a success story, it also shows the danger points at which alliances between ideologically and culturally diverse groups can break down. The most obvious scenario is an irreconcilable dispute over strategy. For example, at the time the Latino housing activists vetoed the proposed Brooklyn-to-Manhattan march, NYPIRG believed the event was critical to defeating the incinerator project. NYPIRG feared the Cuomo administration might issue the permit before public pressure mounted and considered an immediate, high-profile publicity event essential. Fortunately, the state did not immediately act, and the campaign was not hurt by having delayed the march. Nevertheless, one can readily understand how a coalition partner thwarted on what it perceives as a make-or-break issue might be tempted to go forward on its own. Such unilateral action with the approval of the coalition may be permissible; however, groups that move forward over the objections of the their coalition not only risk undermining the entire cause but also sour their partners on future involvement in coalitions.

Coalitions also can fail when the participating organizations have different standards for success. Considering that coalitions of ideological opposites are often alliances of convenience, the coalition's opponents often can undermine unity by neutralizing one or more members. Such members often are chided for having been "bought off," though it may simply be a case in which groups honestly disagree about what constitutes victory. In the example of the Central City Shelter Network described in Chapter 1, the coalition of homeless activists fell apart when certain of the more traditional social service providers became satisfied with the mayor's response to their demands. Some of this satisfaction no doubt was caused by the mayor's decision to fund homeless programs operated by coalition members; other groups simply had different expectations of what constituted a reasonable response to the crisis.

The simplest strategy for maintaining coalitions among groups with diverse agendas is to put decisions in writing. By creating a process for evaluating progress and making decisions (what CAFE called its "Principles of Unity"), coalition members can facilitate mutual trust. The most important step is to establish a written list of demands at the start. This step enables partners with variant perspectives to resolve their differences prior to moving forward on the agenda. Though many social change activists and organizations are not oriented toward putting decisions in writing, documenting a set of agreed-upon demands reduces the risk that a group will backtrack in the future. Such documentation also helps if a recently hired staff member or new leader seeks to revisit a previously agreed-upon aim in the middle of a campaign. A written document showing the organization's original commitment can keep the coalition from returning to square one.

Tactical activists understand that working in coalitions is simply a means to fulfill a constituency's agenda. Like any effective tactic, however, coalition politics can be more hindrance than help if improperly used. For example, social change activists regularly attend meetings of diverse groups to discuss pressing issues. Invariably, someone at the meeting will suggest that "we" need to "bring in" other groups before deciding how to respond to the issue. The development of a strategy on the problem immediately ceases as people go around the room suggesting who should be invited to the next meeting. Someone may suggest that further discussion or decisionmaking be deferred until the subsequent meeting, leaving activists frustrated at having wasted their time. Some of these activists may skip the next meeting, preferring to move forward in solving the problem rather than make a resolution subject to the approval and timetable of other groups.

Unfortunately, coalitions provide a perfect forum for social change activists and organizations who feel more comfortable talking about problems than initiating a prompt and effective response. Action-oriented groups often find themselves penned in by the coalition approach and quickly realize that some, if not most, of the groups involved do not bring anything of political value to the table. In such instances, activists would be foolish to continue working through the coalition format, because the process frustrates rather than advances social change. Tactical activists should accept the risk of being attacked for refusing to work in coalitions rather than sacrifice their constituencies' agendas. It may be in a group's interest to defer substantive discussions until a key constituency can be brought into the process. Too often, however, delay occurs in order to round up the *usual* suspects rather than to round up groups whose diversity may change the political calculus and help ensure victory.

Coalitions are also problematic because decisionmaking is necessarily cumbersome. Most social change organizations are headed by a board of directors or executive committee. Coalition meetings are typically attended by organization members or staff, who do not have final decisionmaking authority. Some organizations vest staff with authority to make decisions consistent with the board's agenda, but others require board approval of every coalition decision or tactic. Such policies may effectively prevent the coalition from making the type of immediate response to events that is often necessary for success and that individual group constituencies often demand. Though organizations often have legitimate reasons for keeping staff and members on a short leash, lengthy approval processes can spell doom for the coalition. This is particularly true where powerful groups like the UJO or El Puente are involved; such groups are not going to enter a coalition that weakens them. Activists can respond to the approval problem either by avoiding coalitions with groups that have impractical decisionmaking procedures or by moving forward in their own name rather than the coalition's. The issue of decisionmaking procedures should be openly discussed and resolved prior to the coalition's beginning its work. In the Williamsburg case, no formal discussion of decisionmaking was necessary because each group understood it could not proceed without the other. Unless similar circumstances exist, groups seeking to work in coalition must reach agreement on decisionmaking procedures that are practical and acceptable to all.

Even when all groups accept the tactical benefit of forming a coalition, agree on a set of demands, and resolve issues of decisionmaking, there remains the problem of finances. My own organization, the Tenderloin Housing Clinic, has never been dependent on foundation support. When the San Francisco Foundation awarded the Clinic grants for organizing and empowering low-income tenants, we were encouraged to work in concert with other groups. Unfortunately, many nonprofit social change groups believe they need to win victories on their own in order to prove their value to foundation or government funders. Such organizations end up choosing smaller, more winnable fights. As a result, foundation funds targeted for community organizing get spent on campaigns to remove unsightly bus stops or to increase the number of trash cans in an area. If such campaigns were the first step toward fulfilling a larger agenda, the funds would be well spent. Unfortunately, the ideology of working independently to prove the value of one's group seems more permanent than transitional. The removal of the bus stop leads to a fight for a stop sign rather than, for example, a broad-based campaign to get downtown corporations to pay for the cost of the transit impacts they cause.

Progressive constituencies do not have the luxury of focusing on trivial though winnable issues. The UJO and El Puente could have worked independently to win all sorts of minor environmental victories instead of taking on a waste incinerator backed by Wall Street, the *New York Times*, construction unions, and city government. Both Niederman and Garden Acosta understood, however, that you do not empower people by backing off from the big fights. As the Reverend Mark Taylor put it, "You can't pursue real social justice by only picking small and winnable fights."[43] They also recognized that the waste incinerator would cause greater environmental harm than could ever be mitigated through a dozen smaller victories. Coalition activism is really about recognizing the mutual self-interest that often exists among diverse and even adversarial groups and then unifying these groups to accomplish a goal none of them could achieve on its own. In most political environments, support from traditional progressive constituencies alone is inadequate to prevail; creating diverse coalitions has therefore become increasingly essential to success.

Ballot Initiatives

THE RULES OF THE GAME

At the turn of the twentieth century, social reformers pursued several strategies for curtailing wealthy interests' growing control of political institutions. One such strategy, a centerpiece of the newly created Progressive Party, was the use of the initiative, the referendum, and the recall. Such measures were designed to regain public control over government by allowing "the people" to legislate directly (the initiative), overturn laws they did not like (the referendum), and remove officeholders who were betraying the public good (the recall). The West Coast led this populist approach. Oregon adopted the initiative process in 1902, and California followed in 1911 as part of the campaign platform of its Progressive Party governor, Hiram Johnson. Nearly half of the states now allow the initiative process. Initiatives increasingly constitute the main subject of political debate, as controversial issues such as term limits, gay rights, and property-tax reduction have appeared on several state ballots, often during the same election. California, for better or worse, has been the national trendsetter for statewide initiatives. By November 1994 Californians had voted on 834 initiatives since 1911—432 of them after 1978. The nationwide "tax revolt" began with the passage of California's Proposition 13 in 1978 and spread as far east as Massachusetts, which passed the less drastic Proposition 2 1/2. California's approval of a term-limits initiative in 1990 made the concept a staple of state ballots throughout the country. California even set the pace with anti-gay ballot measures, voting on the Briggs initiative, which would have barred gays and lesbians from teaching in public schools, among other things, in 1978. The initiative, which failed, arose more than a decade before anti-gay initiatives became a high-profile tactic of the Christian right in such states as Colorado, Oregon, and Idaho.

California's experience has led to skepticism of and even outright opposition to the initiative process, even on the part of progressives. The frequent use of the initiative process by wealthy corporations and other business interests to circumvent legislative obstacles has led some people to ask whether "a populist stick has become a business sledgehammer."[1] Noted pollster Mervin Field claims that Hiram Johnson "would turn over in his grave if he saw how special interests have taken over the initiative process."[2] Other critics have argued that initiatives reduce the "complex public debate" that surrounds the legislative process to "simplistic sloganeering."[3]

Mainstream opposition to initiatives is not surprising. The corporate, media, and political elites who strive to control the terms of political discourse do not want "outsiders" interfering in the process of policy development or implementation. There is something very threatening about citizens' achieving goals without first obtaining approval from elected officials or other powerful interests. Once citizens learn to exercise power independently of politicians or the labyrinthine legislative process, the elite's well-crafted strategy to limit political possibilities becomes suspect. As long as initiatives give people the dangerous idea that they can bring about social change on their own, they will face opposition from those in control of the mediating structures designed to limit such action.

Unfortunately, some progressive critics have come to join political elites in opposing the initiative process. For example, an editor of a progressive publication has attacked initiatives on the grounds that California's Proposition 13 had caused irrevocable damage to the state. He alleged that such initiatives allowed wealthy interests to bypass the deliberate and democratic legislative process in order to govern by advertising slogan and political mailer. Because the side spending the most money usually prevails in initiative campaigns, the writer charged, initiatives were becoming yet another vehicle enabling conservative interests to achieve their goals. The editorial glumly concluded by noting the irony that a procedure originally designed to help the people defeat special interests had instead become the reverse.

Many social change activists share the editorial's critique of the initiative process. It is therefore more important than ever for tactical activists to understand why this critique is misplaced and, more important, why ballot initiatives are increasingly the only viable route left for the attainment of significant social change. Initiatives have skyrocketed in California since 1978, for example, largely because activists on the right and left view the state legislature as entirely unresponsive to real social change. This unresponsiveness seems particularly noticeable with respect to issues of economic fairness, where legislatures across the nation have become virtual captives of major corporate, insurance, banking, and real estate interests.[4] The "complex public debate" surrounding the legislative process primarily involves corporate lobbyists and the politicians under their control; the ability to achieve serious progressive social change through Congress or most state legislatures is increasingly illusory. Social change activists simply cannot afford to forgo initiatives. Yet as most progressive and conservative initiatives go down to defeat in the face of big-money opposition, the feeling persists that the initiative process cannot achieve progressive goals. This chapter will discuss the rules activists must follow to achieve their goals through ballot initiatives.

The discussion will focus on California, whose measures have consistently foreshadowed national trends. In addition to the state's role as a national bellwether, California has three other advantages as a case study. First, tracking one state's response to different measures over time helps demonstrate why some measures succeed and others fail. Second, California is a large, diverse state whose ballot measures regularly become part of national policy debates. For example, California's successful anti-immigrant measure on the November 1994 ballot, Proposition 187, led the president, U.S. attorney general, and two national Republican leaders (Jack Kemp and William Bennett) to become actively involved in the debate over immigration policy. California initiatives do not simply presage initiative battles in other states; they directly influence national policy.

THE FIVE RULES OF PROGRESSIVE INITIATIVES

Rule 1: There Is No Other Way The first rule for progressive ballot initiatives is to examine alternative approaches to achieving the measure's goal. As critics of the initiative process frequently note, progressive ballot measures are difficult to pass. Initiative campaigns are costly and time-consuming and often require activists and organizations to put all other issues on hold during the several months leading up to election day. It simply makes no sense to try to pass an initiative if its objective can be accomplished through the legislative process, direct action, or other less daunting tactics. Most progressive ballot measures have satisfied this test, pursuing goals lacking alternative strategies for achievement. Progressives are more likely to err on the other side, continuing to engage in extensive lobbying or grassroots mobilization despite the slim chance of winning a legislative victory. For example, children's advocates in San Francisco spent three years creating annual "children's budgets" that showed how city funds could be redirected to serve children's needs more efficiently. Despite large public turnouts at budget meetings and support from city department heads, however, the mayor continually failed to include the children's budget in the city's final overall budget. Further, the various revenue-generating proposals necessary to pay for increased children's services were continually ignored. The San Francisco children's advocates then learned of a 1990 Washington state ballot initiative that would have increased funding for children's services. Although the Washington measure was soundly defeated, the San Francisco advocates saw an alternative to their unwinnable legislative fight. The failed budget campaigns also had drained advocates' financial, professional, and emotional resources. The issue finally went to the ballot, and on November 5, 1991, San Francisco became the first city in the United States to guarantee annual increases in funding for children's services in its annual budget. After three years of frustrating attempts to work "through the system," one children's leader concluded that going straight for the ballot may be the best strategy for her movement.[5]

Rule 2: Appeal to Voters' Self-Interest   The second requirement for a tactically successful initiative is that a significant portion of the voters must view its passage as being in their own self-interest. As much as social change activists may decry American society's emphasis on individualism and self-interest, they must accept that most Americans espouse these values. Noted organizer Saul Alinsky made this point, stating, "Political realists see the world as it is: an arena of power politics moved primarily by perceived immediate self-interest, where morality is rhetorical rationale for expedient action and self-interest."[6] My own experience is that even the poorest members of our society, the victims of our capitalist economic system, share the underlying societal belief in the virtue of self-interest as motivation. By contrast, social change organizations include disproportionate numbers of people *not* motivated by economic or personal self-interest. As a result, their ballot measures, legislative campaigns, and direct-action struggles ask the public to act not out of self-interest but rather out of concern for "good government" or "fairness." Although there is certainly nothing wrong with working on issues that cannot be framed as in the self-interest of a major segment of the public, those who lack a personal stake in the outcome of an initiative are more likely to be swayed by misleading commercials and mailers. As a result, initiatives lacking the requisite self-interest component typically fail, and progressive cynicism about the initiative process increases.

The degree to which an initiative appeals to voters' self-interest compellingly predicts electoral results. California, the unparalleled national leader in initiatives, proves this thesis every election. The infamous Proposition 13 of 1978, which launched a nationwide anti-tax revolt that has yet to subside, won because it offered a majority of the electorate a reduction in property taxes. The campaign against Proposition 13 focused on how lost tax revenue would negatively impact schools, social services, and the public infrastructure. This noteworthy and altruistic "do what is good for society" theme could not possibly overcome individuals' desires for lower property taxes. More than fifteen years later, all the fears raised by Proposition 13 opponents have proven correct. California's spending on its schools, social services, and once top-notch infrastructure now rivals the notoriously low levels of Mississippi. Nevertheless, the self-interest motivation remains so strong that polls show continued support for Proposition 13, and no ballot initiative to overturn it has arisen.

Many social change activists responded to Proposition 13 by crafting progressive initiatives appealing to the same philosophical motivation. Proposition 13's passage in 1978 immediately prompted action from tenants, who had been promised during the campaign that their landlords' property-tax saving would be passed on to them in the form of lower rents. When tenants failed to receive the promised benefits, they used local ballot initiatives to enact rent controls in Berkeley, Santa Monica, and West Hollywood. Other cities, such as San Francisco, enacted weak forms of rent control to preempt stronger ballot measures planned by tenant organizations. Although real estate interests consistently spent millions in local races to defeat rent-control, such expenditures failed to convince tenants to vote against their direct financial self-interest.

Harvey Rosenfield, head of the consumer organization Voter Revolt, and Bill Zimmerman, a political consultant with a background in winning rent control campaigns, took the self-interest theme to the state level with an insurance-rollback initiative in November 1988. Rosenfield's Proposition 103 transferred middle-class resentment against property taxes into the auto and property insurance arena. The measure required insurance companies to accept a one-time 20 percent cut in property- and auto-insurance rates and subjected future rate increases to the approval of an elected insurance commissioner. Middle-class voters in Los Angeles were particularly affected by high auto insurance rates, which were well above the state average. Although several factors contributed to Proposition 103's surprising victory, the central one was the prospect of insurance refunds and lower rates for individual voters. The insurance industry and its allies spent over $75 million on insurance-related initiatives in that same election, yet all the commercials could not overcome Proposition 103's appeal to voters' self-interest.

By contrast, a similar effort by Zimmerman in November 1992 failed to make such an appeal. Zimmerman's "Tax the Rich" initiative, Proposition 167, called for the state to increase the revenues collected from wealthy individuals and corporations. Although the measure would have created a more equitable tax system and increased state revenues, it was difficult for individual voters to see how they would gain financially from the initiative. Lacking such clear and direct financial self-interest, Proposition 167 fell prey to its opponents' corporate-funded multimillion-dollar campaign against it. The opposition itself sought to appeal to the self-interest of voters by describing Proposition 167 as "The Jobs Terminator." Commercials had a local auto-parts owner bemoaning the prospect that Proposition 167 would force him to lay off workers just as the state was coming out of a recession. Voters barraged with such ads may have felt their own livelihood depended on Proposition 167's defeat.[7]

California's November 1990 ballot also included two environmental measures that ran aground because, among other reasons, they failed the self-interest test. Both the "Forests Forever" initiative and the "Big Green" multi-issue environmental measure were defeated, the latter soundly. Voters had difficulty concluding that they would directly benefit from the initiatives, and opponents cautioned that tax increases would ensue to pay for the initiatives, giving voters a self-interest reason to vote no. The difficulty of translating environmental issues into self-interest terms has hampered environmentalists seeking to use initiatives, though all too often the need to make such an appeal is ignored.

Rule 3: Keep It Simple   During Bill Clinton's presidential campaign, his top political advisers recognized their candidate's willingness to drift from their central strategic focus: the economy. To ensure that Clinton and his campaign spokespersons stayed on theme, a notorious sign was posted in the "war room": "It's the economy, stupid." This statement had two meanings. First, it sought to ensure that Clinton focused on the issue most likely to win him votes. Second, and less widely noted, the phrase meant that a simple economic theme would more likely persuade voters than would complex plans for a wide range of issues.

Lack of simplicity is the fatal flaw in all too many progressive ballot initiatives. Many social change activists are understandably eager to solve complex problems and often create "Christmas tree" measures designed to achieve wide-ranging goals. They reason that if tremendous energy and resources are to be invested in an initiative campaign, the initiative should really make a difference. Unfortunately, their measures try to solve too many problems at once. They cannot be explained to voters in one sentence and are defeated as much out of voter confusion as on the merits. These attempts to remedy multiple social problems with one measure resemble the panicky strategy of a football team that falls three touchdowns behind and then tries to catch up by throwing long passes into the end zone on every play. This tactic does not work in sports, and it will not work to achieve social change.

For example, many progressives were surprised at the large margin of defeat for Proposition 128, the Big Green initiative, on California's November 1990 ballot. Environmentalists assumed that huge public support for the twentieth anniversary of Earth Day earlier that year would guarantee victory for any environmental measure. The initiative's authors, who included the state's leading environmental groups and longtime activist and state assemblyman Tom Hayden, must have felt likewise, because the Big Green initiative was a multifaceted measure seeking valuable but entirely diverse environmental goals. Big Green included provisions to regulate pesticide use to protect food and agricultural workers; phase out chemicals that potentially depleted the ozone layer; reduce emissions of gases contributing to global warming; limit oil and gas drilling within ocean waters; require oil-spill-prevention plans; establish water-quality criteria; create an elective office of environmental advocate with the power to enforce all state environmental and public-health laws; and issue $300 million in bonds to fund the acquisition of ancient redwood forests and another $40 million for environmental research. The initiative may have been intended to touch upon the self-interest of environmentalists in every field, but its resulting complexity likely confused voters not automatically committed to environmental initiatives. Further, by including provisions creating a new administrative position and issuing bonds, Big Green weakened its support among fiscal conservatives and anti-bureaucracy voters who might otherwise support the initiative's environmental regulatory provisions. Big Green's "Christmas tree" approach allowed opponents to argue that the 39-page, 16,000-word measure tried to do too much and that each of its provisions should be debated and voted upon separately.[8] Voters could oppose the measure on these grounds yet continue to identify themselves as pro-environment.

In contrast to Big Green, Proposition 130, the Forests Forever initiative on the same ballot, contained a message that could be explained in one phrase: preserve ancient forests. Supported by many of the same environmental groups sponsoring Big Green, Proposition 130 sought to impose new restrictions on logging and authorized a $742 million bond issue for state acquisition of old-growth forest lands. By focusing on only one issue and framing the debate as a clear choice between redwood trees and timber companies, Proposition 130 advocates relied on a simple message that should have prevailed at the polls. The measure's narrow defeat can be attributed to two factors unrelated to its drafters' tactical sagacity. First, the election occurred during a period of statewide economic insecurity that caused voter opposition to new bonds (a trend not fully grasped until after the election results). Second, the Big Green measure brought in money to the campaigns opposing both environmental initiatives that would not have emerged if Proposition 130 stood alone. Proposition 130 could have overcome opposition from timber interests despite the voters' fiscal concerns, but Big Green acted like an anchor, pulling its companion initiative down to defeat. Moreover, the two environmental measures competed for pro-environmental campaign contributions. In all, the far stronger electoral performance of Proposition 130 over Big Green confirms the necessity of initiative simplicity.

The need to keep it simple does not mean that an initiative's language cannot be complex. As long as the measure can be explained in one sentence, most voters will not need to review the text carefully. Thus, although Proposition 103's auto insurance rollback used complicated legal language, everyone understood that a "yes" vote meant lower insurance premiums. In 1986 Tom Hayden sponsored an environmental initiative, the Safe Drinking Water and Toxic Enforcement Act (Proposition 165), that was as textually complicated as could be. Yet its message was simple: vote "yes" for protections against toxics. Had Proposition 165 also included provisions to create a state toxics commissioner or issue environmental bonds, à la Big Green, it would likely have gone down to defeat. California's historic and successful Coastal Protection Act of 1972 was another textually complex, "big picture" initiative whose message—protect our coast—could easily be explained in a sentence.

Ease of comprehension is even more critical in light of media trends. It has become increasingly rare for major news organizations to spend resources on detailed analyses of state or local ballot initiatives. Local television news departments typically do only one story (if that) on most measures, and all the viewing public is likely to glean from the story is the initiative's basic content. If you cannot convincingly describe your measure in the one or two sentences television news provides, forget it. Newspapers have so cut back on hard news that one story may discuss several initiatives. Neither television, radio, nor print journalism is likely to provide enough coverage to satisfy many social change activists' desire to use the measure as an educational campaign. And when the media do "educate" voters about the measure, it is not likely to be in the direction initiative advocates expect. There may never have been a single progressive ballot measure created by grassroots activists and opposed by major corporate interests that has received strong mainstream media support. The owners of the major media often align with progressives in opposition to right-wing ballot measures, but they are not in the business of fomenting social justice or redistribution of wealth.

Tactical activists must discard the notion that the media will effectively explain a complex, multifaceted initiative to voters; they should be satisfied if the brief coverage the initiative receives is fair and accurate. A simple-to-understand measure facilitates this result. A reporter assigned to write a story on an initiative is no more likely than the average voter to sort out its complexities. Proponents of complicated initiatives should not be surprised when reporters trying to be fair misstate essential terms. In the current "MTV" world of journalism, issues must be quickly and convincingly conveyed, because audience attention spans are fleeting. The ability to convey the advantage of your measure in one bold sentence has become a necessity in radio and television news.

Keeping it simple has another advantage: forestalling opposition attacks. The easiest way to defeat an initiative is to focus on its most controversial point and talk about nothing else. All political sides use this tactic to defeat measures that violate the rule of simplicity. The opposition to a school-voucher initiative on California's November 1993 ballot is a case in point. Sponsored by the right wing, the complex measure included a provision allowing public financing for schools operated by religious sects, including witches. With the assistance of cooperative members of the Wicca cult, opponents of the voucher initiative pointed out that practicing witches could open schools with taxpayer money. Few people knew how many witches operated private schools in California, but any conscientious voter had to oppose the voucher initiative to ensure that public funds were not spent on such schools. Voucher proponents included many such controversial features in their measure, thus ensuring that even voters upset with the public schools would vote against the initiative.

Opponents of multifaceted initiatives frequently take out full-page newspaper ads in which each and every component of the measure is isolated and questioned. The idea is to ensure that all voters—even those that favor most elements of the measure—find at least one part of the initiative objectionable. The big money interests that oppose progressive initiatives will make sure the media and advertising focus remains on the objectionable parts. Defenders of multifaceted initiatives argue that because opponents will distort even the simplest measure, there is no risk to placing more comprehensive measures on the ballot. However, this reasoning fails to recognize that the distortions included in opposition campaign materials are typically those of emphasis and interpretation, not of fact. Multifaceted initiatives, no matter how popular their central features, give their well-funded opponents more elements to attack, which is why they so rarely pass.

Rule 4: Create the Initiative Through Due Process   The fourth test of a progressive initiative is whether it has been developed with due process. Is the initiative a product of only a small portion of a constituency, or does it have the enthusiastic support of the individuals and groups whose campaign participation is essential for victory? Tactical activists should never promote a measure that does not have the support of the key constituency groups addressing the issue. Such measures are divisive, distracting, and counterproductive and hence never, ever win. Unfortunately, such measures are very commonly set forth, often by well-meaning activists convinced that they alone have seen the light to the Promised Land.

In an earlier era, groups that proceeded without broader constituency support would be labeled "sectarian" or identify themselves as a "vanguard" party. Today they are better described as iconoclasts. I like iconoclasts; they are typically interested in discussing ideas and strongly sup-

port the principle of proactive action. Unfortunately, iconoclasts operate in a fictional world where voters are desperate for radical social
change but deprived of the opportunity to vote their desires by out-of-
touch organization leaders and politicians. Instead of engaging in the
grassroots organizing necessary to create a broad constituency base for
their agenda, iconoclasts skip this step and put their agenda directly on
the ballot. Iconoclastic groups and individuals generally lack the money
or constituency to get their measures on statewide ballots, so their havoc
is largely confined to local elections.

A prime example of how tactical activists should respond to icono-
clast-created initiatives occurred during San Francisco's anti-development
wars of the 1980s. San Francisco's increasing Manhattanization led to
strong support of slow-growth initiatives in 1979 and 1983, although
both narrowly failed. The 1983 defeat led City Hall to try to address voters' concerns by imposing some limitations on downtown growth. Because the city's vaunted "Downtown Plan" was widely viewed as inadequate (except by the *New York Times,* whose front page gushed over
the plan's precedent-setting growth limits), slow-growth activists geared
up for a 1986 ballot showdown in which they were confident of victory.

With every slow-growth organization planning for the 1986 ballot, a
self-styled neighborhood activist gathered enough signatures to put a
poorly conceived slow-growth measure on the 1985 ballot. The initiative was not the product of a broad-based discussion among key constituency groups, yet voters might have viewed it as such because it was
the only slow-growth measure on the ballot. Slow-growth advocates
feared that the inevitable defeat of the measure would hurt the entire
movement and make it harder to come back to the voters with another
initiative the following year. The iconoclast had thus touched all the
bases: he had bypassed due process, started a divisive and distracting ballot fight that could harm the broader campaign, and gained publicity for
himself, an ambition that often drives iconoclastic groups and individuals to initiative efforts.

However, San Francisco's two most prominent slow-growth activists,
Sue Hestor and Calvin Welch, were sharper than the iconoclast. These
tactical activists spoke out against the measure, thus ensuring that the
public would not associate the slow-growth movement with a doomed
and ill-conceived campaign. They opposed the initiative on the grounds
that it was too weak, thus setting the stage for their own more rigorous
measure. Because their critique came from the left, the iconoclast could
not attack the activists for being too "moderate" or "pragmatic." As a

result, the iconoclast's measure lost all credibility and was defeated, and the 1986 slow-growth measure subsequently prevailed.

I do not mean to argue that tactical activists should always oppose initiatives that are not the product of due process. The point is that appropriate action must be taken to prevent iconoclast-driven ballot measures from impairing constituency-based social change activism. Often silence will serve this purpose; the failure of recognized organizations and individuals to support a measure addressing their issue of concern speaks volumes. Credible groups should not feel obligated to follow an iconoclast as he or she leaps with their issue off a cliff. An organization that engages in proactive agenda setting and develops tactics and strategies for implementation should never be sidetracked by one individual's Lone Ranger approach.

Rule 5: Evaluate the Political Context   The process of determining whether to resort to the initiative process must not occur in a political vacuum. This statement may seem obvious, but people actively involved in a particular issue can easily become unmindful of broader political events. Obvious examples of such unmindfulness occur when progressive initiatives requiring a large voter turnout are placed before the voters in off-year elections. It does not take a political genius to figure out that certain elections will have lower turnouts, which, particularly at the state level, ensure an electorate that disproportionately consists of fiscally conservative white homeowners. Placing progressive initiatives such as tax rebates for renters or park-acquisition bond issues on projected low-turnout ballots almost guarantees defeat. Even worse, the defeat of progressive initiatives on off-year ballots can convince proponents and their allies that the public simply opposes such measures. Winnable battles are too often lost due to the failure to understand the importance of political timing.

Unfortunately, even well-timed campaigns can go awry. Consider the fate of California's single-payer health care reform measure, Proposition 186, on the November 1994 ballot. When the signature drive for the initiative was launched in early 1994, there was broad consensus that Congress would pass some form of health care reform before the election. This was to be the year in which the United States finally joined all other industrial nations in guaranteeing health coverage for the vast majority of its residents. As late as June 1994, Representative Vic Fazio, chairman of the Democratic Congressional Campaign Committee, told his colleagues that "health care is the make-or-break issue, the centerpiece of congressional activity" for the fall election.[9] Proponents of California's Proposition 186 were operating on the seemingly safe assumption that health care reform would be strongly on voters' minds during the fall campaign season in California.

However, less than two months after Fazio's prediction, congressional health care reform was dead. Its demise was so tortuously drawn out that voters were left confused by the health care debate and/or disgusted by Congress's failure to act. Polls showed that voters still cared about health care reform but that the issue was being entirely ignored in Senate and House campaigns.[10] In a year of record levels of television campaign advertising, only one commercial committed a candidate for federal office—Senator Ted Kennedy of Massachusetts—to fight for national health care legislation in 1995.

California's Proposition 186 faced an even worse fate than public indifference. Right-wing interests, with the tacit support of California's Republican governor, Pete Wilson, had succeeded in placing on the ballot Proposition 187, an initiative to end all public services to illegal immigrants. This measure, combined with Wilson's campaign focus on the issue, made illegal immigration rather than health care the centerpiece of the fall election initiative debate. Progressive forces who might have joined the drive to pass Proposition 186 instead focused on the unsuccessful campaign to defeat Proposition 187. Conservatives, who frequently use initiatives to frame the public debate around their issues, also had a "three strikes and you're out" bill on the same ballot. The presence of a harsh anti-crime measure and an anti-immigrant measure, combined with Wilson's $25 million reelection campaign emphasizing these two themes, moved Proposition 186 and health care reform almost entirely out of public consciousness.

Because the state Democratic Party opposed single-payer, Proposition 186 proponents could get their measure into the public debate only by taking publicity-generating actions or by spending their limited campaign resources on advertising. A poll taken in early September 1994 found that only 29 percent of those surveyed had even heard of the single-payer measure.[11] Advocates tried to arouse public attention through tactics such as civil disobedience by wheelchair users, but plans to blockade insurance companies and other high-profile actions either never took place or never won media coverage. In the political climate that emerged only months before the November election, the single-payer initiative never had a chance. A campaign that could have weathered the crash-and-burn of congressional health care legislation could not overcome the additional hurdle of an electorate focused on other issues. The single-payer concept was likely too new to win in November 1994 under the best of circumstances; its appearing in what turned out to be the worst possible election cycle led to a landslide defeat that may not be a true measure of its future chances for success in California or other states.

Evaluating the political context also means not promoting a hot-button measure if it will assist conservative political candidates. Californians paid a terrible price for a small group's ill-advised decision to place a weak gun-control measure on the November 1982 ballot. The measure caused a higher-than-projected turnout among gun-owning, largely conservative rural voters. Having made the trip to the polls to vote against the gun-control measure, these traditional nonvoters also voted overwhelmingly for George Deukmejian, the Republican candidate for governor. Deukmejian, a right-wing law-and-order candidate, was expected to lose narrowly to Democrat Tom Bradley, the African-American former mayor of Los Angeles. Unlike crime or tax-cutting measures, which appear in many elections, a gun-control initiative had not previously appeared on the state ballot. It thus brought to the polls precisely the type of people progressives would rather not see on election day. The gun-control measure made every mistake in the book: it was an iconoclast-type initiative, could not be simply explained, appealed to the strong self-interest of opponents rather than supporters, and ignored the November 1982 political context. Further, California had no statewide network of grassroots gun-control activists in 1982, whereas opposition to gun control had a hard-core base in rural and conservative urban areas throughout the state. The measure's proponents were thus out-organized and outspent and had no chance to win. Its strong defeat would be forgotten but for its critical role in electing "the Duke" as governor and moving California politics sharply to the right.

Although weak initiatives can harm other progressive causes and candidates, strong ones can increase turnout among nonvoting progressives. An issue must be selected that is of particular concern to a certain group of nonvoters, who will then vote for other progressive candidates or issues. For example, initiatives requiring police to make the enforcement of marijuana laws a low priority can increase the student vote in local elections in university towns. Many students do not follow politics in the city in which they attend college, but reducing the risk of marijuana use offers the necessary self-interest motivation to get them to the polls. Once they decide to vote, they are likely to rely on a progressive slate card in selecting candidates and positions on issues. Ballot measures seeking to reduce fares or improve service for public transit also have the potential to bring nonvoting progressives to the polls. People who rely on public transit often cannot afford cars, rent rather than own their homes, and have low to moderate incomes.

A key strategy that to my knowledge remains untapped is the use of initiatives to increase voter turnout in lower-income African-American and Latino communities. National and state elected officials increasingly ignore these constituencies in their pursuit of white, suburban voters, sending the message that politicians do not care if low-income racial minorities vote. If candidates are not trying to win their support during the "I'll promise you anything" campaign period, why would minority individuals think they had a stake in the outcome? Of all the various ballot measures that have emerged to circumvent legislative roadblocks, few if any have been primarily geared to the needs of low-income or minority voters. Part of this astonishing absence is attributable to a chicken-and-egg scenario: because low-income and minority voter turnout is light, initiatives do not focus on low-income or minority concerns; because initiatives and candidates do not address their concerns, low-income people do not vote.

Poor and minority communities experience a social disenfranchisement and feeling of disempowerment so vast that their members do not even vote when their own pocketbooks are at stake. For example, California governor Pete Wilson put a measure on the November 1992 state ballot that would further slash already paltry welfare benefits for families. Activists seeking to organize San Francisco public housing tenants whose incomes would be affected by the measure were unable either to obtain many campaign volunteers or noticeably increase voter turnout. By contrast, my organization, the Tenderloin Housing Clinic, has had success getting single indigent adults on county welfare to walk precincts, hand out literature, and vote in high percentages by emphasizing tenant- and welfare-rights initiatives. Our success comes from year-round contact with single-room-occupancy hotel tenants, a process far harder to duplicate in mammoth housing projects like Chicago's Cabrini-Green that virtually constitute separate cities. The Clinic's success in getting low-income people involved at the earliest stages in tenant, welfare, and code-enforcement initiatives shows the possibilities at the local level. The lack of health insurance disproportionately affects low-income and minority communities, so proponents of California's single-payer measure had to achieve high voter turnout among these groups. Their unfortunate political timing kept them from doing so. Because low-income workers have a strong self-interest in single-payer insurance and look more favorably on government's actively solving problems, the ability to increase voter turnout among this group will be critical to the success of future single-payer ballot measures throughout the nation.

In assessing whether the broader political context favors placing an initiative on a particular ballot, tactical activists may discover that the measure can achieve important organizational goals even if defeated at the polls. For example, once the signature drive for California's 1990 Forests Forever initiative began, the lumber industry on the north coast began reducing the all-out clear-cutting that spurred the measure. Initiative proponents estimated that nearly a million old-growth redwoods were temporarily spared between the launching of the initiative and election day. Presumably, the lumber industry's political consultants advised their clients to avoid massive clear-cutting that would outrage voters prior to the election. Launching an initiative thus proved a good tactic because, even in defeat, the measure slowed the elimination of old-growth forests. Similarly, the launching of an urban slow-growth initiative almost always has an immediate impact on unbridled development. The narrow defeat of anti-high-rise measures in San Francisco in 1979 and 1983 led even the ardently pro-development Feinstein administration to impose development and transit impact fees on office developers. These regulations came in response to voter support of the 1983 initiative's demand that downtown pay its fair share of the cost of city services. Although slow-growth advocates were unsatisfied by the mitigations and returned to the ballot in 1986, the failed 1983 initiative played a key role in achieving development restrictions. Further, the initiatives established that even supporters of downtown office development wanted approvals conditioned on payments for affected public services, including child care, housing, and public transit. Establishing this support for impact fees led to movements in other major cities for what former Boston mayor Raymond Flynn described as "linkage"—requiring developers to compensate the city for the public burdens imposed by their projects. The very concept of linkage has its roots in San Francisco's tactically wise but ultimately unsuccessful initiative campaigns.

Gauging the broader political context before pursuing the initiative route also requires honest discussion about money and volunteer resources. Tactical activists must accept that every progressive initiative will meet opposition from private industry groups that will spend whatever they deem necessary to maintain the status quo. Post-election complaints about the opposition's hired-gun consultants, its "dirty" campaign, or its large spending advantage are mere rationalizations; no sympathy need be given to those who are defeated by foreseeable, rather than unexpected, obstacles. This realism also means that proponents of defeated measures should not claim victory based on who got the most votes per dollar or make other excuses to conceal what is in reality a tactical error—failure to include their opposition's financial capabilities in their analysis of whether an initiative is the proper strategy. Activists must also consider their own financial potential, as even the most grassroots-oriented efforts require money for campaign literature or ballot arguments. Launching an initiative drive on a wing and a prayer is no different from starting a business without capital; a hopeful enterprise soon dissolves in bickering and recrimination over a lack of necessary funds.

Honest discussion about volunteer resources may be even more vital than financial projections. Many activists rely on the "field of dreams" approach to initiative campaigns: if they put a progressive initiative on the ballot, active campaign volunteers will come. The initiative world does not so work. In my experience, the vast majority of initiative campaign volunteers are people connected to organizations sponsoring the measure. A handful of people always contact the campaign office to volunteer, but you cannot build a campaign around walk-ins. Each group involved in deciding whether to use an initiative must make an honest assessment at the outset about its volunteer resources. I am not describing this process as requiring a "commitment" of volunteers, because I have seen too many such commitments broken, and they cannot be enforced. Few groups want to douse the excitement that surrounds the early discussions of an initiative by saying something like, "Gee, it's a great idea. My group will endorse it, and tell our members to vote for it, but we are not willing to make phone calls, drop literature, or do anything that is necessary for the initiative to prevail." It may be that a group's members do not like to work on initiative campaigns or are committed to working for a candidate on another issue on the same ballot. All too many progressive initiatives are defeated not because of anything the opposition said or spent but because the expected grassroots campaign never materializes. A real grassroots effort is defined by bodies, not by a shoestring budget and inadequate campaign materials. Many a progressive defeat might have been averted had key constituency groups stated plainly at the idea stage, "Do not rely on us for volunteers." Better this frankness than infighting and recriminations during the campaign over an organization's failure to keep its volunteer commitment.

To summarize: a progressive initiative should do well if it appeals to the self-interest of a significant portion of the electorate, is simple enough to be explained in one sentence, has been developed though a fair and open process involving key constituency groups, is timed to appear in a high-turnout election, and has sufficient money and volunteer resources to withstand a big-money opposition campaign. I had the opportunity in 1992 to test this analysis at the ballot box. Our strategic planning for an initiative resulted not only in one of the biggest surprise victories in San Francisco political history but also, and more important, an unprecedented redistribution of millions of dollars in wealth from the rich to the poor and middle class. The initiative's story serves as an example of what tactical activists can accomplish by adhering to the rules of the initiative process.

SAN FRANCISCO'S PROPOSITION H: WINNING ECONOMIC JUSTICE AT THE BALLOT BOX

In November 1991 I had the misfortune of observing a ballot measure that violated every single rule discussed in this chapter—the vacancy-control measure that contributed to the downfall of Mayor Art Agnos (Chapter 2). The measure asked voters to limit the amount by which landlords could raise the rent when units became vacant. To the surprise of many, it went down to a landslide defeat. I viewed the measure with the same trepidation and sense of helplessness one might feel when watching a brakeless train approaching a cliff. I was surprised by the margin of defeat, but I had always perceived a fundamental flaw in the measure that could be described in five words: vacant units do not vote. The principal requirement for any successful progressive initiative—that a significant percentage of the electorate find a self-interest benefit—was entirely absent. Few people casting a ballot on election day could be sure of receiving any advantage from the measure's passage. All of the claimed benefits were conditioned upon a voter's moving within the city to a new apartment, whose initial rent might be lower if the initiative passed. This remote possibility was understandably dismissed by most voters. Nor was the vacancy-control initiative simple enough to explain in one sentence. The measure was so riddled with loopholes, "good landlord" exceptions, and complicated rent-increase mechanisms that the raw concept no longer said enough. Activists were willing to ignore the complexity of the measure and focus on the big picture; voters were not.

Because the vacancy-control measure was not truly a creation of tenant groups, the necessary due process for ballot measures was also absent. Although all tenant groups endorsed the measure, their members had been entirely left out of the planning stages. This problem manifested itself in the absence of any grassroots election campaign, thus violating the requirement that progressive initiatives have the volunteer base necessary to offset the opposition's financial advantage. Finally, the measure was placed on an off-year ballot that excluded the state and national races necessary for a large turnout of progressive voters.[12] After the election, I was contacted by reporters and activists eager for my opinion on the "death" of San Francisco's tenant movement. My response was that the vacancy-control travesty did not reflect the real power of tenants and that I intended to prove as much by putting a winnable tenant measure on the November 1992 ballot. This vow led a cocky landlord leader to belittle me as "the mouse that roared." The remark encouraged me to begin immediately the time-consuming process necessary to create the first successful tenant initiative in San Francisco history.

My first step was to refocus on the issue that I felt was tenants' chief concern: high rents. San Francisco rents were extremely high despite a decade of rent control because the law guaranteed landlords rent increases of at least 4 percent annually. This automatic raise particularly hurt seniors, persons with disabilities, public assistance recipients, low-income working people, and groups either living on fixed incomes or whose annual salary increase did not approach 4 percent. The 4 percent increase was particularly unfair because the inflation rate for 1991 was about half that amount. To spark discussion of the issue, I authored an article for tenant newsletters arguing for a citywide rent freeze. The idea was that a one-year freeze would compensate tenants for years of rent increases that exceeded the inflation rate. The city's tenant counseling groups met to discuss the idea, and in order to involve the broadest possible constituency, each agreed to hold neighborhood "tenant conventions." The conventions would facilitate participation by people who were not members of any tenants group and perhaps draw new energy into the movement. None of the conventions would have a rigid agenda; everyone attending would feel his or her input was not simply tolerated but strongly encouraged. We planned to hold the five events in March and April 1992. The top two recommendations for ballot measures from each event would proceed to a citywide tenants convention in May. That gathering would vote on whether to proceed with a ballot initiative and, if so, on what issue.

The process, which gave equal decisionmaking power to all convention attendees rather than limiting voting to members of key constituency organizations, had its detractors. There was certainly something reckless about allowing people with no prior involvement in tenant activities to attend a meeting, vote for a particular issue, and then disappear, never to be seen again. There was also a risk that the staff members and governing bodies of organizations would chafe at having their own influence diminished by giving outsiders an equal vote. Tenant leaders were very alert to these dangers but felt it essential to let every tenant in the city know that his or her participation was desired. A far different message is conveyed when you tell people you value their presence but not their judgment; it is a choice between a process of inclusion or exclusion. An open, inclusive process is always preferable, but it is mandatory when the people affected by issues feel estranged from activist leaders. Many of us interpreted the lack of grassroots enthusiasm for the vacancy-control ballot measure as a reflection of its authors' not listening to the concerns of actual tenants; an excessively open process would help rectify this shortcoming. An open process was also necessary to maintain unity among the convening groups themselves. Any process limiting voting to tenant group members would raise debates on the definition of membership; the relative political strength of groups emphasizing membership; the value of nonmembership organizations focused on organizing or direct service; and many other issues that would have diverted energy from our objective. Agreeing to an open, inclusive process does not require groups formally to endorse the outcome, so the risk to organizational autonomy is not as great as might appear. Our reliance on an open process succeeded in clearing the air and burnishing the image of the tenant movement.

Throughout the four-month convention process, the tenant groups engaged in the type of strategic discussions and proactive agenda setting that had virtually disappeared from the movement. This activity clearly raised the spirits of tenant organizations. Because high rents affected all tenants covered by rent control, this was, not surprisingly, the most frequently mentioned concern. Other issues raised at the conventions impacted some tenants but not others. The tenant movement had resoundingly lost all four of its previous ballot initiatives and was in no position to advance a measure excluding any segment of the tenant population from its benefits; our proposed initiative had to appeal to the maximum number of tenants.

At the citywide tenants convention in May 1992, a spirited debate broke out between those who wanted an initiative limiting annual rent increases and those who wanted to focus on both high rents and unfair evictions. Many people in the room had been unfairly evicted, and there seemed no way to reach unity without addressing their concerns. To satisfy those who, like me, strongly opposed combining two distinct ideas in one measure (remember: keep it simple), the convention voted to proceed with two separate initiatives.

This decision illustrated why many activist leaders oppose an open decisionmaking process. In voting to proceed with two measures, there was no discussion of how the necessary signatures for both could be obtained, nor of how we could fund two initiatives or provide sufficient volunteers. Further, it subsequently became clear that some of the people voting to do two initiatives were unwilling to volunteer for either. Yet despite its politically naive outcome, the convention achieved something unprecedented: for the first time, every tenant group felt that the initiatives going to the ballot had been through a fair, democratic process. This was no small accomplishment from a gathering whose participants spoke three languages and whose organizing groups had very different political styles. Progressive initiatives do not often enjoy such unified support and legitimacy, as many activists prefer to draft their measures without consulting less politically sophisticated allies. Our ultimate success was a sharp rebuttal to those espousing the "father knows best" approach.

Following the convention, we had seven weeks to collect 15,000 signatures for each of the two initiatives. We learned a valuable lesson at the outset: many hardworking, committed activists do not like collecting signatures. People who will work tirelessly dropping literature or making phone calls often do not feel comfortable stopping someone on the street and giving a quick sales pitch for a petition. Further, many volunteers from my organization, the Tenderloin Housing Clinic, simply lacked the verbal skills necessary for successful petitioning. Organization leaders must understand the limitations of fellow activists and be careful not to make people feel badly because they lack the ability to perform an important task. Signature gathering is simply a means to an end. If leaders make extensive participation in the petition process a "test" of people's commitment to the cause, those unable to perform the task will feel guilty and distance themselves from the campaign. When their skills are subsequently needed, they will be gone. We did not interpret our unexpected difficulty in getting volunteers to gather signatures as a sign of low interest in the effort. Neither did we view the signature process as a barometer of our capacity to run a strong grassroots campaign in the fall. We simply acknowledged people's unease over signature gathering and hired paid signature gatherers. Virtually all progressive initiative campaigns now use this tactic, as activists in every field of social change have increasingly had trouble getting the necessary signatures strictly through volunteer efforts. The goal of signature gathering is to get the initiative on the ballot, not to educate voters (though some education naturally occurs). With key volunteers excused from the signature drive, the grassroots team enters the actual campaign rested and primed.

Although our volunteers eventually did gather a majority of the signatures necessary to qualify one measure, our need for paid gatherers made the pursuit of two initiatives fiscally unfeasible. Some advocates of the two-initiative approach had felt that the unfair-eviction measure would bring large numbers of new volunteers into the campaign. This influx of volunteers never materialized, however, so there was no chance of qualifying the measure without paid gatherers. Most volunteer petitioners had difficulty getting people to sign their name and address twice, so nearly everyone was relieved when we could focus only on the high-rents measure.

Our campaign ultimately gathered more than 16,000 signatures in seven weeks, easily qualifying the initiative for the November ballot. We also learned which individuals and organizations produced results and which produced little more than promises. Most important, we recognized that the initiative had primarily activated people already connected to existing tenant groups rather than bringing new people into the movement. We were initially disappointed by the absence of new people from the petition drive; we thought the new faces so active at the conventions would continue their involvement. After repeated phone calls and letters brought little new participation, however, we realized that we should not count on newcomers. Our disappointment was more ideological than practical, as we had achieved our goal of creating a large volunteer base. It is always nice to say that you have developed an issue so exciting that new people are joining your cause in droves, but the reality was that the city's tenant counseling groups already had a sufficiently large membership base. Like most social change organizations, the tenant groups had many inactive members; tenant leaders like Ted Gullicksen of the San Francisco Tenants Union succeeded in using the initiative to reenergize volunteers. Gullicksen's success confirmed that the convention process and resulting initiative had succeeded in rebuilding the tenants' activist base.

Initiatives often can serve this purpose; in fact, a progressive initiative that fails to activate one's own base faces certain defeat. Unfortunately, in local elections in California the number of signatures necessary to qualify initiatives is so low that as few as five people working daily for months can obtain the necessary signatures. In other words, activists can qualify initiatives without broad-based constituency support. As tempting as it may seem to qualify an initiative in this way, it is ultimately a waste of everyone's time, because it will go down to defeat without any accompanying benefit. I emphasize this point because some activists wrongly equate ballot qualification with broad-based constituency support. Although we appeared to have the necessary support after our city-wide convention, we would have had to abandon the high-rents initiative if the support was lagging during the petition drive. Our goal was to win in November, not to prove we could simply qualify something for the ballot.

As we began the actual campaign, we had already satisfied all of the requirements for success. First, our measure was simple. The existing law allowed annual rent increases equal to 60 percent of the overall inflation rate, the percentage that constitutes the housing portion of inflation. But the law also stated that "in no event shall the annual rent increase be less than 4%. . . ." Nearly every year in the late 1980s and early 1990s inflation was less than 4 percent, so a formula designed to allow landlords to keep up with inflation was actually giving them a windfall. Our initiative ended rent increases above the inflation rate by simply deleting the 4 percent guarantee from the existing law. The measure not only could be explained in a sentence but also could be illustrated in handouts showing the text of the current law with the 4 percent guarantee crossed out. The simplicity of Proposition H prevented the traditional opposition tactic of focusing on ambiguous phrases or provisions—such as the school voucher proposal's implicit allowance for witches' schools—collateral to the initiative's purpose. Unable to confuse voters over the initiative's content, our opposition was forced to focus on our claim that Proposition H was "fair."[13]

Second, our measure appealed to the self-interest of a significant portion of the electorate: every tenant covered by rent control would save money if our measure passed. Under existing law a tenant paying $500 per month would be subject to automatic 4 percent annual rent increases; rent would increase to $520 a month after the first year, to $541 the next year, and so on. After five years the rent would be $608 a month, $100 more than the initial rent. The tenant would be paying $1,296 more per year in rent than he or she had paid five years previously. Our initiative would save this tenant at least $120 the first year, and savings would increase every year because the rent increase percentage would be levied on a lower prior year level. Further, many apartments in San Francisco rent for more than $1,000 per month, and their tenants would enjoy even greater savings from our initiative. These higher-end apartments housed people who regularly voted, whose political outlook was relatively conservative on economic issues except those affecting their wallets, and whose financial future had suffered because of the lingering recession. Our initiative thus appealed to the economic insecurities and financial self-interest of middle-class and low-income tenants. It also appealed to upper-income people who might not identify themselves as progressive but who always voted in their own financial interest.

Third, and of central importance, our initiative was conceived with the full understanding of the political context of the November 1992 election. This context involved far more than an expected high voter turnout. Two significant factors stood out in my mind. First, the presidential campaign, Bush versus Clinton, would be a highly partisan contest. (California also had two hard-fought senate races in that same election.) All national elections are partisan, but after losing a winnable presidential race in 1988, Democrats had a unified thirst for victory unparalleled since at least 1960. The highly partisan nature of the 1992 election would give a boost to initiatives that could be portrayed in a partisan light. Second, it was clear from the primary debates of early 1992 that the Democratic presidential candidate, whomever it was, would base his November campaign on the economy. This focus would assist a local high-rents initiative in two ways. It would remind voters why the times required that landlords lower rents; also, the emphasis on the unfairness of Republican economic policies could be used to attack a law that unfairly raised rents at more than double the inflation rate.

We subsequently harnessed our campaign to the Democrats' national campaign by making our race—like the Clinton-Bush contest—into a plebiscite on economic fairness. Just as it was not fair that the rich got richer and everyone else got poorer in the 1980s, it was not fair that rich landlords received rent increases in excess of inflation at the expense of working people. Rather than talk about tenants' rights, rent control, or housing policy, our campaign focused on the savage impacts of trickle-down economics on the middle class, families, children, seniors, people with disabilities, and ethnic minorities. Whereas prior tenant ballot campaigns used the official voter handbook to make arguments related to tenant issues, ours had key groups make the case that Proposition H was essential for economic fairness. For example, groups representing seniors emphasized that the total yearly Social Security cost-of-living increase was less than the 4 percent annual rent increase and that seniors were suffering as a result. Children's advocacy groups noted how national economic policies had caused undue hardships for San Francisco's middle- and low income families, many of which were being driven out of their homes and the city by unfairly high rent increases. African-American and Latino organizations emphasized the damage caused to their communities by Reagan-Bush economics and explained how our initiative would help start to turn the process around. These arguments and others helped establish our campaign theme that Proposition H was essential not only for local economic fairness but also to rectify unfair national economic policies.

The focus on economic fairness was critical in attracting votes from homeowners and others who had no self-interest in the initiative. Although tenants constitute 70 percent of San Francisco's population, even in the highest-turnout elections they make up only 55 percent of the voters. Because this percentage includes those living in government-subsidized housing, newly constructed apartments, and other units exempt from the city rent-control ordinance, nearly half of the electorate would not immediately benefit from Proposition H. Our success thus required the support of liberal homeowners and others whose vote would be based on their overall political outlook. This group typically had supported liberal economic and tax policies at the national level but failed to connect these views with the fairness of laws protecting the city's tenants. This failure was understandable, because the plight of local tenants had never been explicitly connected to national politics, and what little homeowners knew about rent-control initiatives tended to come from opposition campaign literature. By connecting our proposition to the Clinton-Gore economic fairness theme, we could win the support of this critical voting bloc.

We also sought to win disinterested voters by identifying Proposition H's opponents with the Republican Party. This kind of tactic can involve both controversy and risk. Controversy arises because many progressive social change activists are uncomfortable about identifying their causes with the Democratic Party. The reasons for this view are legion, but in essence the argument goes that Democrats represent the moderate side of corporate America while falsely claiming to speak for working people. The actual political orientation of the Democratic Party, however, is separate from the tactical question of whether identifying with it will facilitate progressive social change. When your electorate is certain to vote overwhelmingly Democratic in a highly partisan presidential race, it only makes sense to use this association to your advantage. Our campaign emphasized less the universal support we had from the local Democratic Party and clubs and more the fact that the San Francisco Republican Party opposed our measure. Literature delivered to liberal homeowner areas focused entirely on our claim that the Republican Party opposed Proposition H because it was designed to help the victims of the Reagan-Bush years. I even sought to link California's then-unpopular Republican governor, Pete Wilson, to Proposition H's opponents. In my official campaign response to the *San Francisco Chronicle* editorial opposing Proposition H, I noted that the paper's position was not surprising in light of its unwavering support for both Reagan-Bush trickle-down and Governor Wilson's failed economic programs. I felt this argument would win us more votes than were lost by the paper's position.

Our effort to link Proposition H to the Democratic Party reflected the tactical principle of invoking the values and symbols that your target audience understands. Progressive social change is not achieved by the ardent support of only a small minority of the population; identifying progressive causes with widely accepted values and symbols is simply common sense. Despite the apparent obviousness of this strategy, however, many social change activists reduce their chances for success by ignoring, even attacking, popular cultural values. For example, Saul Alinsky felt 1960s antiwar demonstrators' attacks on the American flag were disastrous, because the flag's role as a symbol for American values made the demonstrators, rather than the war, appear anti-American.[14] Sponsors of progressive initiatives should carefully analyze the possible linkages between their measure and values broadly supported by the electorate.

However, equating opposition to Proposition H with support for an unpopular Republican Party had its risks. As Thomas Ferguson and Joel Rogers amply document in *Right Turn: The Decline of the Democrats and the Future of American Politics,*[15] the national Democratic Party of the 1980s was heavily funded by real estate interests. In major cities such as Boston, New York, Los Angeles, Chicago, and San Francisco, battles over rent control or development primarily occurred among Democrats rather than between the two major parties. San Francisco's Democratic mayor, Frank Jordan, opposed Proposition H, and Democratic senator Dianne Feinstein had consistently opposed strengthening rent control while mayor from 1979 to 1987. In other words, our effort to transform

Proposition H into a litmus test for Democratic Party loyalty could have provoked a mailing from "Democrats against H." Our landlord opposition could have self-righteously proclaimed their bona fide Democratic credentials and attacked our cloaking of a "radical" measure in Democratic Party clothing. Rather than so responding, however, they chose to rely on confusion and scare tactics.

Linking ballot measures to notoriously unpopular constituencies is an effective political tactic. If right-wing interests actively oppose your measure, it may be wise to focus your campaign on their agenda so that people will vote "yes" in order to say "no" to your adversaries. We always made sure to include a partial list of Proposition H opponents in our literature. This list was limited to real estate groups and the local Republican Party, entities very unpopular with swing voters. We also emphasized hotel magnate–turned–tax evader Leona Helmsley's role as the leading contributor to the "No on H" campaign. (Helmsley owns one of San Francisco's largest apartment complexes.) A "yes" vote became a way for people to say "no" to Helmsley. Achieving significant social change for the disempowered and disenfranchised is not a civics exercise; with the continued rise of the Christian right, social change activists seeking to focus only on "the issues" should enter a new field. Tactical activists must look for opportunities to use their opposition's goals, symbols, and even personalities as springboards for success at the ballot box.

Although Proposition H had all the characteristics of a successful progressive initiative—simplicity, self-interest benefits, due process, and a favorable political context—the measure could not pass without a sufficient volunteer and financial base. There is no particular number or estimate for what constitutes a "sufficient" volunteer base; a campaign has sufficient volunteers when it has people available to carry out all of the tasks necessary to win. With the signatures already collected and the initiative officially on the ballot, our grassroots effort swung into gear. Our campaign needed volunteers for two tasks: phoning and literature drops. We were able to meet our volunteer goals through the significant participation of unemployed single men receiving county welfare. People living in desperate poverty rarely play such a decisive role in the outcome of an election. The Tenderloin Housing Clinic had long worked with single men living in low-rent hotels, but even we were surprised by the willingness of hotel tenants to drop literature in outlying neighborhoods almost daily. Unlike most progressive initiative campaigns, which rely heavily on Saturday mobilizations, our campaign could utilize people during the week. This made a big difference in our ability to reach voters, because our campaign had decided to forgo expensive mailings and signs in favor of cheaper but more labor-intensive phoning and literature drops.

Our volunteer base also included members of citywide tenant groups, but we did not enlist well-known progressive activists. Our reliance on people unknown to traditional activists and our focus on nuts-and-bolts phoning and literature dropping rather than high-profile media and fundraising events contributed to the pundits' perception that Proposition H did not have a viable campaign. After we won the election, one City Hall "insider" told me she did not see how we could have won, because our campaign had been "invisible." Our goal had been to get information to voters, not prove something to the establishment by running a flashy media campaign.

Proposition H had advantages that most progressive initiatives lack in attracting low-income volunteers. The Tenderloin Housing Clinic had a strong institutional connection to hotel tenants, we had paid organizers focusing on this group, and we had an initiative that directly impacted the meager living expenses of those living on public assistance. Notwithstanding these factors, social change activists miss out on a critical opportunity when they fail even to attempt to bring unemployed single adults into their campaign. Many of our volunteers had a broad progressive political outlook that would lead them to participate in campaigns that might not directly involve their economic self-interest. Organizations having no direct contact with such people can make connections through local anti-poverty groups. For example, if representatives of environmental, health care, or slow-growth initiatives were to express interest in reaching low-income tenants, the Clinic would happily schedule a community meeting to discuss the measures. Many unemployed single adults living in single-room-occupancy hotels or studio apartments are desperate for human contact. They want to be involved working with other people, but they are waiting for an invitation. They have learned not to go where they are not wanted and are unlikely simply to show up at an open campaign meeting and get involved. Tactical activists do not have the luxury of ignoring this key volunteer constituency. We could never have dropped nearly 100,000 pieces of campaign literature without the critical involvement of poor people in every facet of this effort.

For many progressive campaigns, the problem is money, not campaign volunteers. This is particularly true in statewide campaigns in very large states such as California, whose very size has made television advertising almost a must. But as the case of Proposition 103, the auto-insurance initiative, proved, a strong grassroots attack coupled with such factors as a widely publicized Ralph Nader endorsement can enable David to defeat Goliath. In local initiatives, the deemphasis on costly television advertising makes the money differential slightly less determinative. Nevertheless, social change organizations often err by proceeding to the ballot without first achieving the minimum financial backing necessary to mount a winning campaign.

Proposition H was outspent by a 12-to-1 margin—we spent $25,000, our opponents $300,000—yet we prevailed. We won despite the fact that various "experts" had assured me it would take $50,000 to $75,000 to run a campaign with any potential for victory. For our $25,000 we dropped 100,000 pieces of literature, made several thousand phone calls, and distributed 10,000 specially made doorhangers reading "YES ON H" in a key swing neighborhood. We avoided costly glossy literature, used no expensive street signs, and did only one highly targeted mailing. I repeatedly said before and during the campaign that Proposition H would not lose due to a lack of funds, and I remain convinced that we would not have done substantially better at the polls if our budget had doubled. Many proponents of progressive initiatives have become too caught up in imitating their opponents' expensive campaigns. In a San Francisco rent-control campaign in 1979, the ardor to create campaign literature equal in quality to our opponents' predominated over analysis of how our money could best be spent. That campaign spent more than $50,000 in 1979 dollars to achieve glossy color mailers—and barely 40 percent of the vote. Some consultants insist that progressive campaigns need to spend money on top-quality literature to establish "credibility" with voters. These same consultants make the same arguments for expensive street and yard signs, even though such signs are usually torn down by opponents within a week. Credibility is established by the substance of the initiative and how it is framed, not by fancy campaign materials.

Our first campaign expenditure was to hire local political pollster David Binder to evaluate which neighborhoods we should target. After receiving his report, we calculated how much it would cost to reach these target areas through literature drops and phoning. Based on this estimate, we felt confident that $25,000 would be sufficient. Most of the campaign was funded by my organization. I had learned in 1991 that 501(c)(3) nonprofit organizations are permitted to spend money on ballot initiatives, and I could not think of a better use of Clinic funds than to spend them on an initiative that would lower rents. The Tenderloin Housing Clinic generates unrestricted funds by representing tenants in lawsuits against landlords, so we had the money to spend. The fact that we were running a true "outsider," grassroots effort meant we would not attract significant funds from elected officials or well-off individuals who did not feel directly involved in our campaign. Neither did we want to squander precious time on small-scale fundraising events unlikely to make much money. In addition to the Clinic funds, the campaign received a $5,000 contribution from one large tenants organization and individual donations of an equal amount to reach our campaign budget.

I am a big believer in nonprofit advocacy organizations' spending money on ballot measures. If an organization's mission statement or agenda can be fulfilled by a ballot initiative, a refusal to pursue this tactic raises questions about the value of the group's advocacy and its true commitment to achieving social change. Some groups' spending is restricted by various funding sources, leaving no funds for initiatives. But many self-proclaimed advocacy groups do have unrestricted funds, which are invariably spent for additional staff or "services." Is spending from $5,000 to $15,000 on a portion of a staff salary a more effective form of advocacy than contributing the same amount to help initiatives that could, for example, reduce rents, prevent environmental hazards, or widen access to health care? People working in nonprofits need to examine this issue seriously. It should be a required discussion at the organization's annual retreat.

I found the question to be a simple one. If the Clinic had used the funds we spent on Proposition H to hire additional staff, the expenditure would have brought negligible benefits to the city's low-income, senior, and disabled tenants, who would continue to suffer from steeply rising rents. Hiring a staff person to "advocate" for a goal that cannot be achieved without a ballot measure is not a strategic use of resources. With funding so precious, nonprofit social change advocacy organizations should participate in and be counted upon to help fund initiative campaigns seeking to benefit their constituencies. Staff of nonprofit advocacy groups often tell me that spending money directly on ballot measures is too "controversial" or "political." Unfortunately, an organization that fears controversy or politics is not likely to achieve social change.

In the Proposition H campaign, we sought to stretch our funds by creating literature that would stick in the minds of voters. If our literature resembled the dozens of other campaign pieces voters received, our message might be quickly forgotten. Further, whereas our opponents could hammer their message home through several mailings, we would only reach most voters with one piece. We therefore created a campaign theme that raised eyebrows even among people whose judgment I usually trusted.

When I first learned that our proposition had been assigned the letter "H," I was upset. "Proposition H" sounded too much like "Preparation H," the heavily advertised hemorrhoid ointment. I then realized that we had the opportunity to make a memorable impression with voters by connecting Proposition H to that famous medication. After considerable discussion and debate, we came up with the slogan: "Proposition H: For Relief of Rental Pain." Our first piece of literature included a picture of a female doctor, her accompanying words prescribing Proposition H. Our campaign insignia became a tube with the words "Yes on H." We used both humor and an unusual message to pack our lone piece of literature with the punch of several. We hoped to heighten the impact of our message further by distributing this initial piece prior to the start of other campaigns. With this early start we also sought to sway absentee voters, who often cast their ballots before receiving the frenzy of end-of-campaign mailings.

One factor we never considered was the need to act quickly to pre-empt our opponents' use of the same advertising theme. Yet three weeks after we distributed our "relief of rental pain" literature, bus shelters throughout the city sprouted lurid red and yellow posters depicting a large tube emblazoned "Proposition H Means Higher Rents." Dozens of billboards with the same design soon followed, and the Preparation H–type tube became the focal point of opposition literature. If any voters were offended by the linking of Proposition H to an over-the-counter ointment used for a very personal problem, they were surely more likely to blame our opponents than us. Indeed, the *San Francisco Examiner* editorial opposing Proposition H castigated our opponents for their unsavory attempt to portray tenants as needing a hemorrhoidal cream. No one in the media ever commented on our use of the same imagery, although we maintained it throughout the campaign.

Although Proposition H satisfied all of the requirements for a successful progressive initiative, very few people thought it would pass. When reporters asked me whether Proposition H would prevail, I responded truthfully that I felt it would. When I asked their opinion, the hemming and hawing would begin, frequently ending with the assertion that we had really done a good job and that the contest surely would be close. In fact, the skepticism over our grassroots, outsider campaign was so great that, to our disappointment, even alternative newspapers seemed to look forward to our defeat. Apparently they preferred seeing their predictions of Proposition H's failure fulfilled over achieving lower rents for tenants.

On election night, the first results came from the more conservative-leaning absentee voters. These ballots had us trailing only 48 to 52 percent, meaning we would most likely win. Our eventual margin of victory was 53 to 47 percent, a dramatic reversal of the 57–43 margin defeating the preceding November's tenant ballot measure. A review of voting totals by neighborhood showed that Proposition H did well even in conservative parts of the city that had strongly rejected previous progressive initiatives. The broad support for Proposition H reflected support from seniors and upper-income tenants, whose conservative economic views took a back seat to their personal desire to pay less rent. Although San Francisco's overall voter turnout in November 1992 was large, other local results did not reflect an unusually large or disproportionately progressive electorate. We had succeeded in winning the votes of political moderates on behalf of an initiative that would result in an unprecedented progressive redistribution of wealth in our city.

AVOIDING POST-ELECTION SURPRISES

Victorious progressive initiatives cannot always deliver their promised benefits right away. For example, Proposition 103's landmark victory in November 1988 mandated immediate insurance-premium refunds and rate rollbacks and made state insurance commissioner an elected position effective with the November 1990 election. Roxani Gillespie, the incumbent Republican appointee serving as commissioner from 1988 to 1990, did everything in her power to destroy Proposition 103. Gillespie's stonewalling received an assist in 1989 from the California Supreme Court, which ruled that refunds could not proceed until the adoption of regulations ensuring the insurance companies a fair rate of return on their investment. In 1991, with Proposition 103 still effectively in limbo, the new elected commissioner, Democrat John Garamendi, adopted the necessary regulations and ordered the companies to comply. The insurance companies again filed suit and won a lower court ruling that the refund formula was unconstitutional. It was not until August 1994, nearly six years after Proposition 103's approval, that the California Supreme Court upheld the regulations and paved the way for the majority of consumers to begin receiving the initiative's promised benefits.

From 1988 to 1994, the insurance industry and its media allies consistently attacked Harvey Rosenfield for having misled the public about the initiative's benefits. During this period, the only tangible effect Rosenfield could point to was a slight decline in auto insurance rates since 1988. Garamendi fought valiantly to deliver on Proposition 103's promise but was continually frustrated by the insurance companies, which spent more than $100 million to undermine the initiative in the six years after its passage. When Garamendi sought the Democratic nomination for governor in June 1994, voters gave him little credit for his efforts. Rather than seeing him as the consumer's David in a battle against the insurance industry Goliath, voters viewed Garamendi as the insurance commissioner who failed to make Proposition 103 work. He ended up running on a law-and-order platform rather than as a pro-consumer populist. Rosenfield and Garamendi tried everything in their power to focus the public's anger over Proposition 103 delays on the insurance industry but could not prevent the skepticism from being directed at the initiative's backers. The insurance industry's $100 million investment in delaying Proposition 103 likely was calculated to increase public cynicism over reform efforts and forestall future measures. As a result of Proposition 103's delay, the measure created no momentum for initiatives to redistribute wealth. The electorate's eventual receipt of the Proposition 103 refunds in 1995 will improve the prospect for future statewide populist measures, but such initiatives should strive to be self-executing to avoid the possibility of lengthy delays.

A similar post-election surprise occurred following voter approval of an unprecedented "Children's Initiative" in San Francisco in 1991. The Children's Initiative, Proposition J, required that a certain percentage of the city's budget be allocated to children's services. Sponsored and primarily funded by the nonprofit Coleman Advocates for Children and Youth, the Children's Initiative mandated expenditure levels but left the funding allocation process to be established by a newly created Mayor's Office of Children, Youth and Families, headed by a mayoral appointee. The office proceeded to create nearly a dozen administrative positions to evaluate applications for Proposition J funds. The $920,000 spent for these positions came out of the children's budget.

Although an open evaluation process was needed to enable Proposition J to fund new services, critics of the initiative attacked the creation of a new bureaucracy with funds earmarked for children. Moreover, the city's overall budget unexpectedly shrank, which meant that actual funding for children's services would not keep up with inflation despite Proposition J. As with Proposition 103, negative publicity about Proposition J's perceived failure to deliver promised benefits overshadowed the tremendous achievement of the measure. Proposition J increased spending on children's programs by $3 million annually, despite severe cutbacks in the city's overall budget. The measure preserved school music, library, and recreational programs as well as child-abuse prevention and health services during an era when the budget of every city department—other than police—was slashed. Proposition J shows how media-fueled public skepticism about reform can emerge because of initial execution problems, almost blinding the public to the measure's eventual track record of success.

Proposition H was intentionally designed to provide benefits directly, without the potential for tampering by any elected official or appointee. After its passage in November 1992, Proposition H took effect on December 10, 1992. Annual rent increases imposed after this date were limited to 1.9 percent for 1992–93, 1.3 percent for 1994, and 1.1 percent for 1995. With the country's inflation rate stable at under 3 percent, rent increases for the foreseeable future are unlikely to reach the 4 percent figure in effect for the decade before Proposition H. Even if the annual allowable increase rises to 2 percent, a tenant paying $500 per month in 1992 will still have saved more than $2,000 in five years under Proposition H. Because most rental units in the city rent for far more than $500, the total Proposition H savings to tenants is staggering. By giving tenants an immediate and ongoing economic benefit, Proposition H proponents have never been accused of breaking faith with the electorate.

We also have succeeded in keeping millions of dollars every year in the hands of tenants who live and shop in the city, money that would have been sent to the out-of-town landlords who own most of San Francisco's rental properties. We focused on this stark redistributive shift in resources during our campaign by referring to hotel queen and convicted tax evader Leona Helmsley, owner of San Francisco's largest apartment complex. Helmsley's Park Merced was a leading funder of the "No on H" campaign, and for good reason. Most of Helmsley's 1,000-plus apartments rent for more than $750 a month. A 4 percent annual rent increase raised her own wealth by $30 per month per tenant, or $360 per tenant per year. A 4 percent rent increase on 500 apartments would bring an annual gain of $180,000. Proposition H thus immediately reduced Helmsley's profit on these apartments by more than $100,000. Because Proposition H's rent savings multiply year by year, benefits to tenants increase exponentially. Proposition H has already shifted millions of dollars from landlords to tenants. It is difficult to identify any vote a San Francisco tenant could have cast that would have resulted in a more progressive shift in the redistribution of wealth. It is even more difficult to believe that such a redistribution could have occurred through the "complex debate" of the legislative process.

The successful use of the initiative process to achieve progressive redistribution of wealth refutes progressive criticism of the strategy. The insurance industry would never have allowed a law equivalent to Proposition 103 to pass the legislature, and its power has led most Democratic legislators in California and in Congress to oppose single-payer health reform. Because of the nature of the legislative process, measures seeking to increase economic fairness get so watered down and compromised that the redistributive component is often missing in the end. If social change activists follow the rules for initiatives set forth here, their ability to achieve progressive victories will significantly increase. The vast majority of corporate-funded measures are consistently defeated at the polls by wide margins. As for some progressives' ever-popular initiative nemesis, Proposition 13, the measure hardly reflects a one-time aberrational vote that has forever doomed California's public sector. In the nearly two decades since Proposition 13 passed, California voters have elected conservative Republicans in every gubernatorial race, and no elected official or interest group has viewed the electorate as willing to reverse Proposition 13's property-tax limitations. Proposition 13 is less a reflection on the evils of initiatives than an indication of the continued inability of social change constituencies to channel populist frustration toward progressive rather than reactionary ends.

The Media

WINNING MORE
THAN COVERAGE

For social change activists, the golden age of media relations came in the 1960s and early 1970s. News coverage advanced the civil rights and antiwar movements immeasurably. Television footage and newspaper accounts brought home as never before the sheer brutality of white Southerners who set upon peaceful demonstrators with fire hoses, dogs, bare fists, truncheons, and firearms. The combat footage and nightly body counts on the evening news brought into every living room the waste and horror of the Vietnam War. The investigative probing of Bob Woodward and Carl Bernstein of the *Washington Post* led in 1974 to the only resignation ever of a U.S. president. This roughly fifteen-year period was an anomaly in the history of U.S. journalism, however; rarely since advertising became the main source of income for newspapers in the mid-nineteenth century have the mainstream news media done much to advance progressive causes. With advertisers providing most of their revenue, newspapers and television stations face strong external pressures to endorse the status quo. Internal pressure on reporters and editors to self-censor and to exclude minority viewpoints also has increased as media outlets have been gobbled up by chains and corporations intent on increasing profit margins. Ben Bagdikian, a former *Washington Post* reporter and retired dean of the journalism school at the University of California, Berkeley, has explored these issues in depth in his book, *The Media Monopoly*. As Bagdikian writes, "Most [newspaper] owners and editors no longer brutalize the news with the heavy hand dramatized in movies like *Citizen Kane* or *The Front Page*. More common is something more subtle, more professionally respectable and more effective: the power to treat some unliked subjects accurately but briefly, and to treat subjects favorable to the corporate ethic frequently and in depth."

Bagdikian goes on to note that U.S. newspapers throughout the 1930s and early 1940s managed to marginalize coverage of the European Holocaust against the Jews. By running only token, isolated stories largely removed from their socioeconomic context, the media trivialized what ranks as perhaps the greatest atrocity in human history. The technique is still in full flower in today's coverage of social change issues. For example, the media, particularly during the Christmas season, run frequent "hard luck" stories about homeless families or people living on ever-decreasing state disability payments. These mainstream media outlets are careful, however, to link the subject's plight to personal misfortunes rather than social and economic policies. Such stories routinely fail to call federal or state elected officials to account for cutting welfare or disability benefits. Once again, Bagdikian succinctly sums up the problem: "Large classes of people are ignored in the news, are reported as exotic fads, or appear only at their worst—minorities, blue-collar workers, the lower middle class, the poor. They become publicized mainly when they are in spectacular accidents, go on strike, or are arrested.... But since World War I hardly a mainstream American news medium has failed to grant its most favored treatment to corporate life."[1]

The corporate control over "deciding what's news" can readily be seen in the media's incessant updates on the performance of the Dow Jones stock market index. Major national and local news broadcasts invariably include such updates. The phrase "Advancing stocks outnumbered decliners in heavy trading" is no more relevant to the lives of most Americans than the Dow Jones industrial average itself. The media's daily and even hourly tracking of the stock market's performance gives people the entirely misleading impression that there is a connection between a rising market and their personal economic well-being. (Because a corporation's stock tends to rise after layoffs or downsizing, the converse is actually closer to the truth.) Suppose that instead of monitoring the markets, the media updated daily the number of people in food lines across the country? As the number increased steadily, so would public pressure on national leaders to address the problem of hunger in the United States. Or media could monitor the number of families evicted from their homes, the number of children stricken with lead poisoning, or the number of new AIDS cases. These statistics are all readily obtainable by the media but would not send a message supported by the outlet's corporate sponsors. The "news" that is centrally featured in the media is determined by the interests of its corporate owners; as a result, even the most committed reporters are rarely able to find space to cover events of importance to social change organizations.

For all these reasons, social change activists seeking positive media coverage must prepare a strategic plan. As when dealing with elected officials, activists must have clearly in mind demonstrable results they want to achieve through publicity. Contrary to what many activists believe, "media coverage" in and of itself is not a demonstrable result. When I have questioned activists in various fields why they are planning a particular event, the all-too-typical response is "for the media." If my relationship with the activists is sufficiently close, I will gently ask what results they hope will come out of the media coverage. Often the response is that media coverage will help "the public" understand and support the activists' position on the particular issue. The activists rarely assess the true capacity for such coverage to assist in achieving their goals; nor do they usually have a strategic plan that connects the coverage to fulfillment of a specific agenda. Ironically, activists who place their faith in media coverage per se generally understand that the current mainstream media are not allies of social change. From this understanding, it should follow that the media cannot be trusted to cover an event in a manner likely to prompt broad and immediate support for progressive causes. As will be shown, events designed solely for media coverage of their issues can even result in a story that generates public anger against the activists' position.

In this chapter I will discuss media strategies social change activists should use to accomplish their goals. The central rules for successful activism include using media coverage to win a specific, implementable result; selecting the proper media contact; utilizing the skills of trained investigative reporters as a component of a broader campaign; remaining guarded with most journalists and developing key relations with sympathetic reporters; knowing how and when to respond to media bias and stories generated by conservative think tanks; and understanding how best to use the alternative media to accomplish tactical goals. Following these rules will help activists overcome the ever-increasing institutional media opposition to campaigns for progressive social change.

USE THE MEDIA FOR RESULTS, NOT COVERAGE

By using the media not for coverage alone but rather to achieve a specific, implementable result, tactical activists can gain support for their goals. I was fortunate to be involved in a remarkable example of such advocacy journalism soon after I began working full-time at the Tenderloin Housing Clinic in October 1982. Paid through a $12,000 grant from the Berkeley Law Foundation, I soon was talking to dozens of tenants who lived in a wide variety of residential hotels and shared a serious problem: no heat. I went to hotel after hotel during the cold November evenings to verify personally that thousands of San Francisco's poorest tenants, including elderly and disabled people, were living without heat. When three elderly women came to my office complaining of this problem, I figured we had the perfect opportunity to attract media attention to the scandal. Though many of the residents of the heatless hotels were seniors, hotel residents primarily consisted of single men living on welfare, disability checks, or fixed incomes of another sort. Some had drug or alcohol problems. Although all of them needed and deserved heat, the image of shivering seniors was the most likely to provoke the collective outrage of the media and the public. Finding sympathetic subjects can be an essential part of an activist's media strategy. I sent out a press release headlined "Why Must Seniors Freeze?" and scheduled a heat protest in front of the women's hotel for the next day. My release attracted the immediate attention of former *San Francisco Chronicle* reporter Warren Hinckle. Hinckle, former editor of the 1960s *Ramparts* magazine, wrote dramatic exposés on an occasional basis for the *Chronicle*. I took him on a tour of the city's "heatless hotels," and we did not find a single warm radiator on one of the coldest December nights. Hinckle's story—"Our City's Shame"—galvanized San Francisco residents in a way that has not been replicated on poor people's issues to this day.[2] The day Hinckle's article appeared, the Tenderloin Housing Clinic staged a protest with senior citizens and other hotel residents, bringing coverage from nearly every television and radio station in the Bay Area. The story of seniors living without heat was the lead story on all the television news shows, and Hinckle wrote the lead article on the *Chronicle*'s front page for the rest of the week.

The widespread publicity about "heat cheats" led to a variety of actions. Mayor Dianne Feinstein, herself a residential hotel landlord, had been attacked by Hinckle during the 1979 mayor's race for allegedly abusing her tenants. Perhaps to avoid renewed charges of insensitivity,

families lived. The footage was often run over a period of days, and the media clearly viewed the situation as an outrage. However, the social workers and children's advocates who brought the media to the hotels had no specific set of demands. As a result, the villains in the stories became the hotel owners, who typically were accused of getting rich at the expense of vulnerable women and children. However, the real culprits weren't the hotel owners, who had been begged by the city to house the homeless families; those responsible for the deplorable situation were city officials, whose policy was to shelter homeless families in hotels—the cheapest possible housing source—rather than apartments. Because the social workers did not focus media attention on the city's policy, the "solution" to the scandal thus became linked to the landlords' alleged misconduct. Like the Claude Rains character in *Casablanca,* who is "shocked" to find gambling at Humphrey Bogart's bar, local politicians responded to this media coverage by demanding more hotel inspections and threatening to cut off funds to uninhabitable hotels. The media, having won their "victory" in City Hall promises, went on to other stories, while the families continued to live in completely unsuitable housing.

The differences between the media tactics used in the "heatless hotels" case and those used in the "homeless families" story could not be more clear. In the former, activists persuaded the media to pressure City Hall to take definite actions that would—and in retrospect, did—permanently end the widespread lack of heat in residential hotels. Advocates for the homeless families, however, failed to use the media spotlight to press for the only real solution: ending the city's practice of transforming residential hotel rooms into long-term family housing. Whereas the heat campaign shifted the focus away from landlord misconduct and toward the city's complicity, the homeless family coverage made City Hall the hero for its vow to crack down on profiteering slumlords. The fact that the city had failed to monitor conditions in hotel rooms paid for with public funds was lost amid the footage of crying children, angry mothers, and decrepit rooms.

Had the family advocates attacked the use of the hotels from the start and enlisted the unquestionably sympathetic media as their allies, there is little doubt that the city would quickly have replaced the program with a better one. The city's elected officials and social service staff openly expressed embarrassment about the housing of families in SRO hotels and were not about to vigorously defend the policy. Fortunately, in 1988 a more politically savvy group of family advocates again brought the media spotlight on the family hotel program, which continued to operate even though a new political administration was in power. This time the media focused on the program as an expensive and inhumane public policy failure. The new Agnos administration, unlike its predecessors, was itself held responsible for inadequately housing homeless families. Rather than defend the indefensible, the city ended the hotel program and moved the families to subsidized apartments. A new, nonprofit-operated transitional housing facility for homeless families was opened, with an army of on-site services to help families break out of the cycle of homelessness. After six years of arguing that it had no alternative to placing families in run-down hotels, City Hall changed its course overnight in response to tactical activists' media strategy.

The ability to generate media coverage and then provide a specific, implementable solution obviously depends on the issue. Stories on hunger in the United States, which run with particular frequency between Thanksgiving and Christmas, utilize powerful images and evoke viewer empathy. Activists have responded to such stories by focusing on the need to increase welfare payments, food-stamp allocations, and public jobs, but truly reducing hunger requires measures too complex and indirect to arouse immediate media support. Similarly, the intense media coverage in 1994 of the U.S. health care crisis failed to tie in to a specific program that the broader public could understand and support. The single-payer proposal represented a specific solution, but activists found the media exclusively focused on President Clinton's ambiguous "managed care" plan.

As discussed in Chapter 1, bipartisan political forces have been particularly adept at using the media as a springboard for punitive anti-crime measures. The same politicians who continually preach patience to social change organizations leaped at the chance to approve "three strikes and you're out" legislation following the 1993 kidnap/murder of Polly Klaas in Sonoma County, California. Examples abound of high-profile criminal cases that led directly to legislative "solutions" to prevent such conduct in the future. Progressive activists need only look to their opponents to recognize the strategic value of using the media first to uncover a problem and then to ensure fulfillment of specific goals.

CHOOSING A MEDIA CONTACT

Although social change activists and organizations cannot totally control the media's final product, we can significantly influence it by choosing a skilled media spokesperson. There are two contexts in which such a person is essential: when a reporter wants to speak to a member of the affected constituency group, and when the reporter talks to organization staff. A third issue is whether an organization member or staff person should do the speaking. The first context is usually not a problem; the affected constituency typically includes at least one excellent spokesperson, someone whose communication skills have become evident during the organizing process. Many groups devote great effort to preparing residents for media contact, as recommended in standard organizer-training manuals. However, I have never had a problem letting a homeless person, an elderly tenant living without heat, or a similarly situated individual with no prior public speaking or media training simply tell his or her story to reporters. These people need no training or briefing; all I ever tell them is not to hesitate to describe fully how much they have suffered from the problem at issue. On the rare occasions when I feel reporters will be hostile but the interview cannot be avoided, I will warn the interviewee to talk to the reporter as if speaking with an enemy. Otherwise, I have found that many people are natural communicators who would only be made nervous by instructions on what they should say.

Many people believe in media role playing and mock press events to prepare untrained community speakers; I have tried this approach and found it unnecessary. Reporters enjoy interviewing real people with real problems, because so many of their interviews are with skilled spin-control experts. The natural demeanor of community speakers, combined with reporters' sympathy toward them, generally produces a positive story. For example, in the twenty-five-day sit-in by disabled protesters discussed in Chapter 7, many if not most of the participants were interviewed. The activists needed no training to convincingly explain the meaning of their protest; their open discussion of their own life experiences proved a potent weapon in winning public support for their cause.

The more difficult context includes media contact with staff members of activist organizations. As will be discussed in detail, an encounter between the media and a social change organization staff member who lacks media savvy can be quite damaging. To avoid this problem, staff members should not deal with reporters until they have been trained by the organization. Some groups prefer to route all media contact through a designated spokesperson, but such a procedure deprives other committed staff members of the fun and glory of speaking to reporters and seeing their names in print. It also may prevent the person most knowledgeable about an issue or most responsible for a campaign's success from getting the public credit he or she deserves. A better strategy is simply to have the most media-savvy staff person discuss the ins and outs of the reporting/interview process beforehand with other staff members. The most skilled spokesperson fields media requests for general comment on an issue, and other staff members deal with coverage of their specific issues or activities. I usually try to discuss the Clinic's media spin with other staff members before they deal with the press to ensure that everyone's position or perspective accurately reflects the organization's and best advances its agenda. Discussing and strategizing about a media response tend to produce a better result.

The key is to establish at the outset the message you want conveyed and then make sure staff remarks bolster this message. People often have many comments about a particular issue or event. However, some of these may detract from your central message, so raising them with the press could result in a story that misses or undermines your main point. Staff members inexperienced with reporters get into trouble when they engage in lengthy discussions and allow the reporter to direct their attention away from the central message. The staffer may let down his or her guard and begin talking to the reporters as if addressing a trusted friend. When I read quotes from activists that seem curious or ill-conceived, invariably I am told that the remarks emerged in the course of a long, on-the-record discussion that veered from the original focus of the reporter's inquiry. There is no law requiring activists to talk at length to reporters or to provide comments on diverse issues on which they are unprepared to speak. By training staff to stick to the central message, the organization fulfills its media strategy and reduces the risk that its mission or principles will be misrepresented.

After determining who should speak to the media and what they should say, the group often must decide which type of speaker—a member of the community or a staff person—can best accomplish the constituency's goals. This decision appears simple: the representative of the affected constituency should speak instead of paid staff. In fact, many membership organizations never have staff members provide their media response. I generally agree with this policy, which is based on a commitment to member empowerment and the belief that a democratic process requires that only representatives of the membership should speak for the group. However, the practicalities of social change activism make no allowance for hard-and-fast rules. For example, in the case of the three elderly women living without heat, the activist textbook would have one or all of them lead the media campaign. Unfortunately, after their initial media contact that blew open the story, the women were reluctant to talk to the press and granted subsequent interviews only after I spent considerable time convincing them to speak.[3] The women were not dissatisfied with the coverage; rather, they had suddenly been thrust into the limelight after years of living quietly. The spectacle of cameras from every local television station in front of the women's hotel thrilled activists like me, but scared the women. The three thus stayed in the background after the initial media frenzy. Another elderly tenant, living in a different hotel lacking heat, allowed me to set up an interview in his room. The story and accompanying photo appeared above the fold on the front page of the *San Francisco Chronicle,* but this gentleman also begged off from further media contact.

The reluctance of vulnerable, elderly tenants to become media stars was understandable; they wanted heat, not publicity. In my own excitement and inexperience, I accepted reporters' arguments that the scandal would not be sufficiently newsworthy without interviews with the "victims." I also felt that visual images of elderly tenants living without heat were necessary to achieve a legislative solution to the problem. In retrospect, though, I believe the women's initial interview with *Chronicle* reporter Warren Hinckle was all the media contact we needed to accomplish our goals. It also became clear as the heat legislation moved toward enactment that enough tenants of heatless hotels were willing to speak out that convincing reluctant people was unnecessary. The reluctance of the original group of elderly tenants to describe their plight to the media required me to do so instead. Although having activists speak out about the tenants' situation was not ideal, it was the only option under the circumstances.

In most instances, the activists' constituents are ready and able to speak for themselves. For example, in the Luxury Hotel Task Force struggle (Chapter 1), the elderly tenants were eager participants and talked to the media without hesitation. The presence of such willing constituency-based speakers, however, does not mean they will be available to speak when needed. Suppose the press calls an organization for a comment and the staff is unable to reach a member to give the response. Should the organization bypass the opportunity to put its spin on the issue, or should the staff respond instead? There is no right answer to this question. Because reporters regularly claim to need an immediate comment, allowing staff to respond consistently will result in a stack of media quotes from staff rather than members. However, it may be critical for the organization to have its response to a breaking event included in media coverage. If only staff members are available in such cases, they may have to respond. Activists can use a simple test to resolve this possible dilemma. Examine the organization's media coverage over the past year to see if staff and members are satisfied. If the view prevails that group members are not quoted often enough because they are inaccessible, it may make sense to give staff a larger media role. But if the clipping file shows that the staff's domination of media coverage has hampered membership development, then the emphasis should be switched. A balance between staff and constituency responses must be struck to fulfill an overall media strategy.

For an excellent example of such a balance, let us return to the battle over the Brooklyn Navy incinerator (Chapter 3). This struggle involved a coalition primarily comprising Hasidic Jews, Puerto Rican Catholics, African-Americans, and the New York Public Interest Research Group (NYPIRG). Rather than competing for media attention, the groups cooperated to bring their individual strengths to the overall media response. Thus, NYPIRG consistently commented on the technical, procedural, and legal issues surrounding the proposed incinerator, as well as on the scientifically determined health and safety risks. The other groups issued quotes about environmental racism and injustice and the personal impacts that a towering, toxic-spewing incinerator would have on their residential community. This division typifies a tactically savvy media campaign; technical staff members provide the necessary facts and figures, and constituency groups tell the human side of the story. By using all of a movement's media strengths in a combined effort, organizations can avoid disputes over who should do the talking, and a successful media campaign will result.

USING INVESTIGATIVE REPORTERS

The post-Watergate era has seen a decline in investigative journalism's role in achieving progressive social change. The shift in the media climate since the 1980s has been dramatic; investigative reports of twenty years ago on unsafe automobiles, toxic hazards, and dangerous birth-control devices seem as ancient as turn-of-the-century exposés by Jane Addams and Upton Sinclair. Although investigative journalism is still practiced as much as ever, the problem for progressive activists is what is (and is not) being investigated. Today's "investigative journalism" focuses on the private lives of celebrities; television shows such as *A Current Affair* and *Inside Edition* make great profits relying on such work. As celebrity journalism has flourished, mainstream news sources have cut back on policy oriented investigative reporting. Public television, particularly the Corporation for Public Broadcasting, has shied away from investigative reports that might offend corporate sponsors and limit its ability to attract funding. As a result, many of today's activists have little experience with investigative journalists who assist social change.

My own experience working with the nationally acclaimed Center for Investigative Reporting (CIR) has led me to conclude that investigative journalists can have such a powerful impact on social change efforts that organizations should always consider calling upon them. Organizations should even consider funding such reporting if independent financing is unavailable. I learned firsthand of the value of investigative journalism during the Tenderloin Housing Clinic's battle with the late Guenter Kaussen, a man characterized in various news reports as "the world's largest slumlord." This battle began with a small Tenderloin press conference, grew to an international story that received coverage on both West German national television stations and on CBS's *60 Minutes,* and ended with Kaussen's suicide as his real estate empire slid into bankruptcy.

Although there is a certain glamour and excitement that comes from such big-time coverage, attracting the likes of *60 Minutes* to the story didn't yield any special victories for Tenderloin residents or help accomplish any strategic goals. The intense local coverage, however, apparently inspired the German television coverage, all of which contributed to the downfall of Kaussen and the improvement of conditions for his tenants in the Tenderloin, which was our goal. The genesis and development of the story is instructive.

Known as the "German Howard Hughes" for his secretive business practices and his estimated $500 million fortune, Kaussen was Germany's largest apartment owner when the Clinic began its fight with him in 1983. Kaussen also had significant holdings in Vancouver and Atlanta and owned twenty-three large apartment buildings in San Francisco, including fourteen properties containing over 1,100 apartment units in the Tenderloin neighborhood. I became involved with Kaussen after Cambodian tenants living in one of his buildings contacted me. Kaussen's management company had issued eviction notices for nonpayment of rent to many of the Cambodian families. However, all of the families had paid their rent and had the receipts to prove it. The Clinic and some Cambodian tenants held a press conference and rally in front of the apartment building to demand that Kaussen rescind the eviction notices. There was certainly nothing innovative about this strategy, but as a protest by Cambodian tenants—widely but falsely viewed as afraid to fight for their rights—the event had enough of an angle to attract one television reporter.

When I saw the TV crew (more intimidating to wrongdoers than print reporters wielding mere notebooks), I assumed we would win a quick victory. Management would withdraw the notices and apologize for the error, and all would go on with their lives. But events took a different turn. Kaussen's staff refused to speak to the reporters, then barred the television crew from photographing the inside of the building. The result was that instead of an unremarkable clip of yet another landlord-tenant dispute, the evening news showed dramatic footage of apartment managers denying a television crew access to the building. Interspersed with the footage were shots of Kaussen's staff giving evasive "no comment" answers and teary Cambodians holding eviction notices. Something strange was going on, and given that Kaussen had quietly become the Tenderloin's leading property owner, I felt that further investigation into his empire was necessary.

After doing a property search and comparing the list to tenant complaints I had received, I concluded that Kaussen operated his properties unlike any other San Francisco landlord. His rents were the highest in the neighborhood and were about equivalent to the pricier rents of lower Nob Hill, on the Tenderloin's border. I could not understand how Kaussen got tenants to pay such high rents until I discovered that the rent stated in the lease was a myth. Kaussen had an "every-sixth-month-rent-free" policy. A tenant agreeing to pay $600 per month for a studio would actually pay a monthly average of $500 over a year's period. It seemed to make no sense for Kaussen to inflate his rents, then negate his gains by charging *no* rent one month out of every six. Kaussen also had a unique strategy for attracting potential tenants despite the high initial rents: he established a free service for tenants seeking apartments in the city. The service, known as Mr. Apartment, differed from other such services in that it imposed no fee; however, all of the units available through Mr. Apartment were owned by Kaussen.

The inflated rent roll, Mr. Apartment, and other oddities convinced me to seek assistance in figuring out Kaussen's operation. Fortunately, located barely a mile from my office was the CIR, which by 1983 had established a track record for investigative journalism. I met with CIR director Dan Noyes, and he immediately expressed great interest in investigating the secretive German multimillionaire. The CIR had a contract with the local NBC television affiliate to develop stories, and the station's reporter, Evan White, was excited about pursuing the story. I gave Dan all my notes and sources and let him go to work. Eventually, Dan would persuade a *60 Minutes* producer that Kaussen was worthy of attention. As depicted by *60 Minutes*, Kaussen was "the world's worst landlord," a reclusive eccentric who had successfully avoided publicity for years while pioneering condo conversions in his native West Germany. Now he was suddenly the subject of two or three television news reports per week.

The Clinic sought to emphasize Kaussen's strategy for building his real estate empire, a point ultimately deemphasized by *60 Minutes*. Research into the financing of Kaussen's properties revealed three critical facts. First, Kaussen used his buildings as collateral to obtain loans to acquire new properties. He was particularly adept at using the same property as collateral for several different loans. One such property, a 364-unit apartment building located in the heart of the Tenderloin, was worth at most $8 million in 1983; yet Kaussen had used this property to secure nearly $18 million in loans, including a multimillion-dollar guaranteed loan from the US Department of Housing and Urban Development. Second, Kaussen inflated the value of his properties through his "sixth month free" policy, which exaggerated the rental income from each building by $15,000 to $20,000 a year. The inflation of value enabled him to obtain loans that could not be supported by actual revenues. Third, Kaussen's North American empire was created when the West German mark was at a historic high in relation to the dollar. As this margin contracted in the early 1980s, so did Kaussen's cash flow.

Simply put, Kaussen was an early practitioner of the type of real estate chicanery that led to the savings and loan scandal. S&Ls lent him money without paying attention to his lack of up-front capital, determining the actual income from or operating expenses of property used as collateral to secure loans, or investigating whether such property had been similarly used for previous deals. Guenter Kaussen became the Tenderloin's largest property owner solely on the strength of his name; his vast international holdings—rather than proof of equity—were all he needed. Kaussen also made use of shady post-deregulation financing vehicles such as the creatively named Consolidated Capital. These small, speculation-fed institutions must have been thrilled to attract someone of Kaussen's stature.

The publicity we generated about Kaussen's financing practices made some of his more traditional lenders nervous. They began monitoring their Kaussen loans closely, refusing new refinancing efforts and cracking down on delays in mortgage payments. The lenders' concern intensified when they learned from the media that the rent schedule they relied upon in granting Kaussen financing was falsified.

By mid-1984, the San Francisco media were all over the Kaussen story. For several months I had been in almost daily contact with Dan Noyes, and the Clinic had helped fan the flames by filing highly publicized lawsuits over Kaussen's failure to return tenant security deposits and to make necessary repairs. As time went on, stories about Kaussen increasingly involved foreclosures and sales of his properties. Kaussen's problems in San Francisco became a major story in West Germany, and I was repeatedly interviewed at length by both West German national television stations. The German media had long been frustrated by Kaussen and were excited at the prospect that events in San Francisco might spell the end of his empire.

Then *60 Minutes* came to town. I found myself hosting Morley Safer at my office, where we talked for a few hours, and taking him on a tour of the Tenderloin. His producer's interest in the story was not shared by Safer himself, who only became animated when the off-camera discussions turned to rising Manhattan real estate values. My own excitement over the prospect of national attention waned as soon as I saw the finished product, which didn't air until several months after the filming, by which time Kaussen's empire was in a free fall. Significantly, the *60 Minutes* report virtually ignored the real estate practices that Kaussen used to create his empire. Instead, Safer focused on former employees' remarks about Kaussen's bizarre employment and management practices. The context of Kaussen's rise—his leveraging of properties through doctored rent schedules and overcollateralization of properties—was never examined in detail. Although Kaussen's empire was headed inexorably toward collapse when the *60 Minutes* episode finally aired, the show seemed to take credit for pushing him over the edge when, a month after the episode's airing, it announced his suicide.

The main impression left by the *60 Minutes* story was that Kaussen was one strange multimillionaire. I was obviously naive in thinking that his rise and fall would be portrayed as a cautionary tale for the real estate industry of the mid-1980s. As it stood, Kaussen's empire disintegrated three years before the savings and loan scandal toppled other real estate magnates of the 1980s. Had *60 Minutes* compared Kaussen's real estate acquisition strategies to those of American entrepreneurs, the program could have foreshadowed, if not predicted, the urban real estate crash of the late 1980s.

The rapid demise of Kaussen's empire was not an inevitable result of adverse publicity. Kaussen had been subject to media attacks before, including a cover story in *Der Spiegel* (the German equivalent of *Time*), with a cover drawing depicting him as a vulture. Our media strategy achieved greater results because the Center for Investigative Reporting was able to produce one new gem of information after another, keeping the media on the story for months. I helped by timing the lawsuits against Kaussen to maximize media coverage (our filing became the lead story on the local evening news). Kaussen's real estate empire might have fallen eventually, but CIR's work ensured this outcome.

Kaussen's suicide and the wholesale distribution of his properties through foreclosure and/or probate marked the end of CIR's involvement in the case. The local television station that launched the coverage of the Kaussen case subsequently terminated its contract with CIR in a budget-cutting move. CIR no longer has a regular contract with any Bay Area news outlet—none is willing to pay for investigations of major urban problems—making the social change process that much more difficult.

Although the Clinic's media strategy succeeded in destroying the Kaussen empire, our overall goal of improving conditions and reducing rent levels in the thousand-plus Tenderloin units once owned by Kaussen has still not been entirely achieved. Because Kaussen's properties were overfinanced and inflated in value, some continue to experience foreclosures and other problems to this day. One of his most notorious buildings, a 10-story, 100-unit property in the center of the Tenderloin, has experienced several foreclosures since Kaussen's demise. Only recently have some lending institutions acknowledged that their loans on former Kaussen buildings exceed the properties' market value; the subsequent restructuring of the financing has finally brought rent levels down and occupancy up. The press could write great stories on how the real estate practices of Kaussen and suspect lending institutions continue to damage low-income neighborhoods like the Tenderloin, but the current media climate makes such a project unlikely.

TACTICS FOR DEALING WITH REPORTERS

Regrettably, my early experiences with the media on Guenter Kaussen and the heatless hotel scandal were not typical. Over the past fifteen years

I have lost trust in the positive value of the media's final product in assisting social change. I have learned that no matter how sympathetic a reporter may seem toward an activist's position and regardless of how much tape is rolled or how many notes taken, activists can rarely assume that the resulting story will advance their cause. One reason for this shift is that, in economizing moves, daily newspapers have replaced veteran reporters with rookies fresh out of journalism school. Inexperienced reporters usually are more heavily edited by their typically more conservative superiors, and they tend to be unfamiliar with the background of an issue and to have difficulty understanding—despite one's best efforts—the essence of the activist's position. New reporters who do not face heavy editing are thus more likely to get your story wrong. A second reason activists are less certain a story will advance their cause is that conservative editors increasingly select the "spin" in advance and then send a reporter out to cover the story. The activist may connect with the reporter and cooperate fully, only to find that the story ignores the points the activist sought to have conveyed and only includes a quote or two on a peripheral matter.

To use the words of pioneer environmental activist Henry David Thoreau, today's tactical activists must "forever be on the alert" in dealing with reporters. In case anyone still doubts this necessity for eternal vigilance, and before setting forth rules for successful reporter relations, it's worth describing the worst media betrayal of a social change activist that I have ever witnessed.

Not surprisingly, the story involved the homeless. The mainstream media's coverage of the homeless have come to resemble the news trailers used by movie studios to attack Upton Sinclair's 1938 populist campaign for governor of California. In the trailers, actors dressed as hobos were asked where they were headed. "To California," they answered, "because when Upton Sinclair is elected he's going to raise taxes on working people so that I can be housed and fed." The movie audiences, not knowing the hobos were actors reading a script, believed their own scant savings would be taken to support the shiftless if Sinclair were elected. The tactic of using the words of hobos themselves to defeat Sinclair proved successful. Similarly, today's homeless stories often quote self-identified homeless people stating such things as, "Ninety-five percent of the homeless are drug addicts or drunks who voluntarily choose to live on the streets." Quoting homeless people to attack the homeless has become a media staple, even among reporters who personally express support for the homeless population.

My example of media betrayal involves a 1993 Bay Area television news report on the homeless. The report centered entirely on a quote from one homeless advocate, an individual who had no prior media experience and worked full-time for the homeless despite receiving only a small stipend. This individual was not known outside a small core of activists, did not head any organization, and certainly never thought he would become the focus of a two-part series or that one of his quotes would run all week in ads promoting the series.

The activist was quoted as saying: "The homeless are just like you and me." Homeless advocates often make this statement, generally to convey the idea that homeless people, like everyone else, have dreams, aspirations, hopes, fears, and emotional and physical needs. This activist, however, was not "forever on the alert." He did not realize that the producer of the piece, for all his professed concern for the homeless, needed such a quote to fulfill his own agenda. The producer juxtaposed the quote "The homeless are just like you and me" with a video montage of drunks sprawled into gutters and guzzling cheap wine. Added to the montage were quotes from homeless people belittling the idea that the homeless were like "you and me." The entire series, essentially based on *A Nation in Denial* (see Chapter 1), attacked homeless advocates for intentionally misrepresenting their constituency to the public. No homeless person to whom viewers would relate was included in the series. Such an omission was particularly striking from a news outlet that only a few years earlier—using different personnel—ran a five-minute report on how "people like you and me" end up homeless.

Although homeless advocates and media commentators bitterly attacked the series for its depiction of homeless people as intoxicated lowlifes, it won the annual Peabody Award for best investigative local television news story. Whereas a series that exclusively portrayed members of an ethnic group drinking, shooting up, and lolling in gutters would be considered racist, a similar attack on the poor brought an award. The producer took advantage of an activist's attraction to television coverage of homelessness and used him to hurt his own constituency.[4] The episode has at least provided a cautionary message for all tactical activists.

The key to avoiding such errors and fulfilling your media expectations is to determine the reporter's intentions. Be careful when speaking to a journalist who has no track record of fair coverage on your issue. When an unfamiliar reporter calls me, I always ask what angle he or she is pursuing. If the reporter refuses to respond or is evasive, a warning light goes off in my head. Activists must not feel any obligation to assist a journalist with what could well be a negative story. Some reporters are experts at making people feel guilty about refusing to give quotes or to provide information; they claim they only want to hear your side of the story and emphasize that their only commitment is to "the facts." They may also caution that if you fail to speak, only your opponent's views will be expressed. Ignore their pleas. Reporters who refuse to divulge their purpose in seeking your comments will not help your cause and should be rebuffed.

Most reporters will tell you their angle, if for no other reason than to get you to talk. However, this does not mean that your comments will be included in the story or that the piece will be in your constituency's interest. Activists should thus always ask whether the reporter is writing a lengthy story or a brief one. The reason is simple. Reporters often seek out social change activists for lengthy background discussions but never use the information to benefit the activist's agenda. For example, the *60 Minutes* piece on Guenter Kaussen did not serve a major tactical goal of the Clinic, so the significant amount of time I spent on a story that omitted most of my points brought only dismay. It is quite a different matter to work extensively with a reporter on the assumption that he or she will produce a story important to advancing your agenda. Tactical activists must consistently view media contact as a means to further their program, so they must know the reporter's full agenda from the start.

The most effective way of avoiding unproductive and risky contact with the media is to rely as much as possible on reporters known to be sympathetic. Most large media outlets will have at least one reporter interested in producing stories favorable to your constituency's interests. These reporters are readily identified from their prior coverage of similar issues or their discussions with activists. Others may not share a progressive political ideology but may simply be committed to honest and objective reporting on stories of social or economic unfairness. The tactical activist usually must provide the facts necessary for a story. In order to strengthen your relationship with sympathetic reporters, you should give them the first crack at all stories you view as having major public interest. A press release sent out to all media simultaneously does not give any edge to the reporters most likely to produce the best story for your organization. Issuing such a release without having first given it to a helpful reporter is a surefire way of alienating media allies.

Extensive reliance on sympathetic media sources may leave some stories with less than the maximum exposure. A story may even receive no coverage if the sympathetic reporter unexpectedly fails to get it done. Nevertheless, depending on a few key media allies will produce significantly better results over time than the "hit or miss" method of issuing blanket press releases and cooperating with reporters unfamiliar with your goal. Sympathetic reporters are far more likely to produce the necessary follow-up coverage and to include the quotes and overall spin you desire. Moreover, media allies can be counted upon for help should other media sources unfairly attack you or your organization.

I came to appreciate fully the tactical value of relying on media allies when a 1993 front-page story in San Francisco's daily afternoon newspaper, the *Examiner,* attacked me and the Tenderloin Housing Clinic. The story accused the Clinic of referring homeless persons to a residential hotel that was known to be a fire trap. A blaze had occurred at the hotel, resulting in one death. I was quoted extensively in the story, but some passages were entirely fabricated, and most of my quotes were placed at the tail end of the piece (an increasingly common tactic). The key message of the story was that the Clinic, an organization claiming to care about low-income housing conditions, ignored city warnings about the hotel's dangers and intentionally put the lives of tenants in danger.

A front-page newspaper story offering a new angle on an issue often prompts a feeding frenzy from other media sources, because reporters take heat from their editors and news directors for missing the new angle themselves. The Clinic averted a full-fledged media assault on its credibility because I got in touch with all of our trusted media contacts and explained why the *Examiner* story was wrong. I also faxed documents to the media to confirm our position. Reporters with whom I had worked on prior stories and established a relationship of trust were not going to produce false articles about the Clinic. As a result, not a single radio or television station ever followed up on the *Examiner*'s angle. Instead, I diverted the media frenzy toward the city's dismal failure at housing-code enforcement. As media attention shifted from the fire to the city's inadequate housing-inspection process, even the *Examiner* was forced to redirect its own coverage accordingly.

The best was yet to come. On the morning of the fire, I had received a call from Mayor Frank Jordan's office requesting all Clinic documents relating to the burned hotel. Sensing a hidden agenda, I immediately warned city officials against trying to connect the Clinic to the fire.

When I saw the *Examiner* story, it was obvious that the Jordan administration had fed the reporter this material in order to undercut me, a vocal critic of administration policies.[5]

I promptly contacted a reporter for an alternative weekly newspaper with whom I had worked on several stories. In the next issue she revealed how the mayor's chief of staff sought to use the fire to tarnish the Clinic's image as zealous advocates for the poor. When the article came out, the mayor's chief of staff promptly called me to deny any connection to the *Examiner* story or any effort to harm the Clinic. I saw as never before how sympathetic coverage can transform even the worst media attack into an advancement of organizational interests. The fact that the fire resulted in prompt passage of Clinic-supported code-enforcement legislation (previously stalled for lack of votes) only added to my satisfaction.

RESPONDING TO MEDIA BIAS

The media's pro–status quo bias on most issues addressed by social change organizations raises a broad set of tactical concerns. The fundamental issue is how, when, and whether to respond to unfair or slanted media stories about your issue or constituency. When you or your organization are specifically attacked in a front-page story, as in the previous example, responding through sympathetic media is the best strategy. Most cases of media bias, however, do not involve overt attacks on organizations or individuals. The stories most destructive to social change organizations are those like the "homeless are like you and me" series. These appear objective but use quotes, facts, and photos selectively to make invalid points. They also tell the truth about an individual case to support a false thesis about the group as a whole. Homeless advocates could not deny that the homeless persons portrayed in the series were either drunks or drug abusers. As long as reporters are careful not to claim that all members of a particular group have the characteristics of the individual portrayed, they can insulate themselves from charges of bias while conveying their inaccurate perspective. The subtlety of media bias today makes formulating a tactical response even more critical.

I recommend engaging in the following thought process when confronted with an unfair media story. First, consider whether the piece has caused any real harm to your issue or constituency. If it has not, the best response is no response; people are so overloaded with information these days that one unfair story is usually soon forgotten. Although some contend that activists should not wait for harm to occur before responding, there are always risks associated with a response. For example, in most publications the author of an article has the right to reply to letters to the editor. Writing a letter criticizing an unfair but harmless article would give the offending author a second chance to injure your constituency in print. Even worse, your letter and the reporter's reply might cause readers to view you and your organization as hypersensitive crybabies. Such an image would undermine your organization's ability to win public support for its battle against its real opponents.

To determine whether unfair media coverage has caused real harm to your constituency, first consider the author and forum. In San Francisco, a right-wing fanatic regularly distributes a newsletter falsely charging nonprofit organizations and their leaders with stealing public funds and committing other crimes. Having personally been charged with running a multimillion-dollar Ponzi scheme in a 1994 edition, I fully understand the desire to file a libel suit in response. Such a suit would not be wise, however, because it would simply elevate the status of both the attacker and his claims. Because the newsletter's targets do not respond, the publication remains totally irrelevant. A similar tactic applies where the forum is legitimate but the author has little influence with the public. For example, a columnist in the *San Francisco Chronicle* frequently writes about how the homeless, welfare recipients, and the poor cheat the taxpayers. Even though activists are regularly tempted to write letters to the editor to correct the distortions in these columns, the best strategy, and one that advocates for the poor have followed, is simply to ignore such writings, since they appear to cause the poor no real harm.[6]

If the unfair media coverage comes from a credible source in a legitimate medium, activists should then consider whether the bias was central or collateral to the purpose of the story. For example, stories often include references—entirely unrelated to the primary thrust of the story—intended to portray social change advocates negatively. For instance, stories about Alaska in the travel section of a newspaper may include a sentence criticizing environmental groups for seeking to preserve an area they have never visited. Restaurant reviews may include brief attacks on animal-rights activists who preach against meat but wear leather belts. Perhaps most common are articles on all types of subjects whose authors cannot resist throwaway references to feminists as "humorless," "politically correct," or "bra burners." These types of unfair attacks are certainly worthy of criticism, but responses to such collateral comments risk failing the "crybaby" test. Unfair asides that do not involve demonstrably factual errors (such as inaccurate statistics) are unlikely to cause harm and are best ignored.

In contrast, a response is definitely appropriate when derogatory comments appear in articles *focused on your issue*. If an article on legislation to preserve undeveloped Alaskan land includes an unfair attack on environmentalists, readers could well be influenced by the bias and even oppose the legislation as a result. Such an attack demands a response. The same holds true for attacks on animal-rights organizations in articles about the virtues of meat and attacks on feminists in articles pertaining to the feminist agenda. Tactical activists should limit their responses to stories in which the bias is likely to affect people's perception of the core issue and ignore those in which the bias is collateral and likely only to anger the already committed.

After establishing that unfair media bias has caused real harm to one's constituency or organization, a tactical activist must decide how to react. The most common response is to write a letter to the editor of the publication. Effective letters can do much to advance your cause; just be sure to focus on your message rather than reiterate the unfair claims. Avoid making a point-by-point rebuttal. I recommend quickly dismissing the credibility of the unfair story at the outset, then using most of your piece to restate the social, political, and economic reasons for your position. Be careful to consider whether anything you say in the letter can produce a counterresponse that further highlights the area of attack. One strategy is to quote facts from other stories published by the same publication that conflict with the claims in the unfair story. Because your opponents cannot dispute these quotes, the letter has advanced your agenda and given the opposition no grounds for a successful response. Another tactic is to have the letter signed by a respected community figure not directly connected with the cause at issue. Media criticism from an ostensibly disinterested figure enhances the credibility of the objections. Regardless of who signs the letter, it is critical to avoid restating mistruths in your letter for those who missed them the first time. Instead, use the letters page to win additional converts to your cause.

Relying on letters to the editor alone, however, has its limitations. Some publications rarely print letters advocating progressive social change, and others feel free to edit heavily. Still others practice a policy, already mentioned, of giving the author of the story the last word, allowing him or her to spread even greater mistruths against your cause.

Further, a letter to the editor hardly represents "equal time" in response to a column or feature story. You might include a cover letter requesting that your response run as a column rather than in the letters section. As I will discuss, letter writing is particularly valuable in response to think-tank attacks on subjects such as feminism. When the unfair article is part of a broad right-wing media strategy, letter writing is essential to show the public and editors that you are wise to that agenda.

Responding to unfair television stories is more difficult. An angry letter to the producer accompanied by a phone call to the reporter may result in a follow-up story giving your side of the issue. An even better tactic is to contact a competing media source and give it the opportunity to cover the story correctly. Media organizations enjoy the opportunity to demonstrate that their competitor missed critical facts. San Francisco homeless advocates responded to the unfair television series discussed previously by appearing on a nightly radio talk show whose host lambasted the series. They also picketed the television station that produced the series, hoping to attract coverage from other outlets.

Although television is a powerful medium, I have never felt that unfair television news stories could do as much harm to my constituency as bias in the print media. People seem to watch television news while eating or doing something else. When people tell me they have seen me interviewed on the news, they invariably do not recall more than the general subject matter of the story. If people cannot remember the views expressed by someone they know, it's doubtful that they pay close attention to other stories. Television news is most ideologically destructive in its selection of stories; although spending half the news hour covering violent crime may not constitute "unfair coverage," the focus on such stories hurts social change activists by increasing public support for the law-and-order agenda. The media's decisions on what constitutes news are extremely difficult to combat, which is why tactical activists should never entirely rely on ongoing media support to achieve their goals.

Activists wanting to combat biased media coverage can contact Fairness and Accuracy in Reporting (FAIR),[7] a national organization that monitors and exposes the media's corporate and conservative biases. FAIR may be best known for proving statistically that presumably "objective" news shows such as *The MacNeil-Lehrer News Hour* and Ted Koppel's *Nightline* slant the news by relying on guests who are disproportionately conservative white men in official government positions.

FAIR showed that representatives of labor unions, ethnic groups, and women's organizations were rarely included in these shows' "public debates." FAIR was also the first organization to document Rush Limbaugh's "reign of error."[8] Limbaugh's stream of factual inaccuracies had been ignored by such shows as *Nightline,* which even used Limbaugh as an environmental commentator. FAIR's magazine, *Extra!,* should be required reading for all tactical activists.

Although FAIR primarily focuses on the national media, its capacity to influence state or local media coverage is all too often untapped. The corporate owners of state and local media share their national colleagues' defensiveness over accusations of bias. An organization working on a campaign expected to last months or years should send clippings or tapes of strongly biased media coverage to FAIR (and raise the issue directly with local media outlets). Although FAIR is not the arm of a social change organization and is not designed to swoop down and help in particular grassroots struggles, the potential for such assistance exists. The state and local media elite do not want to be viewed on the national stage as lacking professional objectivity, and a story about their bias in a well-researched, amply documented article in *Extra!* could alter their approach.

Grassroots organizations have tried taking direct action to overcome media neglect. Environmental, peace, and Nicaraguan and El Salvadoran support groups have bought costly full-page newspaper advertisements to address the media's lack of coverage of their issues. Most grassroots organizations, however, lack the funding necessary for this approach. Another option is to hold a protest in front of a specific media outlet's offices. Tenants in San Francisco tried this tactic in 1991 to protest the daily newspapers' ignoring a series of press events during a city-declared "Tenants' Week." But the tenants, like the homeless activists protesting in front of the television station, won no media coverage. It may be best to link such protests to an elected official's demanding an investigation into the lack of coverage. Such complaints by elected officials allow the media to write a story about their own alleged failures without directly "rewarding" the affected constituency.

The AIDS Coalition to Unleash Power (ACT UP) may have waged the most valiant direct-action attack on a media giant in its campaign against the *New York Times.* Although headquartered in the city whose strong gay presence led to ACT UP's founding, the *Times* had fallen short of providing "all the news that's fit to print" in its coverage of AIDS. AIDS activists contrasted the *Times*' four front-page stories and fifty-four articles on the 1982 tainted-Tylenol scare with its seven articles, none on the front page, during the first nineteen months of the AIDS epidemic.[9] The *Times* refused to list AIDS as a cause of death or to list gay lovers among surviving family members and did not cover the opening ceremonies of the Fifth International Conference on AIDS in 1989 in Montreal, which won national publicity when it was taken over by ACT UP and other international AIDS activists. Realizing the difficulty of changing the *Times*' approach, ACT UP had decided against targeting the paper until a June 29, 1989 editorial, "Why Make AIDS Worse Than It Is," accused the "powerful gay lobby" of exaggerating the epidemic to obtain funding for a disease that allegedly was "leveling off." Because the editorial attacked the heart of its agenda, ACT UP had no choice but to respond. Its campaign against the nation's most influential newspaper took several forms. Activists placed "Buy Your Lies Here" stickers on newsstands, and "Out of Order" stickers over *Times* vending machines. The organization circulated the *Times*' fax numbers so ACT UP members could use their employers' fax machines to flood editors with their complaints. On the night of July 23, 1989, ACT UP painted the street outside *Times* publisher Arthur Sulzberger's Fifth Avenue residence with outlines of bodies and the phrase, "All the news that's fit to kill." Three days later, 200 ACT UP demonstrators held a protest at the same location and distributed fliers detailing the *Times*' pro-FDA, anti-gay coverage of AIDS.[10]

Despite using all of the above tactics and more, ACT UP achieved no more mainstream media coverage of its actions than did the activists protesting the San Francisco newspapers over Tenants Week. Not a single major outlet covered ACT UP's campaign, and the venerable *Times* would not bow to objections to its editorial policies. As if to further prove its point, the *Times* produced a major attack on AIDS activists in its September 19, 1989 edition. Headlined "Critics fault secret effort to test AIDS drugs," the story accused AIDS activists of causing deaths by attempting to "shortcut" federal drug-trial procedures. The story, by Gina Kolata, was publicly attacked by respected journalists for misrepresenting facts from several key sources and falsely portraying committed physicians, prominent AIDS activist Martin Delaney of Project Inform, and other critics of FDA policy as risking the lives of those they sought to help. Delaney and others wrote letters to the editor criticizing the story; none were printed.[11] Whether Kolata's piece came in retaliation for ACT UP's attack on the *Times* or simply as a continuation of the paper's position on AIDS is unclear; the story did show that ACT

UP's focus on the *Times,* though tactically necessary and well executed, failed to achieve the desired results.

The expression "thick as thieves" explains why the media do not cover grassroots protests against a specific outlet. Simply put, the mainstream media are united in not giving credence to claims of bias; if one outlet covers attacks against another, it will encourage a tactic that might eventually be used against itself. Many reporters learn early in their careers not to write stories critical of other journalists or media sources. When they do so, retaliation from the media fraternity can be swift. Jim Balderston of the *San Francisco Bay Guardian* wrote an important story detailing the personal hypocrisy of *Examiner* reporter Phil Matier, who had falsely accused Dick Hongisto, a progressive candidate for mayor, of remodeling his home without having obtained the necessary permits. As it turned out, Hongisto had his permits in order, but Matier, who was also remodeling his home, did not. The criticism did not sit well with local journalists; Balderston was banned from his weekly appearance on a local cable television news show after Matier and other regulars said they would not appear if the *Bay Guardian* writer did. Not surprisingly, this act of retaliation was only reported in Balderston's own publication.

RESPONDING TO THINK-TANK MEDIA STORIES

A strategic response to an unfair story is most critical when the attack is part of your opposition's attempt to create a climate hostile to your issue. Such attacks began in the late 1970s with the rise of well-funded conservative think tanks, which have worked to create a public-opinion environment hostile to progressive social change. Their resident scholars are employed full-time to write stories, editorials, columns, and news analysis on political issues. The American Enterprise Institute is one of the most prominent of such conservative vehicles at the national level. Meanwhile, the election to the presidency of former Democratic Leadership Council chairman Bill Clinton made the deceptively named, DLC-controlled, and corporate-funded Progressive Policy Institute a major contributor to conservative Democrats' think-tank activities. Think tanks pose great dangers to social change organizations for several reasons. First, their names often conceal their true ideological agendas. People reading an article by someone from the Progressive Policy Institute will likely assume that the author is politically progressive. However, the PPI seeks funding from the same corporate interests solicited by Republican groups. PPI's financial connections to major defense companies such as McDonnell-Douglass, Martin-Marietta, and General Dynamics explain why the institute's "progressive" ideas include opposition to cutting the defense budget.[12] Readers may be more likely to accept factual claims made by a PPI expert than those offered by an unabashedly conservative columnist such as George Will.

In addition to concealing their conservative ideological biases, think-tank scholars frequently enjoy ample space to express their views. A lengthy article in a Sunday newspaper or a prominently placed article on an editorial page can have more influence than dozens of television news stories. A think-tank feature story often first appears in a sympathetic magazine before proceeding to newspaper syndication. Think-tank authors also have access to Sunday news shows to discuss their perspectives. One think-tank article can go a very long way. The appearance of objectivity coupled with wide access enables conservative think tanks to increase public acceptance of their political positions and undermine support of progressive social change.

Think-Tank Voodoo   Recent history is rife with examples of conservatives' use of think tanks to define the political mainstream. The most obvious example of this conservative strategy and of the consequences of progressives' failure to counterattack aggressively is the emergence of supply-side economics. The phrase "supply-side economics" first appeared in the *Wall Street Journal,* which had been arguing for federal tax cuts in its editorial pages since 1978. The idea was the centerpiece of former *Wall Street Journal* editorial writer Jude Wanniski's book *The Way the World Works,* which argued that cutting taxes on the wealthy was the key strategy underlying nations' economic successes throughout history.[13] Supply-side economics thus burst onto the national agenda, and it became the dominant U.S. economic policy upon Ronald Reagan's election to the presidency in 1980. The political value of the policy lay in its offering something new to an electorate battered by both inflation and unemployment. The conservative Republican economic belief in reducing taxes for the rich could not be the centerpiece of an election strategy to win over blue-collar voters. Neither could the phrase "trickle-down economics" be uttered by a presidential candidate vowing to improve the lives of working people. As a result, conservative scholars such as Wanniski and George Gilder worked with their allies at the *Wall Street Journal* to make an economic policy geared entirely toward helping the rich appear populist and even revolutionary. I use the term "worked with" because *Wall Street Journal* editor Robert Bartley was an ardent advocate of supply-side theories who strategized with Wanniski to broaden the audience for his proposal. In a 1989 preface to the third edition of Wanniski's book, Bartley acknowledged his alliance with supply-side proponents and noted that the *"Journal* op-ed page provided a daily bulletin board for such ideas."[14] The wide perception of the *Journal* as an "objective" source of business news gave supply-side policy the credibility it needed to gain acceptance among other media outlets. Supply-side economics became the centerpiece of Ronald Reagan's presidential campaign and of the historically regressive 1981 tax bill. During the 1980 campaign, no concerted media counteroffensive to discredit supply-side emerged, despite criticism of the concept even from the likes of George Bush, who called it "voodoo economics" in a famous exchange. Bush's label notwithstanding, the failure to combat supply-side was probably largely attributable to President Jimmy Carter's abandonment of progressive economic policies. Reporters covering the election were not likely to run articles criticizing one candidate's economic program when the other candidate was not offering alternative proposals.

The full extent of supply-side's unrivaled hold on the media was demonstrated in the famous William Greider interview of David Stockman, Reagan's original budget chief. Stockman's candid admission that "supply-side" was simply another name for "trickle-down" made national headlines. The media acted as if they themselves had believed in the think-tank rhetoric and were now angry at being deceived.

Who Lost Feminism? The think tanks' broadest-based yet least successful strategy for reversing progressive social change concerns their attacks on feminism. Conservative attacks on the progressive feminist agenda paralleled the rise of the movement. However, Susan Faludi's *Backlash: The Undeclared War Against Women*[15] (1991) did such a powerful job establishing the intellectual dishonesty and anti-feminist agenda underlying think-tank feminist criticism that conservatives had to regroup to figure out a new approach. The post-Faludi think-tank anti-feminists introduced a new concept: feminists' love of "victimhood." This new attack on feminism coincided with the increase in public concern over date-rape, sexual assaults on college campuses, domestic violence, and sexual harassment in general. As demands mounted for stronger laws and regulations to protect women from sexual abuse, harassment, and violence, the anti-feminists dismissed such problems as "myths." The right-wing Olin Foundation, which previously had funded Dinesh D'Souza's *Illiberal Education,* an attack on college affirmative action and progressive professors, sought to sway public attitudes by funding two major anti-feminist books.[16] The first, David Brock's *The Real Anita Hill,*[17] vilified Anita Hill and the entire idea of sexual harassment. The second Olin-sponsored work, Christina Hoff Sommers's *Who Stole Feminism? How Women Have Betrayed Women,*[18] hit all the bases by attacking feminists for embracing "victimhood" and the "myths" of widespread campus rape and domestic violence. Although Sommers's work was funded by the right-wing Bradley and Carthage foundations in addition to Olin, reviews of her work insisted she lacked a political agenda. Mainstream publications such as *Time, Newsweek,* and the *Boston Globe* accepted her claim that she was a feminist simply trying to set the factual record straight for the good of the movement.

Sommers's book drew mainstream press support from the usual right-wing commentators, including Rush Limbaugh, Pat Buchanan, and John Leo of *U.S. News and World Report.* The Olin-funded *National Review* featured Sommers's book on its June 21, 1994 cover, under the heading "Why feminism's vital statistics are always wrong." The right wing used Sommers's work as part of an across-the-board media strategy to create a climate hostile to progressive interests. This effort, however, has yet to bring results in the public-policy arena. The reasons are twofold. First, the works of Sommers and Brock, as well as Katie Roiphe's *The Morning After: Sex, Fear and Feminism on Campus,*[19] were devastated by feminist activists. Katha Pollitt in *The Nation,* Laura Flanders in *Extra!,* along with Faludi and dozens of other feminists have so convincingly refuted the anti-feminist analysis that the works have seriously lost credibility.[20] Faludi has observed that feminism's opponents have shifted from using female spokespersons who claim "I'm not a feminist, but . . . " to using Sommers and others who attack feminism while claiming to be feminists. Faludi emphasizes that none of these self-proclaimed feminists use their talk show or media appearances to boost pro-feminist positions, and their hostile attitudes clearly place them in the anti-feminist camp.[21]

Also, the latest round of anti-feminist arguments have failed to impact policy because they defy people's common experience. Why would a college woman fear rape less after reading Roiphe's book or a *New York Times Magazine* article of March 8, 1994 questioning the legitimacy of the campus rape threat? College women evaluate risk based on their own experiences and those of their friends, not on what they read in an article. The demand for safer campuses came out of the concerns raised by college women; it was not handed down to women by Roiphe's so-called "rape crisis" feminists. Similarly, women's own workplace and educational experiences refuted the notion that sexual harassment is a myth, and the O.J. Simpson case likely will bury for years the anti-feminist claim that spousal abuse is not as common as feminists claim. Think-tank-funded efforts to influence public attitudes simply cannot overcome people's personal experience. Feminist activists have done the best job of any social change constituency in issuing point-by-point rebuttals to attacks. These advocates no doubt find it demoralizing and frustrating to have to keep responding to the same old tired clichés and erroneous claims, particularly from anti-feminist sources widely hailed as objective "experts." Nevertheless, public concern over rape, domestic violence, and sexual harassment has only grown since the emergence of the latest think-tank-spawned anti-feminist attacks. Even political conservatives fear opposing new laws to protect women against such conduct. Feminist activists are an excellent model for how social change constituencies should proactively respond to conservative media efforts to shape public attitudes.

ALTERNATIVE VERSUS MAINSTREAM MEDIA

The past two decades have seen the widespread emergence of weekly newspapers targeted to self-identified progressives between the ages of twenty-one and forty-nine. The success of the Manhattan-based *Village Voice* and the *San Francisco Bay Guardian* led to similarly styled weeklies in large and small cities across the country. Many of these publications overtly challenge the mainstream press and thus tend to be openly supportive of social change movements' assaults on the established order.

However, as the gentrification of our major cities has proceeded, the alternative weekly press has grown in size and profitability. Today, the progressive political content of the weeklies often gets lost amid the mass of ads for futons, restaurants, and trendy clothes. Advertisers realized that the weeklies are the prime reading material of young, free-spending urban professionals and target advertising dollars accordingly. The alternative press has seemed to increase its focus on alternative "soft news" that meshes well with its accompanying advertising; lengthy restaurant reviews, features on bed-and-breakfast inns, and fashion articles became more and more common.

The alternative weeklies' shift toward less politicized subject matter has been a mixed blessing for tactical activists. On the plus side, the political material in the weeklies is reaching more people who might not otherwise be exposed to progressive perspectives. Increased circulation means increased political clout for the weeklies' pro-social change positions. On the negative side, many activists wonder whether anyone beyond the already committed is willing to search through to find the political articles in the weeklies. Circulation increase may have come entirely from readers who pick up the weeklies solely for their detailed guides to nightly entertainment or their personal ads. Further, increased advertising revenue has not increased the scope of political reporting. Many of the weeklies continue to rely overly on well-intentioned but inexperienced reporters writing stories too brief to advance the social activist's agenda significantly.

As a source for and reader of the alternative press, I have found one principle that stands out: to assist social change activism, an alternative weekly must run repeated stories on the same issue. I refer to this principle as the "Westway Rule," named for the long-proposed highway for New York's West Side. During much of the 1980s, you could not pick up an issue of the *Village Voice* without reading about the horrors of Westway. As a *Voice* subscriber living 3,000 miles away from the project, I might easily ignore articles about the latest deficiency in the Westway environmental impact report. Yet the constant stream of stories demanded my attention. I eventually took a strong rooting interest in the defeat of Westway and looked forward to reading prominent opponent Marcy Benstock's latest salvo against it. If the *Voice*'s ongoing Westway stories won over someone totally unfamiliar with Manhattan's West Side, I could only imagine their impact on area residents. The defeat of Westway in the 1980s surely resulted from many factors, but the *Voice*'s ongoing coverage had to be one of them.

The *Voice*'s West Coast analogue, the *San Francisco Bay Guardian*, also reflects the Westway Rule. The *Guardian*'s twenty-year attack on San Francisco's "Manhattanization" came to embody a critique of downtown growth that became the city's majority sentiment by the mid-1980s. By writing stories on every facet of Manhattanization, including transit impacts, demolition of historic buildings, loss of open space and view lines, pressure on housing costs, hidden costs to the city's general fund, and negative impacts on the city's neighborhoods, the *Guardian* provided a free, comprehensive political education for its readers. Although its opponents sought to discredit the weekly for its unceasing attacks on growth, the continual influx of new residents to major cities or college towns required ongoing recitation of basic facts. It is difficult to imagine that San Francisco's limited-growth movement would have succeeded without the *Guardian*'s longtime support.

Obviously, every issue is not going to become a focus of ongoing coverage by alternative weeklies. However, tactical activists can work with sympathetic reporters on the weeklies to ensure ongoing coverage over the entire course of a campaign. These ongoing stories will have far greater impact than one major mainstream media article, which may make an initial splash but will probably soon be forgotten. I worked with longtime *Bay Guardian* reporter Jim Balderston over an eight-month campaign to strengthen the city's residential hotel preservation ordinance. A major piece in September 1989 discussed the significance of the proposed legislation in reducing homelessness. Subsequent stories tracked the legislative process and reiterated the measure's importance. The *Guardian*'s continued coverage helped maintain the spirit of our residents' organization and confirmed the importance of fighting until victory was achieved. When a self-identified progressive on the Board of Supervisors stalled our efforts, Balderston came down on her hard, breaking the logjam. The legislation was enacted in April 1990, and the *Guardian*'s several stories fueled our victory.

I became so convinced of the weeklies' potential to promote an agenda through constant coverage that I set up a meeting with an editor on the subject in early 1992, the year that I authored the successful rent-control reform initiative discussed in Chapter 4. The *SF Weekly* primarily catered to readers aged twenty-one to thirty, a group I saw as an untapped base for revitalizing San Francisco's tenant movement. I suggested to the avowedly pro-tenant editor that his paper begin regular coverage of tenant issues as part of an overall strategy to increase tenant power. I left the meeting thinking the editor liked the idea, but I could not have been more wrong. The *Weekly* spent the next several months ignoring tenant issues. The few stories that were written dismissed the idea that tenant activists could revive their allegedly moribund movement. One very hostile article concluded that Proposition H was a risky and foolish endeavor, despite its being backed by every tenant group in San Francisco, and that I "would have a lot of explaining to do" if the initiative failed that November. When it passed, the first pro-tenant initiative in San Francisco ever to win at the ballot box, the victory was not even included in the *SF Weekly*'s yearly list of progressive achievements.

So much for the best-laid plans. My experience did confirm, however, that tactical activists' need to be "forever on the alert" with journalists also applies to the self-identified progressive or alternative press.

6

Lawyers

ALLIES OR OBSTACLES
TO SOCIAL CHANGE?

Many activists involved in social change movements in the 1960s and 1970s went to law school with a conscious desire to use their legal skills to advance progressive change. This flow of committed political activists into the nation's law schools was accompanied by the creation of the federally funded Legal Services Corporation (LSC), which paid attorneys to provide free counsel in fields such as housing, welfare, and income maintenance to indigent clients. In addition, activists were attracted to law school by the numerous Supreme Court decisions from the late 1950s through the early 1970s that promoted progressive social change. Our highest court's willingness to recognize and expand constitutional and, specifically, minority rights fostered the view that the judicial system could be an ally of, rather than obstacle to, social change. The Supreme Court's openness to the arguments of welfare, civil, and constitutional rights litigators reaffirmed social change activists' desire to use the legal system proactively to achieve their goals.

The unprecedented influx of progressive activists into the legal profession from the late 1960s through the end of the 1970s greatly assisted social change advocacy. No group benefited more than poor people (both urban and rural), who suddenly had lawyers to protect and assert their rights. Poverty lawyers' proactive use of the courts became so successful that conservative forces began to create political pressure against public funding for legal services. During Ronald Reagan's tenure as California's governor (1967 to 1974), conservatives unleashed numerous attacks on legal services. Reagan sided with wealthy agricultural interests seeking to defund the California Rural Legal Assistance Foundation (CRLA), whose "radical" efforts to improve the lives of migrant farmworkers had angered agribusiness. Although Reagan's campaign against CRLA failed, he resumed his attacks on legal-service programs during his presidency. In his first year in office, Reagan virtually eliminated the VISTA program, which had funded legal-aid fellowships for recent law school graduates, filled legal-aid staffing needs, and trained attorneys for permanent staff positions. He also waged an eight-year campaign to eliminate entirely federal funds for legal services. Although this effort failed, Reagan's allies did succeed in sharply reducing legal-service funding at the same time that other administration policies, such as the arbitrary termination of disability benefits to long-term recipients, added to the number of people living in poverty and increased the need for free legal aid. Reagan's war on the Legal Services Corporation significantly reduced employment prospects in legal aid and forced cutbacks in existing staff. By 1981 few activists were entering law school assuming future employment in a federal legal-service program. There are still progressive attorneys, but there are fewer opportunities for them to earn a living representing progressive constituencies.

In addition to cutting off federally funded employment opportunities for activist attorneys, President Reagan returned the Supreme Court and most federal courts to their historic positions as opponents of social change movements. Reagan's justices were not simply opposed to expanding constitutional or statutory protections to benefit women, minorities, and the poor; they sought to reverse many Warren Court rulings and return to the pre-1960s legal status quo. It was clear by the mid-1980s that social change movements had far more to lose than to gain by challenging government policies in the federal courts.[1]

Although President Clinton's judicial appointments have improved matters, today's activists still face decreasing access to skilled legal-service attorneys and courts that are indifferent, if not hostile, to their claims. Nevertheless, social change activists and organizations can still benefit from legal resources in seeking to fulfill their goals. Activists must recognize how best to use attorneys and the courts and how to avoid the tensions and conflicts that often mar activist-attorney relationships. As both a practicing attorney and a practicing tactical activist, I have experienced these sources of friction firsthand. By understanding the areas of potential conflict, activists and attorneys can establish the positive relationships necessary to achieve progressive change.

PREVENTING ATTORNEYS FROM ENCROACHING
UPON STRATEGIC DECISIONMAKING

During the summer of 1980, while still a law student, I worked both at the Tenderloin Housing Clinic and as a law clerk for a legal-aid agency serving senior citizens. The summer began with the announcement of the proposed luxury high-rise hotels in the Tenderloin. I soon also became involved in an unrelated fight, helping tenants in the residential Glenburn Hotel who were threatened with eviction from their homes by a new owner. The owner, a British physician, wanted to turn the Glenburn into an English-style bed-and-breakfast inn for tourists. Although the hotel had numerous vacancies, the owner did not want his tourists to have to share living space with the hotel's long-term elderly and disabled residents. The owner started a two-pronged strategy to get rid of the tenants, whom he disparagingly described as "squatters." First, he engaged in psychological warfare against the vulnerable residents, telling them they were not wanted at the hotel and should move. He bolstered this illegal strategy by issuing eviction notices to all of the tenants, stating that they must vacate for upgrading of the property. Little did I know when I met with the tenants to discuss the landlord's efforts to displace them that the Tenderloin Housing Clinic would spend the next fourteen years in court fights with the hotel owner.

Many similar hotel conversions had already occurred in San Francisco, resulting in the loss of more than 5,000 low-cost residential hotel rooms during the 1970s. To prevent further losses, the city enacted a Residential Hotel Ordinance in 1979 that restricted the conversion or demolition of residential hotel rooms. Legal-aid attorneys representing elderly tenants had been involved in drafting the new law. Because the Glenburn Hotel tenants were facing formal evictions in addition to psychological threats to force them to move, a legal-aid agency for seniors and the federally funded San Francisco Neighborhood Legal Assistance Foundation (SFNLAF) both agreed to represent the tenants. I was involved both as a law clerk for the legal-aid agency for seniors and as staff for the Tenderloin Housing Clinic.

The British physician displayed open contempt for the Glenburn tenants, describing them as "vagrants" and creating an atmosphere designed to make them feel so unwelcome that they would "voluntarily" vacate their homes. Many of the tenants were under great stress from their landlord's psychological assault, but the attorneys kept looking for signs that he would be "reasonable." This focus on reasonableness is ingrained during law school and even influences progressive attorneys. Nonlawyers seeking social change are far less likely to expect adversaries to act reasonably. The attorneys did not want to contest the issue in court, seeking instead to negotiate an agreement under which the landlord would end his eviction actions. Reaching such an agreement was difficult, however, because the hotel owner was slow and contradictory in setting forth his positions—in other words, he was not acting reasonably. Further, settling the formal eviction actions was less important than deterring the landlord's abusive conduct; a jury would never have voted to evict the tenants, but the abuse might compel them to leave before any settlement could be reached. As the owner continued to delay an agreement, the strain on tenants mounted. Some began drinking heavily, and others experienced stress-caused medical problems. The tenants, the attorneys, and I agreed that we needed to pressure the owner to end his eviction attempts. We decided a good way to get the owner's attention was to schedule a demonstration in front of his medical office. Because the Tenderloin Housing Clinic did not yet have lawyers and thus was not the legal counsel for the tenants, I was charged with organizing the event. This would insulate the tenants' attorneys from being implicated in such "unreasonable" conduct.

As the demonstration approached, I observed a renewed sense of vigor and excitement among the hotel tenants. After months of being on the receiving end of the landlord's abuse, they were now going to get the chance to fight back. We all liked the idea of going after him at his medical office, where his patients and employees would learn of his conduct. Our press release, titled "Landlord Malpractice," connected the doctor/landlord's mistreatment of tenants to his treatment of patients; we felt that people reading about the former would not feel comfortable getting medical care from this physician.

After sending out the press releases, I learned that the attorneys had called a tenants' meeting for the night before the demonstration. Apparently, the hotel owner was once again appearing reasonable and was now interested in negotiating. The attorneys, who had kept their distance from the proposed demonstration, felt that holding the event would jeopardize the possibility for a negotiated settlement. Of course, the attorneys would leave the decision on whether to proceed with the protest up to the tenants; the nighttime meeting would allow the attorneys to explain their position so that the tenants could make the best decision.

I knew as soon as the meeting was scheduled what the result would be; the scene has likely been repeated thousands of times, explaining why so many organizers have come to distrust and even despise their attorney "allies." The attorneys set forth the facts so as to guarantee that the tenants would cancel the demonstration. The tenants' legal position in any future legal action, the lawyers said, had suddenly become precarious, making it essential to reach a negotiated settlement; the landlord was exhibiting a new openness to compromise, but this window of opportunity could quickly close if the protest angered him. The attorneys did not emphasize that the landlord had so far agreed to nothing; nor did they focus on the landlord's pattern of promising compromise, only to renege. Those facts were not stressed because they undermined the attorneys' position. I was permitted to give a dissenting view, but there was no way tenants were going to trust a law student over their own lawyers. The tenants accepted their attorneys' recommendation and canceled the protest.

In my opinion, the legal-aid attorneys had wrongly interfered with the tenants' decisionmaking process. Rather than objectively laying out all the options, the attorneys treated the tenants as if they were a jury, rather than clients. A lawyer must persuade a jury to accept his or her perspective on the case, but an attorney should not treat a client in the same fashion. I would not have objected had the attorneys laid out the facts fairly and expressed their own strategic preference. There is a difference, however, between expressing a viewpoint and falsely implying that any other perspective could spell disaster.

The attorneys' chief failure was their misunderstanding of the tenants' needs. Lawyers, including those who support social change, look for solutions in the law. In the Glenburn Hotel case, this outlook led the tenants' attorneys to focus on resolving the specific legal problem confronting their clients: the eviction notice. They were unable or unwilling to understand the greater risk that tenants would be displaced by the landlord's psychological attacks, which would not end with the resolution of the eviction issue but would cease only when the tenants made it clear that they could not be pushed around.

Although the tenants had voted to cancel the protest, most of them deeply regretted the act. They had been excited about going after the doctor on his own turf, and now they were again reduced to passive participation in the ongoing drama affecting their lives. The tenants had lost a sense of personal empowerment and, more critically, a sense of unity. The legal-aid attorneys ultimately obtained the withdrawal of the eviction notices, but the settlement merely confirmed the legal reality that a San Francisco jury would never have allowed the landlord to evict the

Glenburn tenants. More significant, the number of tenants benefiting from this legal "victory" steadily declined, as tenants moved anyway, convinced the landlord would ultimately be able to evict them and not wanting to postpone the inevitable. That the tenants incorrectly assessed their legal position was irrelevant; few low-income people are willing to trust the legal system to protect them. What the tenants needed was a sense of control based on their own perceived power. By carrying out the protest, the tenants would have said to the landlord: "Our power over you is based on our strength, not simply our attorneys." Had the attorneys understood and been willing to accommodate the tenants' psychological and emotional needs, they not only would have advocated the demonstration but would have actively encouraged such actions in the future.

The story of the Glenburn Hotel tenants illustrates some of the reasons community organizers traditionally distrust attorneys. Social change activists typically criticize attorneys for relying on the legal system instead of direct actions designed to strengthen the constituency's sense of empowerment. But the Glenburn story has a deeper lesson for tactical activists who interact with attorneys: tenant activists made a fundamental error in granting the legal-aid attorneys too large a role in the decisionmaking process. Although organizers from the local Gray Panthers chapter and other community groups were centrally involved in the fight against hotel conversions, the issuance of eviction notices at the Glenburn suddenly transformed the tenants from autonomous members of the community into "clients" represented by attorneys. The informal relationship between a social change organization and its constituency was supplanted by a powerful and legally recognized "attorney-client" relationship. The decision of whether to proceed with the protest at the landlord's clinic was made in an attorney-client setting rather than in a strategic meeting between nonattorney organizers and tenants.

This transfer of influence to attorneys and away from the social change organizers and the affected constituency itself is at the heart of the problem. Unfortunately, overcoming attorneys' undue influence in tactical and strategic decisionmaking is not easy. Attorneys can't be eliminated from the social change process, because legal issues and the need for technical legal skills emerge constantly. But the very creation of an attorney-client relationship necessitates formalized legal and ethical procedures, including confidentiality of communications, and gives most low-income "clients" a sense of obligation to their attorney that outweighs their informal ties to their constituency group.

Fortunately, strategies exist to prevent the creation of an attorney-client relationship from eroding constituents' strategic power. First, attorneys who are not actively involved in a social change organization should be brought in for technical assistance only. Attorneys defending Black Panther Party members in criminal cases did not receive a voice in party decisions; nor were attorneys defending antiwar protesters involved in planning future demonstrations or protests. This model should equally apply in cases like the Glenburn Hotel eviction battle involving low-income clients, who typically lack a college education and are not political activists. It is the responsibility of tactical activists working with such low-income groups to ensure that attorneys do not encroach upon constituents' strategic decisionmaking power.

Second, tactical activists must ensure that all decisions on nonlegal tactics are made in the presence of community organizers and acknowledged resident leaders. Such individuals have the ability to equal if not exceed the influence of attorneys when all are in attendance. To facilitate nonattorney input, activists should hold meetings at a social change organization's office or another familiar setting rather than in a law office conference room; even longtime activists can be intimidated in unfamiliar and formal surroundings. Attorneys may try to discourage the selection of a familiar site by raising the fear of compromising attorney-client confidentiality. In truth, the substance of strategic meetings held on the eve of planned protests such as the Glenburn Hotel tenants' rarely if ever reveals useful legal information not otherwise obtainable by your adversary in a lawsuit.

A third tactic to keep attorneys from becoming too involved in decisionmaking is to work only with those who understand the limits of their role. Most legal-aid organizations have more than one attorney in each subject area, and the lawyers eagerly seek cases that have a broad impact. Social change activists should select the attorneys with whom their organization can best work and avoid those who view "impact" litigation as a personal power trip. Legal-aid attorneys need access to exciting cases, and this need gives activists the upper hand; too many activists err in focusing only on the organization's need for an attorney and forget that, in the legal-aid context, it is often the attorney who needs the client.

The problems that can arise after the creation of an attorney-client relationship, however, are not eliminated by limiting attorneys' involvement in strategic decisions. Additional attorney-organization friction may arise. Most participants in community-based social change organizations—and nearly all individuals or groups eligible for free legal services—have less education, income, self-esteem, and self-confidence than the average attorney. When tenants who have come to me for legal advice start asking me whether they should move, where they should move, or what they should do about nonlegal matters, my response is always that they can answer these questions themselves better than I can. Yet despite widespread public distrust and even dislike of attorneys, people of all income levels tend to defer to them even on issues of common sense or personal preference.

Assume the Glenburn Hotel meeting between attorneys and clients had taken place at a community center with community organizers and neighborhood leaders present. Further assume that the attorneys had no desire to steer the tenants toward a certain outcome and had objectively laid out the pros and cons of holding the scheduled protest. Also assume that, when asked for their opinion, the attorneys had expressed a preference for canceling the demonstration. Based on my long experience working with low-income, elderly, and disabled people such as those who lived at the Glenburn Hotel, I think the residents would probably have sided with their attorneys. They would have done so even if the attorneys involved had exhibited no understanding of the political environment, the social, psychological, and emotional value of the protest, or the social change organization's broader strategy. Such unwarranted deference to attorneys incenses community activists and often motivates organizations to forgo potentially effective strategies by refusing to work with lawyers.

How, then, can a social change organization reach decisions untainted by attorney influence? Returning to the modified Glenburn Hotel example, assume that, when asked for their opinion, the attorneys had stated that the group was in the best position to determine whether the protest should be held. The attorneys might have emphasized that it was the landlord's intimidating behavior, rather than his issuance of eviction notices, that posed the greatest risk to the tenants' future in their homes. They could have added that they were involved for their legal skills only and would stand behind whatever decision was made. By expressly renouncing the opportunity to sway the outcome, the attorneys would have encouraged the group to make its own decision. This process not only best serves the group but also increases the attorney's credibility and trust within the organization.

A successful model thus exists by which social change organizations can obtain legal assistance without sacrificing a measure of control over their agenda to outsiders. The model clearly presupposes organizational discussion and agreement about the proper scope of the attorneys' role. As in other areas of tactical activism, the absence of such internal discussions can cause unfortunate results, as in the Glenburn Hotel example. It is easy to blame attorneys for overstepping their bounds, but activists also bear responsibility for not taking the steps necessary to forestall this result.

WHEN ATTORNEY CONTROL IS UNAVOIDABLE

Activists' concern with attorney influence over community decision-making is heightened where such influence is unavoidable. This circumstance typically arises when a social change organization seeks a legislative response to a problem. Though a basic legislative framework can be developed through a community-, neighborhood-, or constituency-based process, attorneys are left to draft the actual language. This unavoidable reliance on attorneys raises two issues. First, deciding which words to include in legislation involves substantive and not simply procedural issues. The person doing the actual writing must make decisions that relate to the political effect of the legislation. Second, the attorney is often the only person who can assess the substantive impact of changes made to the original legislation as it travels through the political process. Such changes are often negotiated literally at the last minute. Because the timing of such decisions does not allow for open decisionmaking, the group's attorney typically makes the call.

Social change activists frequently complain about attorneys' often inevitable control over drafting decisions. I have heard numerous organizers complain that their attorneys "sold out" the community organization as victory approached. This suspicion arises when the organization's involvement in the redrafting process becomes so attenuated that its members do not witness the true cause of the unsatisfactory result. A last-minute lobbying blitz by the opposition may weaken legislation on the eve of enactment; unless activists are present to see the process, they may blame their attorneys and not their opposition.

An excellent example of how community organizations and attorneys can avoid ill feelings during the drafting and legislative processes arose during the Tenderloin Housing Clinic's year-long campaign to strengthen San Francisco's Residential Hotel Ordinance (RHO). Although the ordinance was enacted in 1979, it was so riddled with loopholes that it was failing to serve its goal of preventing the conversion of residential hotels to tourist lodgings. In 1989 the Clinic joined neighborhood groups throughout the city in redrafting the ordinance to facilitate and ensure vigorous enforcement. The Clinic participated both in organizing around the issue and in drafting the proposed legislation. The campaign began with community meetings in the Tenderloin neighborhood, whose residents proposed the necessary reforms. Subsequent meetings brought a consensus on how to proceed, and the community's proposal was introduced to the city's Board of Supervisors. In August 1989 hundreds of low-income residents turned out for a committee hearing on the proposed legislation. Our hopes for quick legislative approval were dashed, however, when the "progressive" committee chair stated at the outset that the issue was "too complex" to be voted upon that day. The issue seemed to have increased in complexity after one of her financial supporters privately requested that she delay the matter until he could resolve the concerns of his wealthy, hotel-owning clients. This initial delay kicked off a series of additional hearings and postponements that stretched until the measure was finally enacted into law in April 1990.[2] The various delays were designed to give our opposition a full opportunity to weaken the legislation.

These delays put the community-based organizations supporting the legislation in a difficult position, because few of their members could attend hearing after hearing over a period of several months. In order to avoid having members feel alienated from the process, backers of the legislation established a small network of residents and organizers to keep each other informed. The network's small size served three functions. First, it enabled residents to continue their psychological investment in the campaign without feeling guilty about missing some hearings. Second, it ensured that the political base behind the legislation remained at the ready should a larger mobilization become necessary. Third, the smaller network allowed me, the attorney responsible for drafting the amendments, to receive quick feedback on changes to the legislation proposed during the lengthy campaign.

As frequently happens when legislation that really makes a difference approaches a final vote, the opponents offered a continual stream of revisions and technical amendments to the ordinance. It was my job as attorney to understand the substantive impact of the proposed changes, but the network retained the authority to decide whether to accept or reject them. We were thus able to avoid the scenario in which attorneys make a deal on statutory language without receiving the constituency's prior assent. Because some community residents and their organizational representatives were always present during hearings and legislative votes, we also avoided the more common scenario of a group's having to rely exclusively on information provided to its attorneys by elected officials. In such cases, the politician often tells the attorney what language is politically acceptable; the attorney then tells the group that unless it agrees to this language the bill will fail. Constituency members have no time to meet with other officials to verify this assessment, nor can they be certain that their attorney has not already promised that the group will accept the change. With the constituency group removed from the sources of primary information, the attorney's knowledge becomes power—and this power can be used to influence decisionmakers. Tactical activists should thus always insist on hearing from the source any information material to a decision. They also should rely on strategies that force elected officials to deal with the constituency directly rather than through an attorney or paid staff. Unfortunately, even well-intentioned attorneys can become so vested in reaching a "reasonable" agreement on legislative language that they fail to consider whether a compromise might upset their constituency group. All too often, attorneys' acceptance of an agreement the community opposes provokes anger.

The attorney's own self-interest demands that the constituency group make critical decisions about legislation. An attorney jeopardizes his or her future credibility with both the constituency group and the legislators by usurping decisionmaking authority, which belongs with the people actually affected by the outcome. Legislators may be attracted to an attorney willing to compromise constituency interests but will soon learn that their ally has lost the group's confidence. Also, ongoing grassroots support for laws is critical to their enforcement and, potentially, their continued existence. Because community residents shared in the victory of the strengthened Residential Hotel Ordinance, they were ready to lend support when the law was subjected to a lengthy federal court challenge. The courtroom presence of low-income tenants may not have affected the appellate judges' decision to uphold the ordinance, but their attendance certainly gave a psychological boost to me and the other attorneys who were defending the law. When constituencies affected by laws retain decisionmaking power throughout the legislative process, their attorneys retain the backing necessary to ensure the measure's continued potency.

Maintaining personal contact with legislators is more difficult at the state or national level. Because many organizations operate hundreds or thousands of miles from the state capital or Washington, D.C., it is even more imperative that grassroots activists use the type of representative network we used in the local RHO battle. These networks provide attorneys with immediate access to the people affected by the outcome of the legislative process. During passage of some of the most important national progressive legislation, grassroots activists maintained ongoing control of the process through their Washington, D.C.-based legal advocates. Such positive activist-attorney relationships have been evident even during legislation of such complex and far-reaching measures as the Americans with Disabilities Act (ADA). The grassroots support for the ADA will prove critical as political and business assaults on the measure gather steam in the years ahead.

WHEN SOCIAL CHANGE ADVOCATES SHOULD USE THE COURTS

Many social change activists unquestioningly view the courts as the ultimate protector of individual and minority rights. This perspective exists even among people who can provide a complete Marxist analysis of the role of the legal system in a capitalist society; it persists despite strong contradictory evidence over the past decade. Inaccurate assessments of the court system are perpetuated because there is no forum in which to educate activists about when, how, and why to use litigation to achieve goals. Perhaps legal-service attorneys feel that laypeople would be bored discussing the law or that such discussion is too complex. Whatever the reason for this failure, it is essential that tactical activists understand how the legal system can help or hinder their agenda.

An example from California captures the complexity of the legal/political environment confronting social change activists and attorneys. California law has traditionally required that welfare payments be linked to the actual costs of housing, food, clothing, and other essential services. In the fiscally austere post–Proposition 13 world, California's counties tried to save money by failing to raise welfare payments to single indigent adults in accordance with the rising cost of necessities. In response, legal-aid attorneys throughout the state filed lawsuits and won appellate court rulings requiring counties to ensure that grant levels accurately reflected the cost of living. These lawsuit victories resulted in annual grant raises in many counties, though the payments never rose enough to match the steep increase in rents throughout the 1980s. Nevertheless, there was no question in anyone's mind that lawsuits were the only way to enforce state funding requirements.

In January 1991 legal advocates for the poor hit the jackpot. In a suit brought by private attorneys, a state court of appeal ruled that Alameda County must raise welfare levels to reflect the true cost of housing.[3] The judges had the courage to ignore county arguments that state mandates for provision of aid to indigent persons should be ignored because of their alleged fiscal impact. After several years of inadequate grant levels, which forced many welfare recipients into homelessness, justice for the poor apparently was at hand. The Tenderloin Housing Clinic's housing survey established that in San Francisco, also bound by the court's decision, the ruling would require a monthly grant increase of at least $25. These increases would be even larger in other Bay Area counties. Because the ruling was based on the plain language of a state statute, chances for reversal even by the ultraconservative California Supreme Court seemed slim.

County governments, however, were not focusing on a legal reversal. Instead, they went right to the state legislature and six months after the court ruling succeeded in abolishing the state mandate linking aid levels to the cost of necessities. The new regulation established minimum dollar amounts for aid with no provision for increases in the cost of living. Some of the counties sought to use the adverse court decision as a springboard for eliminating county welfare obligations altogether; only opposition from San Francisco's officials doomed this draconian result. The counties subsequently obtained the authority to lower grant levels even further with the approval of a state review agency. The counties steamrolled their bills through a legislature facing a huge state budget deficit. Not a single article in a Bay Area daily newspaper or television news report publicized this effort. The resulting legislation left welfare recipients in their worst position in two decades and probably eliminated the prospect of grant increases for the foreseeable future.

I relate this story not to castigate the attorneys for having filed their lawsuit. On the contrary, their legal strategy brought, albeit very temporarily, a prospect of economic justice for welfare recipients that could never have been achieved through the political process. But this episode illustrates that social change activists and their advocates are operating in the most dangerous legal/political climate in decades. The impulse to roll back the gains of the 1960s and 1970s is so great that even a lawsuit likely to succeed must be examined for potential repercussions prior to filing. Activist attorneys and their constituency groups should go through a checklist of factors, including the potential negative impacts of losing at the trial and/or appellate level; the prospect of a court victory's being overturned by legislators or by the voters through an initiative; the ability to achieve a comparable result without litigation; the capacity of a court to provide the specific relief sought; the value of expending resources on litigation as opposed to some other strategy;[4] the potential that a resort to the courts will reduce participation in grassroots political action; and the length of time for a final victory to be achieved. Initiating a lawsuit to achieve progressive social change without carefully evaluating these factors can place a constituency's security and future at risk.

Even taking these caveats under consideration, the legal system often represents the best or only option for social change activists. Some prominent examples include lawsuits challenging voting systems that deny minority representation, suits filed to halt development projects, and suits seeking protection of civil rights.

Many African-Americans in the South and Latinos in Texas, California, and the Southwest are permanently disempowered because at-large voting systems and runoff elections virtually guarantee all-white local representation. The Reverend Jesse Jackson focused on this issue during his presidential campaigns but failed to sway the white officeholders who benefit from and control particular regions' "democratic" processes. Because the political process itself is the problem, the goal of African-American empowerment and representation in these areas can only be achieved through legal challenges. Lawyers for similarly disempowered Latino communities have won court challenges to at-large voting practices, and it seemed that the revised federal Voting Rights Act of 1982 would bring a flurry of lawsuits to finally topple this undemocratic facade. The U.S. Supreme Court may have different ideas, however. Some current justices have argued that race must be irrelevant to the political process. The court not only has appeared unwilling to grant relief to racial minorities disenfranchised at the local level but also has actively intervened to reverse historic gains in African-American congressional representation in the South. Having won a strengthened civil rights bill from Congress in 1991, it is doubtful that civil rights activists can return to even a Democrat-controlled Congress for a stronger voting rights measure anytime soon. Even the enactment of such a law would not prevent a hostile Supreme Court from striking down the measure. Although our highest court appears to have returned to its historic role of denying or ignoring, rather than fostering, civil rights, a significant change in its composition may provide the best opportunity for racial minorities to achieve the political representation they have long sought.

A second prominent area where litigation represents the best or only strategy is in stopping development projects that have won approval through the planning process. Once a development project obtains such approval, progressive activists have only two options. In a jurisdiction that allows initiatives or referenda, activists can gather the necessary signatures and try to defeat the project at the ballot box. More commonly, activists resort to the courts to stop the project, usually basing their objection on the grounds that the environmental impacts caused by the proposed project were insufficiently explored in the planning review process. The threat of such lawsuits is often the only way activists can rein in ardently pro-development government bodies. In the 1980s environmental impact litigation focused on the effects of intensive high-rise office construction in our nation's major cities. Other suits addressed urban sprawl, as new housing developments encroached on agricultural land and open space, increasing traffic, creating problems with sewage disposal, and so on. The rise of Wal-Mart and large-scale suburban malls in the 1990s has expanded the scope of environmental impact litigation to smaller towns desperate for the employment opportunities the stores offer. Rural and suburban communities continue to be split over the benefits of such projects, and potential litigation over defective environmental analysis is an important strategy for preventing them.

Actual or threatened litigation over development is particularly effective because activists can achieve success simply by delaying the project. When a court rules that a development project has a defective environmental impact statement, the developer must create a new, legally sufficient report. The project cannot commence until the new report is approved by the local planning agency. This new report also can be challenged in court, and because few developers are willing to risk resuming construction until the final challenge is resolved, there is further delay. There was a well-publicized case in Hawaii in the 1980s in which a developer completed a condominium tower while the local residents' court challenge to the project's height was still pending. Presumably, the developer assumed that he would either win the case or, if he lost, simply have to pay a fine for exceeding the height limit. The court instead ordered the developer to remove the illegally erected eight stories. Most developers are unwilling to risk such a costly result and choose to delay construction until lawsuits are resolved.

Delay can kill a development project for several reasons. Financing can disappear, the business purpose of the development can change, or a corporate merger, reorganization, or bankruptcy can render the project moot. During delays, project opponents can elect officials opposed to the venture, the overall business climate can change, interest rates can rise, and new problems with the project can be discovered. There is also what I have called the "aggravation factor" caused by the filing of a lawsuit. After going through the time-consuming process of planning the project and perhaps hiring expensive lobbyists to help remove political hurdles, some developers simply get fed up and abandon their plans once the new roadblock of a lawsuit emerges. The University of California, long accustomed to getting its way whenever it wanted to expand one of its campuses, ran into strong opposition in the 1980s over its plan to build new facilities at its San Francisco medical school. Neighborhood groups, concerned about adverse health effects from the activities proposed for the facilities, filed a lawsuit claiming the environmental impact statement failed to address health risks. Although the university brought in high-priced legal talent, the state Court of Appeals ruled for the neighbors. A new environmental report was written, challenged in court, and found to have additional defects. The university, aggravated by one legal delay after another, eventually looked to expand elsewhere. A project that ultimately would have obtained legal approval was thus defeated.

Anti-development lawsuits may also challenge the legal basis of the project's approval process. These cases typically charge that a local planning commission or other approval agency has ignored or violated the law or evidence in order to fulfill a political agenda. A lawsuit exposing such administrative abuses can achieve two goals. First, it can keep the project under a cloud of uncertainty despite its victory in the political process. Second, such a lawsuit sends a message to the approval agency and to developers that social change organizations will not tolerate circumvention of the law. Neighborhood residents can yell and scream about agency wrongdoing at a public hearing, but filing a lawsuit gets the attention of agency commissioners like the ring of a cash register. Legal challenges require the agency to pay for legal defense. Agency chiefs and commissioners do not like to see their budgets spent in such fashion and are less likely to approve development projects illegally in the future.

Gay rights advocates also must often resort to the courts because of their inability to prevail politically. Federal legislation barring anti-gay discrimination is but a pipe dream in the current political climate. Federal law does prevent discrimination against people with AIDS, but, as some gay activists have noted, this provision only protects people who have a life-threatening disease. Lawsuits have been necessary not only to obtain federal protection for gay rights but also to prevent the repeal of local anti-discrimination statutes. Colorado's repeal of such statutes in the November 1992 election was overturned by the state's highest court,[5] and the same result was achieved in Oregon courts. As for discrimination against gays and lesbians in the military, it will be generations before political conditions permit a legislative solution. This discrimination will end earlier only through a ruling from the U.S. Supreme Court.

It would be heartening to think that the political process could safeguard gay and other minority rights, but the Colorado vote in particular dispels this idea. Colorado has never been viewed as a bastion of anti-gay zealotry, and its vote to repeal local laws protecting gays and lesbians may not reflect particular anti-gay fervor as much as the difficulty of any minority's winning a majority vote at the polls. California voters in 1964 upheld racial discrimination in housing. Federal anti-discrimination statutes never were subjected to popular vote or they might not be with us today. The Equal Rights Amendment was never passed, and Arizona voters once rejected a measure creating a state holiday to commemorate Martin Luther King, Jr.'s birthday. (The vote occurred after the federal holiday for him was enacted.) In Colorado, conservatives persuaded voters that anti-discrimination measures afforded "special rights" to gays; the same argument is now being used, with similar success, against all groups protected under the federal Title VII anti-discrimination statute. Efforts in California and at the national level are underway to prohibit all affirmative action by public entities. The misguided idea that affirmative action violates the civil rights of white people has caused even many Democrats to question the continuation of such "special rights" for women and racial minorities. Because court-ordered affirmative action plans are immune from politically imposed restrictions, civil rights activists will have to rely more on the legal system to remedy past discrimination. Unlike women and racial minorities, however, gays are not even protected from open discrimination by the majority will. Because repeal measures can wipe out local or state anti-bias laws, court rulings may be the only means to guarantee ongoing legal protection of gay rights.[6]

When progressive political movements or social change organizations are forced to turn to the courts to achieve a central goal, conflict between organizers and lawyers can easily emerge. This conflict differs from that described in the Glenburn Hotel example, because the tension is not based on attorneys' improper intervention into a fundamentally nonlegal struggle. Nor is there competition between organizers and attorneys over who speaks for the client or over how decisions at meetings with clients are made. The conflict that can emerge once a litigation strategy takes center stage is far deeper and potentially even more divisive. It frequently arises when activists skeptical of participating with government bodies are forced to work with attorneys who are seeking social change within the government's courts. This chasm between people organizing for change at the grassroots and those advocating from inside the legal system can best be bridged when the two groups have an ongoing and equal relationship. Without a prior relationship of trust, serious conflict can emerge. For example, in his Pulitzer Prize–winning history, *Parting the Waters: America in the King Years 1954–63,* Taylor Branch details the rancor in the 1950s and 1960s between Roy Wilkins and Thurgood Marshall, respectively executive director and chief counsel of the NAACP, and Martin Luther King, Jr.[7] Whereas the NAACP was intent on pursuing a legal strategy to achieve civil rights for African-Americans by way of Supreme Court rulings, King and his allies preferred the direct-action tactics of sit-ins, bus boycotts, and Freedom Rides. Wilkins/Marshall and King not only saw little value in each other's tactical approach but believed the other was interfering with his own camp's strategy and reducing the potential for its success.

It is easy to understand how even two of the leading forces for civil rights of this century could fail to create a unified approach. The differences revolved around issues of power between ministers and lawyers, between people who suffered under Jim Crow laws on a daily basis and those living outside the South, and between people of different ages, educational backgrounds, and economic classes. King's strategy was based on the willful violation of state laws, whereas Marshall and the NAACP assumed the legitimacy of the legal system.[8] The conflict between the activist and legal factions of the civil rights movement typifies the tensions underlying many social change movements. The media have often created a false impression of a unified and harmonious civil rights movement; for example, media coverage of Thurgood Marshall's death in 1994 included almost no focus on the split between legal and activist forces. Instead, journalists and broadcasters commenting on Marshall's life acted as if the NAACP and King's Southern Christian Leadership

Conference had worked hand-in-hand for civil rights. Social change activists cannot afford to idealize the past this way. Those who naively expect that everyone supporting their agenda will unite in one big happy family may abandon political involvement when reality sets in. To avoid such disillusionment, activists and attorneys must recognize the need to reach agreement on their respective roles. Such an accord may not emerge, but the dialogue will at least reduce the tensions and enhance the prospects for success.

A more recent example of conflict between social change organizations over litigation occurred during a suit brought by a disparate alliance of environmental groups in the Pacific Northwest over the effect of logging on the habitat of the spotted owl. The suit developed during the Bush administration, which viewed efforts to save the endangered spotted owl from extinction as environmental overzealousness. Because Bush's Environmental Protection Agency would not enforce its own laws, litigation became essential. Twelve environmental groups filed suit, and in 1991 Seattle federal court judge William Dwyer issued an injunction that virtually ended logging on millions of acres of forest land that served as the owl's habitat.

As long as the organizations could subsume their different political and strategic perspectives under their unified opposition to Bush policy, they avoided internal conflict. But the election of Bill Clinton changed this dynamic. The Clinton administration put forth one of its notorious "compromise" plans; known as "Option Nine," it rewarded the very timber interests that had strongly opposed Clinton in the 1992 election. Clinton's plan allowed the continuation of logging in federal forests in the Northwest, though at a lesser rate than was permitted prior to the court injunction. Convinced by the Clinton administration and major environmental groups that Option Nine provided adequate protection for the spotted owl's habitat, the federal court judge lifted his injunction in June 1994. Clinton's environmental team persuaded eleven of the twelve original plaintiffs, including such mainstream organizations as the Wilderness Society, the Sierra Club Legal Defense Fund, and the National Audubon Society, to accept Option Nine. The Forest Conservation Council was the only plaintiff that opposed the plan. The executive director of the Oregon-based Native Forest Council, which was not a party to the suit, also opposed the compromise, claiming it "set the environmental movement back 20 years."[9] Groups opposed to Option Nine soon announced plans to file new lawsuits. Their chance of success, however, was undercut by the mainstream environmentalists' position that the Clinton plan was acceptable. On December 21, 1994, Judge Dwyer voided further challenges to Option Nine.[10]

Given the Clinton Interior Department's success in extracting concessions from mainstream environmental groups in the spotted owl case, local environmentalists would have been better off litigating independently. The failure of most of the national environmental organizations to adopt a "fear and loathing" approach to national Democratic Party officials reduces their ability to litigate effectively on many environmental issues. Although the prospects for successfully preserving the spotted owl's habitat through new lawsuits may be dim, it is a positive sign that the progressive environmental groups betrayed by the settlement are still exploring legal strategies.

Social change organizations can best avoid conflict with legal organizations working for similar goals either by hiring their own legal staff or by relying exclusively on a small circle of attorneys they trust. The great model for the former approach is the United Farmworkers of the 1960s and 1970s. UFW founder Cesar Chavez built a movement for social and economic justice that attracted some of the best young legal minds of that generation. With low-paid but high-quality in-house legal talent on hand, Chavez retained complete control over the UFW's litigation strategy. The organization's top-notch legal staff and hard work enabled the UFW to overcome the greater resources of its agribusiness adversaries. Although few, if any, contemporary causes can engender the type of commitment given by lawyers to the farmworkers movement of the 1960s and 1970s, social change organizations can at least approximate the UFW's strategy simply by hiring a staff person with a law degree. For example, NYPIRG's lawsuits against the Brooklyn Navy Yard incinerator project (Chapter 3) were filed by an in-house lawyer, allowing CAFE to retain total control of the litigation process. Many top-quality, committed activists cannot obtain progressive legal jobs after becoming attorneys, and if they have other useful skills they can bring an extra dimension to social change organizations. As litigation has increasingly become part of many environmental disputes, even grassroots organizations hostile to the legal system should try to hire staff with legal training. This staff could at the very least monitor environmental litigation so that grassroots activists could get crucial information from someone they trust.

Social change organizations having in-house staff with legal training can avoid unnecessary disputes between activists and attorneys over litigation. For example, lawsuits filed amid great publicity and optimism for success can hit unanticipated snags. The attorneys may recognize these problems and realize that a compromise settlement is necessary. Activists who have stayed out of discussions of the litigation since the press conference announcing its filing may not understand why the attorneys now seem unwilling to take the case to trial. Discussion of complex legal issues or case precedents may seem little more than a coverup for a sellout. If an organization's own staff understands the legal issues, there may be agreement on the need to accept a disappointing result. Conversely, the activist group may have the analytical ammunition needed to counter the attorney's claims and avert a bad settlement. In either case, having a staff member with legal training can help bridge the chasm between the two forces. Those social change activists who prefer to avoid any involvement with litigation might still consider the benefits of having an in-house legal monitor.

The other strategy for reducing conflict between social change activists and attorneys is for an organization to work only with one or a few law offices it trusts. For example, the Tenderloin Housing Clinic provides legal services for various neighborhood or tenant-based organizations in San Francisco. Numerous other nonprofit law offices promise similar services to constituencies throughout the country. Some private law offices will undertake such cases on a one-time basis, but misunderstanding and distrust often result from the lack of a prior working relationship. There are also prominent and respected civil rights legal organizations, such as the NAACP Legal Defense Fund, the American Civil Liberties Union, and the Center for Constitutional Rights, whose focus on complex litigation involving such issues as desegregation require years of close contact with social change activists. However, few activists, and even fewer organizations, seek significant personal involvement in lengthy, intricate federal litigation. Members of social change organizations prefer strategies in which they, not attorneys, are the key players and where success can be achieved quickly rather than after years in the courts. Neighborhood-based social change organizations that engage in proactive strategic planning are therefore unlikely to make a long-term legal fight the centerpiece of their agenda. When such a commitment is made, organization members have little or no role to play in what inevitably becomes an attorney-controlled litigation strategy. Groups choosing to participate in major court actions cannot survive without conducting other campaigns pending the results of the litigation. Because most social change groups who act as plaintiffs in major cases do not expect to have their members actively participate, conflicts are less likely to emerge.

LAWSUITS AS PART OF A BROAD STRATEGY

Lawsuits also play a critical role when they are included as part of a broader strategic effort. In CAFE's campaign against the Brooklyn Navy Yard incinerator (Chapter 3), NYPIRG filed a federal lawsuit on October 29, 1992, alleging that the state had denied Williamsburg residents' "due process right" to "meaningfully participate" in the permitting process. The obvious purpose in filing the suit was to increase public scrutiny of the state's conduct only two weeks before the November 15, 1992, deadline for issuing permits exempt from the new federal Clean Air Act regulations. A lawsuit challenging "due process" provoked more serious scrutiny than would have resulted from a press conference making the same points. Further, because the lawsuit was a new angle, it was more likely to generate media coverage of the coalition's position. State environmental chief Thomas Jorling, who appeared to be trying desperately to avoid the limelight on this issue, now found himself a defendant in a highly publicized case. Because media coverage of lawsuits typically quotes verbatim from the complaint, CAFE's strategy had the additional benefit of exposing the public to the exact spin the coalition sought. An October 30, 1992 story in *New York Newsday* quoted the lawsuit's claim that Jorling "devastated the administrative review process" in order to "add more pollution to the environment." Also quoted verbatim was the claim that Jorling's administrative law judge "ordered a truncated schedule in spite of the extraordinary tactical and legal complexities involved." Had the coalition raised these points at a press conference or in some other forum, reporters might have heard the quotes incorrectly or failed to grasp the key points. By making allegations in a lawsuit, organizations can help control what quotes appear.[11]

In the absence of a broader strategy, the legal challenge against Jorling would have had little impact because it probably would not have prevailed. But NYPIRG and its allies did not need to meet a legal test; they only needed to establish a violation of due process in the public mind. In this they unquestionably succeeded. Less than a week after the lawsuit filing, Jorling announced that the permitting process would be delayed until after the November 15 deadline. The lawsuit had served its purpose, and CAFE achieved its goal without court action.

CAFE's resort to the courts served further notice on pro-incinerator forces that it would fight this battle on every possible front. When activists are using several strategies simultaneously to achieve their goals, a critically timed lawsuit can help push their adversary over the edge.

NYPIRG's suit had this "last straw" effect on Jorling; strategically timed lawsuits had a similar impact in the Tenderloin Housing Clinic's battle against slumlord Guenter Kaussen (Chapter 5). The key in this instance was a class-action suit challenging Kaussen's policy of failing to refund tenants' security deposits. Two factors increased public interest both in the lawsuit and in Kaussen. First, both plaintiffs were refugees—one from Cambodia, the other from Ethiopia—who had sought the Clinic's assistance. They and their families had fled terror and starvation in their native lands to come to the United States. One could not have invented more sympathetic plaintiffs, and Kaussen's mistreatment of them bolstered his image as an unscrupulous profiteer. Second, by filing the tenants' case as a class-action suit, the THC greatly magnified the scope of Kaussen's wrongdoing. Evidence existed that hundreds, if not thousands, of San Francisco tenants had been cheated out of their deposits, so that a huge sum of money was potentially at stake. The media would want Kaussen's former tenants to know of the suit, thus increasing the likelihood of widespread press coverage.

The local NBC affiliate, whose contract with the Center for Investigative Reporting had led it to produce dozens of Kaussen stories, led off its evening news with a piece on the class-action suit. It described the suit as yet another Kaussen-related scandal and reiterated the string of abuses connected to the mysterious slumlord. The story primarily focused on the fate of the refugee/plaintiffs, who had fled oppression abroad only to be cheated in the United States. The fact that people so distrustful of legal systems would nevertheless turn to the courts for justice highlighted the degree of Kaussen's wrongdoing. The lawsuit helped reconnect human faces to Kaussen's abuses and gave an always-hungry media the additional fuel necessary to justify their continued investigation into his practices. The refugee plaintiffs ended up recovering all of their deposits plus additional compensation, so the lawsuit succeeded in achieving both specific and more comprehensive objectives.

LAWSUITS AS DETERRENTS

Social change activists should also consider litigation for its deterrent effects. A lawsuit can help activists achieve their goals even if the suit itself is ultimately lost. For example, lawsuits have long been filed throughout the country challenging a pattern and practice of discriminatory treatment of racial minorities by local police. Although U.S. Supreme

Court rulings have made it difficult for such suits to prevail, litigation of this type places a spotlight on police treatment of minority residents. This attention puts the police on notice that future claims of abuse will not simply be ignored. On the contrary, media outlets covering such suits can make subsequent claims of misconduct the subject of follow-up stories. Scrutiny of police practices thus continues even beyond the life of the case. Police departments understand that lawsuits give victims a public forum for complaints and are more likely to avoid future conduct that substantiates the lawsuit's allegations. Defense lawyers may even recommend changes in department practices that will either reduce the likelihood of future misconduct or at least give the impression of trying to do so. If the defense lawyer does not believe a jury will find an ongoing police practice "reasonable," the department will have the necessary motivation to change the policy.

With elected officials, even self-described progressives, eager to win endorsements from police officer associations to bolster their anti-crime image, reforming law-enforcement practices through the political process is increasingly difficult. Few if any big-city mayors will accept the political risks of seriously challenging police conduct. Voters once willing to create civilian oversight commissions for the police are increasingly likely to oppose such measures on the grounds that they "tie the hands" of the officers. Some minority neighborhoods once critical of police tactics now see the police as valuable allies in the war against drugs and gang violence. Litigation has therefore become the leading strategy for changing unfair or unconstitutional police practices. Federal court judges, whose life tenure insulates them from anti-crime political pressure, may be in the best position to afford relief to victims of illegal police activity.

Recently, several lawsuits have been brought by social change organizations to deter police enforcement of local laws prohibiting loitering, blocking the sidewalk, and panhandling. Municipalities throughout the country have sought to deter the entry of poor and homeless persons by criminalizing such conduct as sitting on a bench next to a bedroll or pack, resting with one's back leaning against a building, or even carrying possessions in a shopping cart. Critics have understandably viewed these laws as unconstitutional anti-loitering measures disguised under a different name. Such measures also have been challenged for violating poor people's constitutional right to travel and for illegally transforming homelessness and poverty into crimes.

Unfortunately, lawsuits brought to prevent or deter police enforcement of such laws have achieved only limited success. A California court of appeal issued a sweeping indictment in striking down a measure enacted by the conservative Southern California city of Santa Ana, but the law was subsequently upheld by the California Supreme Court. Similarly, a partial victory in Miami, in which a trial court temporarily deterred some of the challenged police conduct, was reversed by the federal appellate court. In 1993 San Francisco homeless activists filed a federal suit challenging the widespread arrest of poor and homeless people under the city's "Matrix" program. The trial court refused to stop the program, and the arrests continued. The reluctance of courts to intervene in what they perceive as a social policy question rather than a legal dispute has hampered legal challenges to the "poor laws" of the 1990s.[12]

Lawsuits that deter challenged conduct, even if ultimately unsuccessful, should only be pursued if a meritorious claim exists. Grassroots activists must recognize this point or else risk financial sanctions for filing what in legal terms is called a "frivolous" claim. Filing an unwarranted lawsuit to stop a particular act or to attack a specific official undermines the credibility of both the organization and its attorneys. Such cases do not deter anything because their target does not take them seriously. Newspapers commonly report on lawsuits that are so ridiculous on their face that both the parties and attorneys filing the cases look foolish. Social change organizations should be careful to avoid such litigation.

Activists and attorneys can differ on what constitutes a meritorious case, and serious conflict can result. Early in my career, I was involved in a campaign to ensure that the police responded properly to calls from tenants who were illegally locked out of their homes. Lockouts were commonly used to oust without due process tenants who were behind in their rent. Some police consistently sided with the landlord; others erroneously told tenants that lockouts were "a civil matter." Our campaign was quite successful and featured a picket of a police station and the arrest and handcuffing—in front of cameras—of a prominent landlord with a history of utilizing illegal lockouts.

During the anti-lockout campaign, the following situation occurred. A person moved into a nonprofit-owned residential hotel primarily serving seniors. During his first month of residency, he was seen walking around the lobby carrying a gun. Tenants expressed alarm at this behavior and reported the conduct to management. Management confronted the man, an argument ensued, and the hotel handed him a refund and ordered him to leave. He proceeded to seek assistance from a neighborhood community organizer, who felt I should file a lawsuit against the hotel for perpetrating an illegal lockout. I refused to initiate such action on the grounds that the hotel had seemed to act reasonably in response to a gun-waving resident who had only recently arrived. I saw no value in suing the most popular hotel in the neighborhood for conduct that might technically violate the law but that most people would agree was proper. The hotel's tenants supported the management's action, indicating that a lawsuit on behalf of this short-term resident would be opposed by the constituency my office claimed to represent. The organizer's position was that the law was the same for everyone and that attorneys could not pick and choose when to enforce it. He felt I was betraying my obligation to the community, and we did not speak for several months as a result of the dispute.

My decision not to file the lockout case was not difficult, as the case was legally questionable and would have undermined tenant and neighborhood support for the THC's anti-lockout campaign. A lawsuit would also have focused on an incident that was atypical of the problem, thus confusing the message. Although my conflict with the organizer was in part a tactical disagreement, another aspect of it was that he, like some other activists, had little conception of what constitutes a meritorious case. Unfortunately, this lack of knowledge may not impede activists' zeal for filing legally doubtful cases in an attempt to achieve their goals. In the mid-1980s, a small meeting was held to discuss possible legal challenges to San Francisco's homeless program. The one nonlawyer at the meeting, a newly hired executive director of a shelter, insisted that there had to be grounds for a lawsuit. A few of us carefully explained that, as much as we disagreed with city homeless policy, we saw no basis for a suit, but the shelter director thought we were in effect "letting down the cause" by not proceeding to court. We later heard that the director had concluded from our comments that we "were not interested in dealing with the problem"; he equated our failure to sue with political indifference.

A ready solution to this type of friction exists. Tactical activists in all fields can and should readily become familiar with the basic legal principles applicable to their work. Activists who insist that they do not want to read about laws or the legal system make two key errors. First, they limit their understanding of possible strategies to achieve their goals, because many strategies may relate to legislation or legal interpretations. Second, they cede power to the very attorneys of whom they are so suspicious. When grassroots activists meet with their lawyers to discuss potential litigation, they should not hesitate to ask to read the cases on which the attorneys are relying to reach their conclusions. This request does not imply any distrust of the attorneys; it is no different from activists' asking for a line-by-line itemization of the budget during a fight over spending cuts. Most attorneys have the relevant cases in their offices and can distribute copies. After reading and discussing them with the attorneys, the activist will have a better sense of whether his or her legal position is justified. More commonly, activists dissatisfied with their attorney's tactical approach ignore legal issues and try to find an attorney who agrees with them. This process not only wastes time but continues to place the activist in a subordinate role. Activists should also strive to have at least the same level of information as their opponents. By becoming informed about legal issues affecting their agenda, activists can deal with attorneys on a more equal footing. Differences of opinion on the strategic value of filing a lawsuit may still emerge, but the dispute will not arise out of distrust based on misinformation.

Direct Action

ACTING UP AND
SITTING IN

Although people commonly describe marches, rallies, or other public protest tactics as "direct action," this term is more appropriately limited to events that immediately confront a specific individual or organization with a set of specific demands. Direct actions are distinct from protest activities such as bridge or road blockades that are designed to send a political message to the broader public. These protest activities are particularly valuable as spontaneous responses to sudden events and, like annual "solidarity day" marches, build social bonds, reduce feelings of political isolation and demonstrate the constituency's strength to the public and media.

Public protests are important, but they are no substitute for developing a proactive program for social change. Direct actions, however, are often central to such a purpose. Confronting an adversary on his or her own turf creates a rush of excitement often missing from political activity. Activists looking back on prior struggles tend to remember such incidents fondly, even if the tactic brought only mixed success. The thrill of taking direct action, however, should not be equated with the achievement of specific goals. For example, picketing and chanting in front of your adversary's corporate headquarters may create community spirit, but if the activity is not connected to specific demands, then the action does not advance the organization's agenda. Just as enacting hollow environmental legislation ultimately hurts environmentalists, engaging in unfocused direct actions drains organizational and volunteer energy and creates a false sense that people are working for social change.

Two movements in the past twenty years stand out for their strategic expertise in using direct actions to achieve specific results. The AIDS Coalition to Unleash Power (ACT UP) has utilized innovative and strategic direct action, with success rivaling that of the civil rights movement of the 1950s and 1960s. The disability rights movement, though less well publicized, has also used direct action tactics to achieve successes that few would have imagined possible a generation or two ago. Both movements show the potential power as well as the limitations of direct action as a proactive strategy for achieving social change. Both movements also have benefited from the groundwork laid by the civil rights movement, which not only pioneered new tactics but also tested the public's sense of justice and its response to direct actions.

"SILENCE EQUALS DEATH"

ACT UP was created in March 1987 for the express purpose of using direct action to ensure an adequate government response to the AIDS crisis. An aggressive, confrontational approach to the AIDS epidemic was long overdue for several reasons.[1] First, AIDS emerged during the decade of the greatest progress for gay and lesbian rights in U.S. history. This progress brought a reaction from conservative religious figures and their political allies. Homophobia became a centerpiece of Republican political campaigns, and anti-gay political forces overwhelmingly supported Ronald Reagan in his victorious 1980 and 1984 campaigns. Although Reagan's political handlers frequently claimed that his years in Hollywood had made him personally tolerant of gays, his chief political base was prone to view AIDS as God's punishment for immoral behavior. The Reagan administration thus ignored the mounting evidence of a burgeoning AIDS crisis; Reagan himself refused to use the term *AIDS* until his friend Rock Hudson died of the disease in 1985. AIDS emerged during a presidency committed to slashing rather than increasing any category of domestic spending (other than defense), one that saw political value in government hostility to gay rights. This circumstance alone could have necessitated reliance on direct action. AIDS activists, however, faced obstacles even greater than presidential opposition to their cause. The nation's medical and scientific establishment may ultimately have been more destructive than hostile political administrations in delaying AIDS research. Activists wanted people with AIDS to have access to experimental drugs that could treat the disease, whereas the interlocking empire of private drug companies, the scientists they funded, and government research agencies seemed to view AIDS as an opportunity for huge profits, Nobel prizes, and dramatic funding increases.

The medical and research establishment's hostility to the goals of AIDS activists meant that success in the political arena did not necessarily translate into better medical options for people with AIDS. Although grassroots and legislative political advocacy eventually forced the Reagan administration to increase AIDS funding to the National Institute of Allergies and Infectious Diseases (NIAID) from $297,000 in 1982 to $63 million in 1986 and $146 million in 1987, few people with AIDS ever benefited from the additional research funds. NIAID was thrilled to receive such significant budget increases but seemed more concerned with bureaucratic empire building than with offering treatment to gay men facing premature death. NIAID received a major funding increase in 1986 but did nothing with the funds for nine months. When confronted with his failure to use $20 million appropriated to set up a network of testing facilities for AIDS drugs, NIAID director Dr. Anthony Fauci claimed that he needed additional money for staff to write the necessary protocols. When AIDS activists pushed Congress to provide the additional funds, still no action resulted. Fauci explained that he had not had the time to interview for the new positions, nor did he have funds for office space and desks. Soon after this admission, AIDS activists would conclude that a strategy focusing on direct action was essential.[2]

The support for direct action to overcome political and medical/bureaucratic obstacles strengthened in the face of yet another major hurdle: corporate greed. The Burroughs Wellcome company used its financial control over scientists in and out of government to ensure that its own drug, AZT, would be the centerpiece of federally funded clinical AIDS tests, even though other drugs appeared to provide better results. The government's limitation of experimentation to a single drug whose chief merit appeared to be the financial clout of its corporate sponsor infuriated AIDS activists. Their anger intensified when, after AZT became the only drug legally available to treat AIDS, Burroughs Wellcome announced on February 13, 1987, that the cost of AZT would be $10,000 per person per year. Thus did the tortuous battle to ensure access to treatment for AIDS come to parallel the fight against the disease itself.

An additional factor, internal to the gay community, led to the creation of an AIDS organization dedicated to direct action. In 1982 Larry Kramer, a New York City–based playwright, joined with other people in establishing an organization named Gay Men's Health Crisis (GMHC). At this time the term *AIDS* had yet to be commonly used to describe the mysterious illnesses suddenly afflicting gay men. This was also a period when many gay activists and organizations ardently supported bathhouses and viewed criticism of gay promiscuity from gay figures such as Kramer as evidence of self-hatred. GMHC eventually became the largest AIDS service organization in the country. Its approach, however, reflected the upscale, professional backgrounds of its founders, some of whom were still in the closet. GMHC sought to become part of city health care systems rather than openly criticize health care policies. Kramer's confrontational style had distinguished him from other GMHC founders, and his efforts to lead the organization into political opposition to government inaction on AIDS had proved unsuccessful. In the mid-1980s Kramer and others publicly attacked GMHC for its unwillingness to engage in an all-out war against the medical/scientific establishment and argued for establishing a more militant advocacy group. Calling GMHC a "sad organization of sissies,"[3] Kramer gave a speech on March 10, 1987, calling for "lobbying, advocacy, public relations people to get the word out, and increased political activities."[4] He asked his audience, "Do we want to start a new organization devoted solely to political action?" The crowd answered with a resounding "yes." Two days later more than 300 people met to form ACT UP.

ACT UP's creation thus reflected a growing consensus in the gay community that politely accepting government, scientific, and corporate inaction was equivalent to accepting death sentences for thousands of people potentially infected with or already suffering from AIDS. The consequences of continuing to work patiently through "the system" could not be more stark. People were dying, and the health care delivery system was unconcerned about their fate. Six gay men created the motto "Silence = Death," put it on a pink triangle against a black background, and printed and posted the message at their own expense. The men, who were members of the Silence = Death Project, were present at the founding of ACT UP and lent the organization the design it became identified with.[5] The motto spawned direct action in two ways. First, people who themselves faced death from AIDS were motivated to wage any type of battle that might save their lives. Second, ACT UP was able to attract activists motivated not by the personal fear of contracting AIDS but by the absolute gravity of the issue. This second factor contributed to ACT UP's unparalleled success in attracting young people to its cause.

ACT UP IN ACTION

ACT UP sent a powerful message about its commitment to a direct-action agenda when it held its first action less than two weeks after forming. On March 24, 1987, more than 250 ACT UP members invaded Wall Street to protest the Food and Drug Administration's decision five days before to license Burroughs Wellcome's AZT as the only government-approved therapy for AIDS patients. The granting of monopoly status to a drug whose $10,000-per-patient annual cost made it the most expensive treatment in history created a theme that would remain central to ACT UP events: big business was making unconscionable profits off terminally ill patients. ACT UP snarled traffic for several hours and hung an effigy of FDA chief Frank Young in front of Trinity Church. Seventeen people were arrested for civil disobedience. Kramer had written an op-ed piece in the *New York Times* the previous day laying out the basis for ACT UP's anger at the FDA; thousands of copies were handed out on Wall Street, along with a fact sheet detailing "Why We Are Angry." The demonstration made national news, and ACT UP was publicly given credit for having forced Young's subsequent promise to broaden drug testing.[6]

This national attention spawned ACT UP chapters throughout the nation, many of them in places like Shreveport, Louisiana, that were not commonly known for a substantial gay presence. Such a tactically and technically sophisticated direct action was likely unprecedented for a newly formed group. The event was effective for three key reasons. First, both the action and the accompanying handouts clearly conveyed the message of the event: an AIDS protest at Wall Street automatically linked a growing medical problem to big business practices. Second, the direct action occurred only five days after the FDA announcement on AZT, enabling the media easily to connect the two events and to accept ACT UP's framing of its action as a response to the FDA's. Media-savvy ACT UP members no doubt understood that delaying the action for even a few weeks could jeopardize media understanding of the context of the protest. (Many activists wrongly assume that media outlets have a collective memory or that editors are capable of making the obvious linkage between events; a quick response can ensure that the same reporter stays on the story and perhaps convinces his or her editor to grant space for a follow-up report.) The third reason the event succeeded was that it used local activists to nationalize ACT UP's demands. Clearly, gaining national news coverage is easier when network television news departments are headquartered in the city of the event, but ACT UP's focus on national targets such as the FDA, National Institutes of Health (NIH), and the president made the group's protest a national issue. ACT UP consistently proved that local activists can use direct action to influence national politics to a far greater extent than previously thought.

ACT UP's second demonstration occurred on the night of April 15, 1987, at New York City's main post office. Post offices are always mobbed on April 15 with taxpayers filing last-minute returns. The setting was thus a perfect one for ACT UP's argument that taxpayer money for AIDS was both inadequate and misspent. Attracting media to the event was easier than usual; most local television broadcasts regularly cover the frantic scene of last-minute filers. Even stations uninterested in the protest could not avoid showing a crowd holding "Silence = Death" placards.

ACT UP's first two direct actions proved so successful that support for its confrontational approach grew. The group's participation in the October 1987 March on Washington for Lesbian and Gay Rights served as a recruiting tool, as ACT UP members were distinguished among the 500,000 marchers by their "Silence = Death" t-shirts. Attendance doubled at the next ACT UP meeting, clearly demonstrating that the group's direct-action strategy had filled a void in the community. Social change organizations strategizing over how to attract new participants should note the ability of successful direct-action tactics to create a sense of excitement.

ACT UP continued its successful strategy of staging subsequent direct actions at sites connected to its demands. The group held a vigil July 21–24, 1987, at New York's Memorial Sloan-Kettering Hospital to protest the fact that the hospital was receiving $1.2 million from the National Institutes of Health to treat only thirty-one patients, a statistic that proved how few people with AIDS were actually benefiting from increased government funding. Similarly, on January 19, 1988, ACT UP went to the Hearst Magazine Building in New York City, the headquarters of *Cosmopolitan. Cosmo*'s January 1988 issue had printed an article claiming that heterosexual women had little risk of contracting AIDS and that condom use was therefore generally unnecessary. The article prompted the creation of an ACT UP Women's Committee, whose demonstration in front of *Cosmo*'s offices protested the misinformation the magazine had conveyed to its readers. The action brought national attention and countered the prevailing media dogma that the AIDS crisis affected only gay men. ACT UP's poster to support its Women's

Committee's campaign, titled "AIDS: 1 in 61," was based on studies showing that one out of sixty-one babies in New York City was born with AIDS or HIV.

One year after its first action, ACT UP returned to Wall Street. Returning to the scene of a successful direct action can be an excellent way to remind the public how little progress has been made on a group's demands. Because the media favor "one year later" stories of all types, obtaining coverage for the anniversary event is fairly easy. However, groups seeking to revisit a previous theme run the risk that the follow-up event will fall short of the original. Social change activists hoping for a story emphasizing how little has changed may find instead that the media focus on the decline in the number of demonstrators. ACT UP had a spectacularly successful first year from a strategic and tactical standpoint, but this very success had the potential of confusing the public, which might erroneously equate the group's ability to obtain publicity with actual progress on its demands. It was therefore essential for ACT UP to remind the public how little had been done to alleviate the AIDS epidemic. ACT UP thus returned to Wall Street on March 24, 1988. Its members now had greater skills in tying up traffic, and the number of those arrested for civil disobedience increased from 17 to 111. The event emphasized that one year had passed without any new drug approvals by the FDA, without significant new funding for AIDS research or treatment, without the promised national AIDS education campaign, and without any new emphasis on AIDS by the president. ACT UP activists added a colorful new twist to its anniversary action, scattering thousands of photocopies of $10, $50, and $100 bills bearing slogans critical of Wall Street.

ACT UP's first-year offensive primarily drew participation from white, middle-class gay men. As the number of drug-related AIDS cases rose among both male and female African-Americans and Latinos, most of whom were straight, low-income individuals, ACT UP recognized the need to focus on the unmet needs of these groups. For example, the Women's Committee organized several events highlighting measures to educate and protect women from the sexual transmission of AIDS. In a particularly creative action, ACT UP members went to a New York Mets game and unfurled banners bearing such slogans as "No Glove, No Love," and "Don't Balk at Safe Sex." They also handed out information and condoms to the overwhelmingly male crowd. ACT UP undertook actions against health care facilities such as University Hospital in Newark and Cook County Hospital in Chicago for failing to offer necessary services to women with AIDS. Although 5 percent of babies in University Hospital were born HIV-positive, the facility was conducting no clinical trials for people with AIDS. Cook County Hospital, the main public hospital in Chicago, had established an AIDS clinic, but women were not allowed to use it. ACT UP responded to this discriminatory policy by placing mattresses down the street in front of the hospital's administrative offices. The instant the mattresses hit the ground, Chicago's finest swooped down and arrested more than 100 people. The predominantly female ACT UP members were charged with "mob action" and treated with the brutality and intolerance associated with the Chicago police. The action achieved its goal, however, as Cook County Hospital reversed its exclusionary policy a week after ACT UP's protest.[7]

ACT UP sought the Reverend Jesse Jackson's support of its efforts to enhance AIDS education in New York's minority communities. Jackson endorsed ACT UP's work with New York's African-American and Latino churches to fight AIDS. ACT UP distributed a flier emphasizing the disproportionate impact of AIDS on both of these minority groups and offered to plan AIDS awareness and outreach programs for church members. ACT UP's willingness to expand its base to politically unpopular intravenous-drug users exposed to HIV would have been unheard of in a less principled organization; its eagerness to work with women and minorities, who were often straight, and its focus on substance abusers and people with AIDS in prisons showed that ACT UP was not only interested in gay white men. The group's outreach efforts also demonstrated its strong political commitment to social and economic justice. As will be discussed below, such passion can help organizations attract volunteers and broaden their political support. Neighborhood organizations and community groups throughout the country have used direct actions without attracting a continual influx of excited new volunteers; it was the combination of direct action and ideological zeal, not direct action alone, that led to ACT UP's success.

On October 11, 1988, ACT UP undertook its most ambitious direct action yet. More than 1,000 ACT UP members from around the country staged a mass "die-in" at FDA headquarters in Rockville, Maryland. The action brought massive publicity and an exaggerated police response. The protesters attacked the FDA for its refusal to legalize experimental drugs, its failure to conduct sufficient drug trials, and its insistence on trials that gave half of the participants placebos rather than medication. The die-in participants lay down in the street holding paper tombstones blaming the FDA for their "death." Chalk outlines on the street represented people who had died of AIDS. The die-in was met by a force of some 360 police officers, many of whom wore riot gear. The primary impact of this massive police response was to elevate the significance of the event. The police tried to keep arrests low to minimize media attention; people who blocked buses holding the 176 protesters that *were* arrested or who tried to enter the headquarters were dragged out of the street rather than arrested themselves. This effort to reduce publicity clearly failed, as the constant street theater and the presence of ACT UP banners covering the building's exterior gave television cameras everything they needed for a great story.[8] The FDA was not a frequent target of mass protests, which further contributed to the media's interest in the event. Further, police officers wore rubber gloves when making arrests at this and other ACT UP events, bolstering ACT UP's contention that the government, the American Medical Association, and the scientific community had utterly failed to provide even the most basic education about AIDS transmission. Newspaper and television coverage of the gloves no doubt caused some people to inquire about AIDS, so the tactic of arrest may also have served an educational purpose.

Direct actions always carry the risk that some participants will "go too far." This risk increases when a series of carefully strategized events bring widespread media coverage yet fail to produce tangible policy results. Just as the frustration of 1960s activists led to the formation of the tactically suspect Weather Underground, so did anger at the lack of progress lead some AIDS activists to engage in high-profile but strategically suspect protest activities. Three such highly controversial events occurred in 1989.

On January 31 of that year, fifty-five protesters stepped into traffic at the height of the morning commute on the Bay Area's world-renowned Golden Gate Bridge. The group, using the "Silence = Death" slogan and focusing its protest on demands associated with ACT UP, identified itself as "Stop AIDS Now or Else" (SANOE). The protesters blocked traffic in both directions, causing a standstill that lasted almost an hour. It was the first time ever that demonstrators had closed the bridge, then fifty-two years old. To ensure that their message was conveyed, the protesters strung a banner across the span reading "AIDS = Genocide/Silence = Death/Fight Back." They also distributed leaflets calling on drivers to demand more government funding for AIDS and to end mandatory testing for the HIV virus.

Was interfering with people's morning commute a wise or effective tactic for accomplishing the protesters' goals? Most of the affected commuters who were quoted in news stories did not think so. Nor did San Francisco's mayor, newspaper columnists, or even Pat Christen, director of policy for the region's largest AIDS organization, the San Francisco AIDS Foundation. Christen told the press that the protest could hurt support for AIDS patients; already, people were threatening to withhold donations to AIDS support groups.[9] The common complaint was that the protesters had picked "the wrong target." Many noted that the commuters affected were likely to be already supportive of the protesters' concerns. Nor were the drivers in a position to alter federal AIDS policy. One columnist thus argued, "If they want Washington to do more about AIDS, they should block the 14th Street Bridge over the Potomac."[10] At a press conference after the demonstration, the protesters defended their actions on the grounds that they had forced people to spend time "thinking about AIDS." Their spokesperson noted that it was their goal to be as disruptive as possible because "AIDS is disrupting our lives, and until people's lives are disrupted, they don't pay attention."[11]

On September 8, 1989, SANOE struck again. At the opening night performance of the San Francisco Opera, about seventy-five protesters rushed through the crowd shouting, "We're here! We're queer! Stop AIDS now!" SANOE's spokesperson argued that no progress had been made since the group's Golden Gate Bridge blockade and that members of the politically and economically powerful crowd could "use their influence to do something about AIDS."[12]

The third and most controversial action involved ACT UP's confrontation with New York's Cardinal O'Connor at St. Patrick's Cathedral on December 10, 1989, likely the most famous action in ACT UP's history. Cardinal O'Connor had been a staunch opponent of the gay and lesbian movement ever since his appointment as archbishop of New York in 1984. He banned the gay Catholic group Dignity from Catholic churches, led opposition to New York City's 1986 Gay Rights Bill, and, most important, advanced an agenda hostile to that of AIDS activists. O'Connor opposed safe-sex education in schools and the use of condoms to prevent HIV transmission, and he attacked assertions that condoms and clean needles could decrease the risk of infection as "lies" perpetuated by public health officials. Graphic artists affiliated with ACT UP created a subway poster and placard picturing O'Connor next to a condom under the boldly printed words, "Know Your Scumbags." The caption under the condom read, "This one prevents AIDS."

Despite widespread belief among ACT UP members that O'Connor constituted a menace to people with AIDS, many group activists questioned the value of an action against the Cardinal. People felt that ACT UP would not influence the Church's anti-gay posture, and it could be assumed that the media would portray an attack on the Cardinal as an attack on the Catholic Church or all Catholics. Nevertheless, a consensus was reached that O'Connor had to be publicly confronted over his anti-gay stance. The Cardinal's open support of the anti-abortion group Operation Rescue, known for its harassment of women visiting family planning clinics, also angered ACT UP, and so ACT UP joined with the New York Women's Health Action and Mobilization (WHAM!) on December 10, 1989 in a demonstration to "Stop the Church." The plan called for a legal picketing protest to turn into a mass die-in around St. Patrick's Cathedral. ACT UP affinity groups would engage in secretly planned civil disobedience inside the church while O'Connor said mass. More than 4,500 people attended the picketing, carrying signs and chanting slogans attacking O'Connor's anti-gay, anti-abortion agenda. Those inside disrupted the mass and forced O'Connor to abandon his sermon. People lay down in the aisles, threw condoms, chained themselves to pews, and verbally attacked the man the placards outside identified as a "public health menace." One participant, a former altar boy, threw a communion wafer on the church floor. The police, who knew of the event in advance, converged on the activists with a brutality that reflected their own pro-Catholic, anti-gay fervor. They arrested 131 people and beat at least one demonstrator repeatedly.[13]

The media coverage of the event was overwhelmingly critical of ACT UP. Cardinal O'Connor was portrayed as a martyr, and ACT UP was accused of violating Catholics' freedom of religion by interfering with the mass and the distribution of the sacrament. The coverage most prominently featured the person who threw the wafer; this act became transformed into "homosexual activists desecrating the host." Randy Shilts, author of the national bestseller on the AIDS epidemic, *And the Band Played On*, viewed the "Stop the Church" event as so "strategically stupid" that the activists must have been "paid by some diabolical reactionary group dedicated to discrediting the gay community."[14] In their post-action meeting, ACT UP members agreed they should more rigorously analyze their choice of targets in the future. The group concluded, however, that the O'Connor attack was a success. The event had forged a coalition with women's health and reproductive rights groups, had shown the country that there was no barrier that ACT UP would not cross to save lives, and had served as a clear reminder that gay activists continued to be targets for police-sanctioned violence.

The bridge blockade, opera protest, and "Stop the Church" actions all were heavily criticized. However, the strategic underpinnings of the first two actions clearly differed from those of the last. The first two events were public protests rather than direct actions because neither involved a confrontation with the target of their demands. Even assuming that powerful people attended the opera's opening night, nobody among the crowd was identified specifically as having a role in federal AIDS policy. The SANOE protests were similar to other disruptions demanding that there be "no business as usual" while the AIDS crisis grew. Such events are rarely as counterproductive as their critics fear, but they should not be confused with direct actions designed to force a target to change its policy.

The Cardinal O'Connor action requires more careful scrutiny. ACT UP knew going in that the event would be unlikely to influence its target; the same argument could have been made about attacks against the Reagan administration. Yet unlike the bridge drivers and opera-goers, Cardinal O'Connor had injected himself and the church he controlled into a political dispute in opposition to ACT UP's agenda. National media coverage of the action ignored O'Connor's actual role in fomenting anti-gay, anti-abortion, anti-ACT UP political advocacy. Because the media used the vandalized communion wafer to create the dominant "spin" on the event, the action came to be perceived as an attack on a religious ceremony rather than on a political advocate. However, the "Stop the Church" protest differed from actions by gay activists seeking to prevent conservative ministers from preaching that homosexuality is evil; it was a political, not religious, attack.

ACT UP knew in advance that the media would side with O'Connor. Should it have proceeded with an event likely to create a media backlash against the organization and having no prospect of influencing its target's policy? Prominent ACT UP members were divided on the question. However, two factors seem to support ACT UP's decision to proceed with the confrontation. First, progressive activists cannot allow themselves to remain on the defensive because of the identity or power of their adversary. Cardinal O'Connor's claim that he "wished he could join Operation Rescue"[15] was an overt effort to encourage people to harass women seeking to exercise their legal right to an abortion. His vocal opposition to any education about safe sex, AIDS, or condoms in schools increased public health risks. These were political rather than religious stances. Having assumed the role of a politician, the Cardinal became fair game for direct political action. ACT UP could not allow a political opponent to avoid confrontation by disguising his political message as religious teaching.

The second and perhaps more important factor justifying the "Stop the Church" action relates to ACT UP's organizational culture and identity. The acronym "ACT UP" was so frequently used that people may have forgotten the organization's full name: the AIDS Coalition to Unleash Power. ACT UP was supposed to harness the rage, fury, and passion of AIDS activists committed to achieving their goals "by all means necessary." Group founder Kramer even wore a shirt with this slogan, above Malcolm X's picture, during his video address to the Sixth International AIDS Conference.[16] Given this organizational culture, ACT UP could hardly forsake actions against certain enemies for fear of a media backlash. ACT UP's formation became necessary precisely because nonconfrontational measures had failed. Placing Cardinal O'Connor off limits to confrontational attack would have reflected this failed approach and imposed artificial limits on ACT UP's power. Activists must sometimes use tactics that may not produce direct results but that are necessary for organizational growth, morale, and development. The "Stop the Church" action had to be done; it should be seen as just one in a continual stream of actions that ACT UP staged in pursuit of its agenda.

During the same year in which the tactics of AIDS activists became the subject of national controversy, ACT UP finally achieved a political breakthrough. At the Fifth International Conference on AIDS in Montreal in June 1989, more than 250 AIDS activists stormed the convention center just prior to the opening ceremonies. Carrying placards and charts as they mounted the stage, the activists announced their twelve-point plan for government AIDS efforts, urging the scientist-dominated audience to "read the manifesto." The audience initially applauded the activist takeover but grew restive as what started as a well-orchestrated direct action broke down into isolated yelling and disruption. After refusing to leave the meeting hall for ninety minutes, the protesters were permitted to remain following extensive negotiations with conference organizers. For the balance of the conference, the protesters did not hesitate to heckle speakers and engage in street theater–type activities. Scientists attending the conference resented this intrusion of "patients" into a scientific meeting and argued against holding future meetings unless a "more productive format" was arranged.

Most news coverage of the conference emphasized the open warfare between scientists and AIDS activists. Randy Shilts's speech at the closing ceremony articulated the prevailing sentiment, criticizing the application of anger unconnected to "intelligence about its best tactical timing and best strategic targets." Despite the consensus that what began as a strategic direct action became transformed into "tantrums" by an "irresponsible few,"[17] ACT UP's initial action represented a watershed in the history of its struggle; its presentation ultimately served to reverse the government and scientific establishment's longtime unwillingness to take the group seriously. The group's unveiling of its comprehensive model for change no doubt contributed to NIAID director Anthony Fauci's acceptance, a few months after the event, of ACT UP's demands for greater input from people with AIDS in policy setting, greater access to treatment and experimental drugs, and more cost-effective use of government funds. Fauci's conversion validated activists' reliance on direct action to achieve their goals. The positive developments following the conference also demonstrate that even actions that "go too far" do not necessarily damage the fundamental message. Despite tactics that were sophomoric rather than strategic, ACT UP's orchestrated opening presentation clearly made a powerful impression on Fauci and other influential figures. This dynamic should be kept in mind by activists who fear that a few thoughtless participants have undermined an otherwise successful action.

ACT UP AND ELECTED OFFICIALS

As befits an organization willing to confront New York's most powerful Catholic official, ACT UP understood and established the necessary "fear and loathing" relationship with elected officials. The group often attacked politicians by crashing events and obtaining a public dialogue. For example, on AIDS Awareness Day at Georgetown University Medical Center in November 1993, ACT UP hecklers forced a nationally televised, person-to-person "debate" with President Clinton. During a speech designed to showcase Clinton's "unprecedented commitment" to AIDS and gay and lesbian rights, a member of ACT UP courageously stood up and challenged the president's record on these issues, yelling, "You promised during your campaign that you would establish a 'Manhattan Project' for AIDS, and all we got was another task force." That sentence distilled the fundamental reality of Clinton's approach to AIDS. Although Clinton responded by talking about how much he had done, how much was still left to do, and how he understood the speaker's frustration and impatience, the powerful impact of the heckler's true, succinct statement already had set in. Everyone familiar with Clinton's AIDS record knew that although he was more committed to the issue than his Republican predecessors, he had not attempted to maximize government resources used in the fight against AIDS. Clinton had promised during his campaign, "When it comes to AIDS, there should be a Manhattan Project." A "Manhattan Project" would entail more than increased funding; like the effort to split the atom, it would bring together experts from multiple disciplines to work in an environment that encouraged cooperation and innovation over competition and secrecy. Such a project would facilitate the testing of treatments lacking industry financial backing and investigate possibilities rejected by corporate interests. Clinton no doubt recognized that the activist had raised an uncomfortable fact during what was supposed to be a back-patting affair; although his administration began doing more on the AIDS issue shortly after the event, Clinton made no effort to encourage passage of the bill introduced to create an AIDS Manhattan Project.[18]

The tactical advantage of directly confronting the president becomes evident when we evaluate other means that could have been used to make the same point. ACT UP could have called a press conference attacking Clinton for substituting a task force for his promised AIDS Manhattan Project. Some ACT UP chapter may well have held such an event; if so, it failed to get the attention of either its target or the national press. Picketing the White House would also probably fail to spark national press interest. Strategies such as marches, rallies, or die-ins might attract national media attention, but whether the coverage conveyed the desired message would depend on the whim of news editors. In light of ACT UP's mixed record in winning positive mainstream press coverage, the protests' message would likely be ignored.

I can think of no strategy other than direct confrontation that would let ACT UP express its position to the president exactly as desired. Further, no other strategy would have forced Clinton to respond immediately. Other types of events probably would only have produced responses from White House spokespersons or cabinet officials; if the protest was so successful that the national media asked Clinton to comment, he would have had time to anticipate the questions and to fudge the issue. ACT UP's willingness to hold its supposed ally accountable for his Manhattan Project commitment was essential. Unlike most of the mainstream environmental groups, ACT UP refused to accept the oft-repeated argument that progressive groups should not pressure a Democratic president for fear of turning government over to Republicans in the next election. The group sent a clear message during Clinton's first year that it would not cut him any slack until he delivered on his commitment to gay rights and the fight against AIDS.

Although best known for its attacks on federal officials, ACT UP recognized that many problems facing people with AIDS were products of local government policies. Activists have often bemoaned the fact that AIDS emerged under Ronald Reagan's presidency, but ACT UP's New York chapter, the largest in the country, faced an equally intractable nemesis: Mayor Ed Koch. Koch consistently blamed the state and federal governments for their failed response to AIDS while allowing his city's health care system virtually to collapse. On March 28, 1989, more than 5,000 ACT UP members launched a "Target City Hall" action in front of Koch's office. Publicity for the action included twelve posters, each stating a reason why people should "act up" that day. The action emphasized that the total amount of city funds requested by community-based AIDS groups was only one-sixth the amount of the city's typical tax rebates to private corporations; that city cutbacks in drug treatment programs resulted in far more costly acute care treatment after drug users contracted AIDS; and that increased funding for education and prevention efforts would save the city hundreds of millions of dollars in hospital costs. The action tied up traffic and City Hall for several hours and resulted in more than 200 arrests. A large media contingent was present at the event, and ACT UP took no chances that its message would be misconstrued: a four-page newspaper, "The New York Crimes," was surreptitiously inserted into that morning's New York Times to ensure that the nation's paper of record would finally tell the truth about the city's dismal record on AIDS.

ACT UP's New York chapter did not limit its attacks to longtime political opponents such as Koch. After the organization helped David Dinkins defeat Koch in the 1989 Democratic mayoral primary and then to prevail in the close general election, Dinkins expressed his gratitude by appointing a city health commissioner who had endorsed putting people with AIDS in quarantine. ACT UP held a large rally in front of City Hall to protest the appointment; a New York Times editorial urged Dinkins to ignore such "hypothetical fears of a vocal minority."[19] There may be no more effective tactic for dealing with politicians than to rally against broken commitments early in their terms. These early conflicts get particularly strong media attention, as news outlets typically cover a new political administration's first steps more closely than its moves after reaching maturity. ACT UP's dispute was described as Dinkins's "first serious political crisis." ACT UP's public attack on the new mayor led Dinkins to insist publicly, "We have not come to a parting of the ways."[20] He immediately made efforts to patch up the conflict. Had ACT UP remained publicly silent and given Dinkins the benefit of the doubt while he got his administration organized, the resulting message would have hampered the group for the balance of Dinkins's term.

INFORMED ACTION

ACT UP's media image as a no-holds-barred direct-action organization conceals a truth central to its success: ACT UP knows what it is talking about. Mere opposition to drugs and testing procedures could not have succeeded if ACT UP had not provided accompanying alternative strategies credible to the government, medical establishment, and more mainstream gay organizations. Although the FDA and other proponents of AZT and the status quo initially accused ACT UP members of being poorly informed, they soon learned otherwise.[21] For example, ACT UP's Treatment and Data Subcommittee acquired the information necessary to prove that the government's testing program was significantly underenrolled. ACT UP then created its own registry of these tests so that people with AIDS could know how and where to sign up. The FDA came out with a similar registry in August 1989, but it was missing so much information that ACT UP's continued to be the main source. ACT UP also discovered that the millions of dollars procured to fight AIDS were being spent testing only one drug: AZT. ACT UP's knowledge of this critical fact fueled direct-action efforts demanding broader drug experimentation. By 1989, ACT UP's investigation enabled it to develop and propose a specific twelve-point plan for government AIDS efforts. It thus became clear to their adversaries that ACT UP members knew what was actually happening in the real-world fight against AIDS.

Knowledge *is* power. This fact runs as a continuous thread through social change organizations' victories over hostile bureaucracies. In the example of the Neighbors for a New Fratney described in Chapter 2, the parent-teacher coalition made sure it had all the facts necessary to justify its support for a multicultural school. This meant developing a realistic program for the new Fratney, one that could actually be implemented in time for the fall school term. The school district bureaucracy would not provide the parents with the necessary information, and school board members, though sympathetic to the neighbors, would never have overruled their superintendent for a proposal they felt could not be carried out. Thus, parents and teachers spent long hours learning everything necessary both to create a new school and to oppose the school bureaucrats' plan. Without this knowledge, direct action and public pressure would have been insufficient.

In the fight against the Brooklyn Navy Yard incinerator discussed in Chapter 3, NYPIRG's knowledge of all of the points at which the project could be denied enabled proactive tactical planning to take place before each stage of the conflict. Its understanding of the complex approval process created opportunities for battles over procedures and public officials virtually unknown to the public. Williamsburg's Satmar and Latino leaders also had to acquire and disseminate information about the serious threat the incinerator posed. El Puente's Luis Garden Acosta had a long-term commitment to educating his community about environmental justice and toxic hazards. He and Rabbi Niederman understood that the incinerator's health impacts could dwarf those of all previous projects, and they successfully transmitted this knowledge to their communities. Williamsburg residents would not have committed themselves to years of struggle unless they were absolutely convinced, emotionally and intellectually, that the incinerator was a serious hazard that could and must be stopped.

The expertise of ACT UP and connected AIDS activists have so convinced the government of their expertise that many view them as now having "veto power" over government AIDS policy.[22] Some pharmaceutical and biotechnology firms contend that ACT UP objections to testing of a particular drug ensure government opposition. This astonishing ascension to power and influence in only a few years is largely attributable to ACT UP's credibility as an organization that effectively mobilizes facts as well as bodies. The group's composition has facilitated its ability to obtain power through knowledge. There may never have been another social change movement including such a high percentage of participants with media, public relations, advertising, and, most important, graphic arts and computer expertise. ACT UP members created the AIDS treatment registry and developed software for people with AIDS. Because the disease knows no class boundaries, ACT UP included people who ran successful businesses, had office and secretarial support, and knew how to get things done. It is difficult to see how a movement lacking people so well versed in information technology could have successfully tackled the government's multibillion-dollar, scientist-dominated health system.

Though ACT UP in the 1980s could not match the medical establishment in professional credentials, it could argue that it was equally well informed, because none of the leaders of government AIDS efforts had learned about the disease in medical school. The knowledge that is critical to AIDS policy is derived from the time-consuming and nonmedical effort of obtaining and interpreting data. Other key information, such as the willingness of people with AIDS to enroll in particular types of testing, is best obtained at the street or local clinic level. In retrospect, it seems obvious that AIDS activists eventually would have a major voice in setting government AIDS policy, but it is equally obvious that they would never have gained this voice without direct action.

THE ACT UP GENERATION

ACT UP's successful implementation of technically proficient, strategically sound direct-action confrontations against powerful corporate and government opponents is unprecedented in recent U.S. history. Any social change activist who has planned a major direct action knows the logistical difficulties inherent in such events. Additionally, most organizations could not attract enough participants to engage in a series of high-profile actions requiring large turnouts. Conventional political analyses of the ACT UP era have generally overlooked the organization's success in attracting and mobilizing dedicated young activists. Examining the factors that led to this success can be instructive for social change organizations suffering from a lack of participation.

The generation born in the 1960s has had to endure an unprecedented level of media disparagement. The over-sixty generation proved its mettle by surviving the Depression and winning World War II, and the baby-boomers earned their stripes marching for civil rights and against the Vietnam War. But the ACT UP generation is portrayed as spoiled by prosperity and uninterested in, if not opposed to, social change activism. It is a testament to how little the mainstream media reflect reality that these assessments of the so-called Generation X could be made even as young people in droves were dedicating themselves to AIDS activism. A more objective journalistic assessment of ACT UP's success might have noted that when the twenty-somethings were confronted with a struggle as grave as those facing their parents' and grandparents' generations, they, too, heeded the call. But such an assessment would conflict with the media's depiction of this as a generation of "slackers."

I have not done a formal survey, but I would bet that, since ACT UP was founded in 1987, there have been far more books and mainstream media stories on the trials and tribulations of civil rights activists of thirty years ago than on the personal hardships currently endured by young ACT UP activists. Generation X should really be described as the "ACT UP Generation."

A direct-action organization can attract dedicated young people when it is seen as addressing an issue of real gravity. In the period of ACT UP's creation, social change organizations created an avalanche of direct-mail campaigns trying to raise funds to oppose the latest Reagan-led assault on this or that interest. Most of these organizations wanted young people's money, not their participation. These mailings often relied on sophisticated techniques of persuasion to elicit contributions. A striking example was a piece that included a separately enclosed envelope with a photograph of a lynched man hanging from a tree. Other mailings relied on inflammatory quotes from Moral Majority leader Jerry Falwell to scare up donors. Although many important organizations rely on direct-mail solicitations, one gets the impression that they sometimes artificially create a sense of urgency to meet their financial needs.

Moreover, effective direct-mail appeals and door-to-door canvassing efforts often urge people to contribute to an organization by becoming a member. The organizations then confuse their rising membership lists with increased public commitment to their cause. These "paper" memberships are rarely mobilized, and many "members" are probably unaware that their contribution conferred membership status. They play no role in organizational policymaking, cannot hold anyone accountable, and are primarily used by groups needing to prove they have a real constituency. When the economy slows, these paper members do not renew. Stories then appear, as with the national environmental groups, linking membership decline to diminished public concern about the issue.

ACT UP did not want paper members and did not need to create a sense of crisis. Nobody needed an expensive mailing to be convinced of the importance of ACT UP's agenda. ACT UP needed money, but its very existence and success depended on personal participation in its events. ACT UP chiefly wanted young people's bodies, minds, and souls, not their bank accounts or "membership." The underlying issues of life and death certainly fueled young activists' passionate involvement in ACT UP; the nature of the issue also facilitated a seriousness of intention that social change organizations in all fields should seek to replicate.

Successful direct action may well require people to exhibit considerable if not extraordinary courage. Such acts send a dual message to their adversaries and the public. The first idea conveyed is the particular demand at issue; the second and more lasting impression is of a group that will not rest until it achieves its goals. When civil rights activists like current congressman and former organizer John Lewis rode buses on the Freedom Rides, knowing they would be viciously beaten, they sent a message that nothing short of their murder would deter them. Cesar Chavez and the farmworkers movement took a similar approach, using tactics such as lengthy hunger strikes and massive civil disobedience. The farmworkers' opponents gradually realized that they could not outlast a group that would give up their lives for their cause if necessary. ACT UP's campaigns had a similar impact. It soon became clear to government, scientific, medical, and corporate officials that ACT UP would use whatever tactics necessary to ensure wider access and better treatment for people with AIDS. If this meant publicly comparing NIAID director Fauci to Nazi war criminal Adolph Eichmann, as Larry Kramer did in a 1988 *Village Voice* article, so be it. Many activists would be unwilling publicly to describe their adversary as a murderer, even if the epithet fit; Kramer and ACT UP recognized no such boundaries.

ACT UP's nationwide success at enlisting and mobilizing young people during a period of national political stupor was not unique. Central American support groups like the Committee in Solidarity with the People of El Salvador (CISPES) and those opposing U.S. intervention in Nicaragua also attracted young activist energy during the ACT UP years. Since the late 1980s, the People for Ethical Treatment of Animals (PETA) has registered astronomical growth in participation and media coverage of its campaigns for animal rights. These activist organizations relied primarily on direct action to achieve their goals, offering young people a meaningful vehicle for working for social change. PETA may be the organization most similar to ACT UP, as it engages in a constant barrage of demonstrations, rallies, sit-ins, boycotts, and other confrontational attacks against its opponents. PETA's enemies are the same triumvirate—government, the medical/scientific establishment, and corporate profiteers—targeted by ACT UP. One reason PETA continues to grow in strength is that, like ACT UP, it consciously uses graphics and creativity to build a sense of excitement into its events.

People committed to progressive social change, like everybody else, want to work on campaigns that are meaningful, strategically savvy, and fun. They also want to feel as if their personal involvement makes a difference. ACT UP facilitated this feeling by pioneering the tactic of using phone calls and faxes to overwhelm its target's normal business operations. These phone or fax "zaps" allowed even the busiest activist to do something concrete to help the cause. PETA's monthly magazine includes dozens of different activities people can engage in to help the cause. These range from participating in a direct action in one's community to writing letters to corporate presidents to returning for refunds products that have been tested on animals. PETA has even succeeded in establishing a "cruelty-free" label for consumer goods. The essence of PETA, however, is the willingness of its participants to risk their personal safety, often in undercover, quasi-legal actions, on behalf of animal rights. PETA uses direct mail as a tool for organizing and mobilizing, not simply to raise funds or to create artificial constituency bases.

The proven ability of direct-action-oriented organizations to enlist large numbers of participants—and to turn people into activists—reflects a powerful truth: progressive constituencies and social change organizations need a direct-action component. The terrible problems besetting the urban poor in general, and African-Americans in particular; the decreased visibility of environmental issues in the national policy debate; and the decline in public schools and health care will not begin to be addressed successfully until direct action becomes a central instrument for organizing and mobilizing people around these issues. Though some contend that ACT UP's model cannot successfully be applied to such complex political subjects, recent experience has again shown that even electing a Democratic president and a Democratic Congress does not produce results when grassroots mobilization is lacking. Had Larry Kramer not issued his siren call in March 1987, observers might still be arguing whether direct action could be effective in the fight against AIDS. Organizations and constituencies looking outside themselves for the source of declining participation and interest in their issues should instead examine what they do to encourage such activities.

THE FUTURE OF ACT UP

As a result of its effective direct-action strategy, by the early 1990s ACT UP had become accepted as an indispensable party to government AIDS policy making. ACT UP's changing role at the annual International Conference on AIDS provides a significant measure of the group's rise in status. In 1989 ACT UP protesters had to storm the fifth annual conference to announce their twelve-point AIDS plan; five years later, at the tenth conference, ACT UP and people with AIDS were invited guests. ACT UP's emergence during Reagan's presidency and its growth during the Bush administration came in response to obvious government stonewalling on AIDS. In contrast, the Clinton administration and the Democratic Party as a whole are consistently open to talking about AIDS. Although their performance has fallen short of ACT UP's expectations, the group has rarely felt it necessary to stage mass acts of protest. Having become a vital part of the policymaking process, ACT UP can hardly call for mass protests against government decisions. ACT UP in the Clinton era can achieve sound bites without direct action and meet directly with government officials whose predecessors refused such contact; articles about AIDS policy include AIDS activists in an "interlocking triumvirate" with their former opponents. A group once forced to shout to be heard now has a seat at the table of power.[23]

ACT UP's success in giving AIDS patients a major role in determining the government's approach to potential treatments or cures was an historic achievement. Federal spending on AIDS rose from $234 million in 1986 to nearly $2 billion in 1992, a nearly tenfold increase in only six years.[24] ACT UP's astonishing effectiveness and success, however, also resulted in the group's decline. ACT UP was always more an alliance of independent local chapters than a national organization, and by 1994 most of the chapters outside New York City were seldom involved in the type of direct actions that once typified ACT UP. In a *New York Times* article titled "Larry Kramer's Roar Turns to Contented Purr,"[25] Kramer's own turn inward became a metaphor for ACT UP's declining reliance on boisterous confrontations to achieve its goals. Although Kramer's status as a gay man may forestall his receiving his just due as an innovative, historically significant political strategist, the *Times*'s willingness to provide positive commentary on its longtime adversary reflects the respect ACT UP has earned for its accomplishments.

Movements and organizations often lose steam after achieving their goals. The strong movement against government aid to the Nicaraguan contras ended when political changes made such aid a nonissue. The grassroots advocacy group Neighbor-to-Neighbor switched its emphasis from El Salvador to U.S. health care reform after similar changes in the political landscape; CISPES remained focused on El Salvador but emphasized ways of assisting the peacetime economy rather than battling

Congress over military aid to the beleaguered nation. The movement for a nuclear freeze, which in the early 1980s concerned millions of Americans, has almost disappeared from the political map.

The critical difference between ACT UP's success and that of other social change organizations, however, is that the ultimate goal—a cure for AIDS, or at least a vaccine that will slow its spread—appears as far off as ever. Because direct action is no longer crucial to achieving this ultimate goal, the continued need for ACT UP's existence is unclear. AIDS activism will certainly continue, but it is doubtful that the cause will attract anywhere close to the numbers of committed young activists previously attracted to it. With a national backlash against the civil rights gains of the 1970s and 1980s in full swing, the emergence of a national equivalent to ACT UP focused on such issues may become essential. For example, businesses who refuse to hire people because they are gay, or who terminate employees discovered to be gay, can increasingly be targeted for direct action. Some local groups already engage in such tactics, but the wrongs of particular businesses will rarely, if ever, have the universal attraction or gravity of the AIDS issue. Nevertheless, ACT UP's tactics likely will find their way into an increasingly powerful lesbian and gay civil rights movement in the coming years.

"STOP STEALING OUR CIVIL RIGHTS"— DIRECT ACTION FOR DISABILITY RIGHTS[26]

AIDS activists adopted a direct-action strategy after it became clear that their use of less confrontational tactics brought no response. Those who personally dislike confrontational politics are more likely to support them after all else has failed. The idea that one's opponents have "forced" a group into direct action fuels activism as well as militancy. One would suppose that officials at the highest level of government would understand this psychological dynamic; the last problem a government needs is an uprising of its own creation. The disability rights movement stands as a striking example of how government can fuel direct-action opposition by leaving social change activists no alternative. Although less well known than other social change movements, the disability rights movement engaged in perhaps the single most impressive act of civil disobedience in the United States over the last quarter-century. It not only used direct action to humiliate a newly elected presidential administration but also sent a message across the country that people with disabilities were a powerful and active political force.

The struggle that eventually involved the longest occupation of a federal building in U.S. history began quietly. In 1973 Congress enacted a comprehensive Rehabilitation Act. Section 504 of the act prohibited discrimination against disabled persons by any institution or agency receiving federal funds. As the *New York Times* consistently reminded readers during the occupation, Section 504 was enacted "without hearings or formal debate."[27] One reason for this lack of debate may have been that the law would not take effect until implementing regulations had been drafted. Universities, hospitals, and other institutions hostile to Section 504 could avoid the bad publicity associated with opposing civil rights for disabled persons by quietly derailing the Rehabilitation Act through the regulatory process. As discussed in Chapter 2, polluters have effectively used this tactic to circumvent environmental protection laws, and the proponents of Section 504 were likely considered less powerful than national environmental groups. It was therefore not surprising when the process for developing implementing regulations for the one-sentence Section 504 was put in a deep freeze by the federal government.

The lead agency for developing the Section 504 regulations was the former Department of Health, Education and Welfare (HEW, which became the Department of Health and Human Services after Jimmy Carter made Education a separate department). HEW's regulations were critical because they would govern the approach of all other federal agencies. After it became apparent that HEW was making no progress, disability rights groups filed a federal lawsuit to force the agency to act. In July 1976 a federal court judge ruled that there had been unusual delay and ordered HEW to issue final regulations immediately. After extensive discussions with both Section 504 proponents and opponents, final regulations were sent to President Gerald Ford's HEW secretary, David Mathews, eight days prior to his replacement by the incoming Carter appointee. All Mathews had to do was sign the regulations, and legal discrimination against people with disabilities would come to an end in federally funded employment, health, and social services and educational institutions.

To the dismay of the disability rights community, Mathews did not sign the regulations. Instead he sent them to Congress, asking it to decide whether it wanted the regulations to apply equally to people whose disability was alcoholism or drug addiction. Although Mathews justified his action by claiming that HEW had no legislative intent to guide it and did not want continued battles over this particular issue, disability rights groups saw the unusual action as simply another delaying tactic.[28] Congress could spend years fighting over the meaning of the one provision while schools, hospitals, universities, and day-care centers continued to discriminate. Disability rights groups thus responded to Mathews's action by returning to federal court. On January 18, 1977, the court agreed with activists' claims that Mathews had unreasonably delayed the final regulations and ordered HEW to issue the rulings immediately. HEW appealed, however, and Mathews left office with the regulations unsigned.

When the Carter administration took over on January 20, 1977, the appeal remained in court, and incoming HEW secretary Joseph Califano pleaded for time to review the rules. As far as the disability rights activists were concerned, the fix was clearly in: at the last minute, opponents of the 504 regulations had obtained a reprieve. The new secretary may have thought that disability rights activists would hesitate to protest in the hoopla of a new, Democratic administration. Regardless of what he believed at the time, Califano claimed after leaving office that he welcomed the prospect of nationwide demonstrations against him, hoping that such protests would raise the public's awareness of the pending regulations and ultimately facilitate compliance.[29] However, considering that Califano viewed the disability rights activists as "rather one-dimensional in their views" and admittedly sought to "restructure" the regulations, his subsequent justification for his actions seems merely a means to explain away a significant strategic miscalculation.

Organizations working for the Section 504 regulations had created an umbrella group called the American Coalition of Citizens with Disabilities (ACCD). ACCD learned soon after Califano's refusal to sign the regulations that he had created a task force to study the rules and make recommendations. No people with disabilities were included on the task force, nor were there any representatives from the organizations making up ACCD. Although the task force meetings were secret, word soon filtered out to ACCD that a major watering-down of Section 504 was underway. ACCD director Frank Bowe learned that one proposal changed the regulations applying to the education of disabled children.[30] The entire thrust of those regulations, which mandated integration of disabled persons into mainstream institutions, was being shifted toward a "separate but equal" approach. Upon hearing these reports, ACCD indirectly contacted President Carter, who in a highly publicized campaign speech at the federal rehabilitation center in Warm Springs, Georgia, had promised to sign the regulations. Carter now refused to intervene, however, leaving ACCD to battle with Secretary Califano.

ACCD began its struggle with an extremely savvy technical move. Rather than waiting for the task force's recommendations to become public, ACCD took the proactive approach and announced that if the regulations were not signed by April 4, 1977, it would launch nationwide demonstrations. ACCD thus regained control of the agenda, forcing Califano either to accept its timetable for review or face protests. The April 4 deadline was near enough to maintain the pressure on Califano but still gave ACCD enough time to plan nationwide protests. Organizing for the events began in March under the motto "Sign 504 Unchanged." ACCD planned protests at HEW headquarters in Washington, D.C., and at regional offices in New York City, Boston, Seattle, Dallas, Denver, Chicago, Philadelphia, and San Francisco. Califano, along with most Americans, was likely unaware that the disability rights movement did not fit the erroneous stereotypes of a constituency dependent on public sympathy or handouts. Disabled activists were demanding their civil rights, which included an end to separate-but-equal accommodations for disabled persons, particularly when the separate facilities were no more "equal" than schools for African-Americans had been in the pre-*Brown vs. Board of Education* era. Many disability rights activists were veterans of the civil rights and antiwar movements and understood how the tactics of those struggles could apply to their own. Their strong identification with the political movements of the 1960s fueled their response to Califano's tactics and was a major factor in their ultimate success.

Judy Heumann, a disabled person who later became an undersecretary of education in the Clinton administration, served in 1977 as a board member of ACCD and deputy director of the Center for Independent Living in Berkeley. She took responsibility for planning the San Francisco component of the nationwide April 5 protest. Heumann and fellow CIL staffer and wheelchair-user Kitty Cone, who had spent most of their adult lives as political organizers, focused on expanding political support for the protest to include other civil rights organizations, the religious community, labor unions, and progressive activists and officials. This was not simply a rounding up of the usual suspects; the disability rights movement had traditionally operated apart from other movements for social change. Attempts to build networks had been geared toward unifying people with diverse disabilities rather than on creating alliances with the nondisabled. Heumann and Cone's strategic approach came out of their experiences as organizers for progressive change, and their tactical decision gave the San Francisco protest a power that was lacking in the other events around the nation.

The ACCD activists made another critical strategic decision to advance the disability rights agenda. A one-day nationwide protest would focus national attention on the Section 504 regulations, but the public's interest in the issue would then evaporate. No follow-up protests had been planned, so Califano would only have to weather one day of negative press before continuing his efforts to weaken the regulations. Further, getting disabled persons to demonstrations on short notice was no simple matter. For the ACCD to maximize its pressure on Califano, a tactic had to be utilized that did not require additional events with their accompanying logistical complexities. The solution to this challenge was to hold sit-ins in HEW's offices until the regulations were signed. Heumann, working through Berkeley's Center for Independent Living with allies throughout the Bay Area, was charged with organizing the San Francisco protest. She did not want the press or Califano to know about the planned sit-ins. If HEW had advance knowledge, it would ensure that the protesters did not gain access to its offices. The organizers thus quietly took people aside and told them to bring sleeping bags or blankets to the rallies across the country.

As the San Francisco demonstration began on April 5, 1977, the sit-in remained under wraps. A crowd of more than 500 people listened to a series of speeches; then Heumann took the stage. She urged the audience to "go and tell Mr. Maldonado [HEW regional secretary] that the federal government cannot steal our civil rights." Most of the crowd followed Heumann's direction and entered the floor of the federal building containing HEW's offices. The unexpectedness of this relatively harmless tactic increased its value. Thus, HEW's Joseph Maldonado, who probably saw the regional secretary position as a plum job free from controversy, was in his office when the protesters entered. His presence made for the type of confrontation that ensures good coverage on the evening news. Had the rally organizers allowed Maldonado to learn of their plan, he could have found a reason to be away from the office that day. Alternatively, he could have been briefed on the Section 504 issue and given the protesters a prepared statement presenting HEW's position in the most favorable light. Apparently taken by surprise, however, Maldonado did not appear even to know about the existence of Section

504. As cameras rolled, protesters demanded to know why the regulations were not being signed unchanged. Maldonado's obvious confusion reflected poorly on HEW's stance. The regional secretary's inability to justify Califano's position, and the sense he conveyed of being overwhelmed by the protesters, fueled a sense of empowerment throughout the group. When the San Francisco protesters had matters well in hand, they used HEW's phones to call other cities to check on the progress of other events.

Having flooded HEW's San Francisco office with protesters, the organizers announced they would not be leaving. When confronted by security guards, the group's security committee simply told them that the protesters refused to leave. The first night more than 200 people, most of them disabled, slept in HEW's offices, hallways, and meeting rooms. There were no showers, bathtubs, or cooking facilities, and there was only one accessible toilet for men and women. The absence of such amenities further strengthened solidarity, as people with different disabilities helped each other. Though the protesters could get by without maintaining normal standards of cleanliness, they had to eat. In Washington, D.C., more than 75 disabled demonstrators remained in the building overnight but were effectively starved out of their sit-in after twenty-six hours. HEW's national headquarters had allowed only one cup of coffee and one doughnut per protester during the first day of the occupation. After HEW announced that no more food would be provided, the protesters decided to leave as a group rather than have individuals leave on their own because of hunger-induced medical problems. A sit-in by six disabled protesters at HEW's New York City office also succumbed to the lack of food.

What had Cone, Heumann, and other organizers done to prevent hunger from ending the San Francisco protest? The answer lies in their initial strategic decision to build a broad base of progressive support for the Section 504 protest. Cone and company had established a network of volunteers who would have risked arrest to bring food to the sit-in. These people were affiliated with various organizations, including the Delancey Street Foundation, a nationally recognized rehabilitation program for ex-convicts and drug and alcohol abusers. The Black Panthers, who operated food programs in nearby Oakland, also regularly brought meals to the protesters. Once the sit-in became established, even corporate giants like Safeway and McDonald's contributed food. The organizers of the San Francisco sit-in had laid the political and practical groundwork to support as long a siege as necessary. It was not simply the rights of disabled persons at issue; the issue had been transformed into one of the federal government's attempt to steal a group's civil rights.

HEW recognized early on that any attempt to starve out the San Francisco protesters could create the potential for massive civil disobedience against other federal institutions by several constituencies unaffiliated with disability rights. Allowing such escalation would put further pressure on HEW to explain or justify its attempt to weaken Section 504. Further, the last thing an incoming Democratic administration needed was a pitched battle in the Bay Area, one of the most heavily Democratic areas of the country. The Washington, D.C. protesters did not have a local political base to oppose or circumvent the starvation strategy, so the Carter administration was not inhibited in its tactics. In San Francisco, though, passions ran so high among the protesters that a serious attempt to deny food could easily have created a riot.

The San Francisco sit-in had become the disabled community's last and best hope for ensuring that HEW Secretary Califano would in fact sign Section 504 unchanged. Califano was continuing to take a hard-line position. A former trial attorney, Califano had dramatically stood on his office coffee table during the Washington, D.C. sit-in to announce that he would not sign the regulations until he could study them and understand their implications.[31] HEW's general counsel had taken an even more confrontational stance, stating that the regulations would "have to be changed" before Califano signed them.[32] HEW officials would have been better off keeping silent; their statements only added to the fervor of the disability rights community.

To Heumann, Cone, and the other strategists, HEW's obstinacy simply meant that ACCD had to flex additional political muscles. Two weeks into the sit-in, with virtually every politician and progressive political group in the region now ardently supporting the protest, two San Francisco Bay Area congressmen held a special hearing in the occupied HEW offices. San Francisco's legendary representative, Phil Burton, a burly bear of a man, presided over the hearing and was brought to tears by the testimony of disabled activists. Ed Roberts, who used an iron lung and was serving as head of California's Department of Rehabilitation, captured the prevailing mood, claiming, "We are not even second-class citizens, we're third-class citizens." A HEW bureaucrat sent to the hearing to explain why the Section 504 regulations had to be changed made the terrible mistake of using the phrase "separate but equal," thus confirming everybody's suspicions about HEW's retrograde agenda. After completing his testimony, the official left the hearing, went into an office, and locked the door. Burton, wanting Califano's emissary to continue to hear from the protesters, ran to the office and began kicking on the door, demanding that the official return. A social change organization rarely gets a powerful political leader so emotionally involved in its cause.

As the local and national media continued regular coverage of the San Francisco sit-in, millions of Americans received their first real exposure to the life experiences of persons with disabilities. The media did individual profiles of many sit-in participants, increasing the public's understanding of why discrimination against disabled persons must end. People who were deaf, blind, or who used wheelchairs were now seen not as wanting special help but as simply seeking equal access to employment, schools, housing, medical care, and public transportation. The positive press, however, could easily have obscured a critical fact: the sit-in could not last forever. Although morale was strong and people had been willing to experience serious pain in order to continue, the protest strategists recognized that Califano had to be forced to act sooner rather than later. Heumann, Cone, and several other leaders thus flew to Washington, D.C. after the sit-in had lasted two weeks. They realized that Califano needed more to worry about than an embarrassing protest 3,000 miles away.

Upon arriving in the capital, the activists again reaped the benefits of their initial decision to create alliances with other progressive organizations. An official of the International Association of Machinists (IAM) became particularly interested in the Section 504 struggle, and the union gave the visiting activists free use of its Washington, D.C. office as a base from which to organize their capital-based strategy. The IAM also provided unlimited food and put a wheelchair-accessible van at the activists' disposal. The IAM's assistance should not be seen as a result of pure luck; the organizers of the Section 504 protest in San Francisco had made overtures necessary to win labor union support. Unions were not directly impacted by the Section 504 regulations and had not been involved in the legislative or administrative struggles surrounding the legislation. Yet the disability rights activists received more assistance from labor organizations than they ever expected. Such unanticipated assistance is a natural product of successful coalition building.

Although weary from the sit-in and the cross-country flight, Cone and Heumann coordinated an astonishing array of activities in Washington, D.C. They moved to shore up their national political support by seeking assistance from the original sponsors of Section 504, Senators Harrison Williams of New Jersey and Alan Cranston of California. Williams's support was firm, but Cranston was waffling. The activists therefore held a meeting with him in the presence of the national press. As Cranston tried to explain HEW's position, people with different disabilities responded to every change in Section 504 sought by Califano. By the end of the exchange, Cranston was convinced that the activists were right. Winning over Cranston might not have been a decisive victory, but California's senior senator was then among the most powerful Democrats in government. His support for signing Section 504 unchanged sent a powerful message to HEW and the entire Carter administration that they would have to tangle with a critical senatorial ally if they insisted on weakening the regulations.

In addition to reestablishing their "inside" power, the disabled activists took to the streets of Washington, D.C. Their strategy was to confront Carter and Califano at various places in the hope that the HEW chief would sign Section 504 unchanged if for no other reason than to end the harassment. This strategy required mobilizing many activists with limited mobility; the IAM's van and escort service became essential. Califano's luxurious house was picketed day and night. His neighbors must have wondered what he had done to provoke twenty-five people in wheelchairs to hold candles outside his home while singing "We want 504" to the tune of "We Shall Overcome." The activists also sat in front of President Carter's church, only to have him exit through a rear door. Califano could not even find refuge at the Press Club. Evan White, a San Francisco television news reporter who had accompanied the activists to Washington, obtained access to the Press Club and questioned Califano about the Section 504 regulations. It was becoming obvious even to the politically arrogant Califano that he would never be free to conduct business until he had signed Section 504 unchanged. After a White House meeting between activists and Stuart Eizenstat, Carter's top domestic adviser, Califano surrendered. On April 28, 1977, he signed the Section 504 regulations virtually unchanged and ended the struggle prior to his own May deadline.[33] Califano claimed the regulations would "usher in a new era of civil rights" and would be implemented with "flexibility" and "common sense."[34] The San Francisco sit-in ended two days later. After twenty-five days of sleeping on floors, eschewing baths or showers, and eating mostly fast food, the 150 remaining protesters were exhausted. Most were filthy, and many had lice. Two sign-language interpreters had stayed throughout, as did a handful of attendants. The protesters had become like family, with HEW's offices as their home. A determined group of people traditionally portrayed as weak and helpless had engaged in the longest occupation of a federal office building in U.S. history and had forced a newly elected political administration and the bureaucracy it controlled to meet their demands. As Kitty Cone told the media, "Nobody gave us anything. We showed we could wage a struggle at the highest level of government and win."[35]

The successful Section 504 campaign used tactical strategies that affirm the tenets of social change activism recommended throughout this book. First, the disability rights movement did not allow the election of a Democratic president to sidetrack its agenda and maintained a proper fear-and-loathing attitude. Despite having supported Carter in the campaign, ACCD held a press conference thirteen days prior to his inauguration, charging the president-elect with failing to make good on his campaign promise to consult with disabled people during his transition period.[36] The activists' subsequent willingness to embarrass and even humiliate Califano further showed they understood that hardball politics is often necessary for activist groups to fulfill their agendas. Not a single disability rights organization broke ranks on the Section 504 demand, a remarkable show of unity in light of the movement's representation of diverse disabilities and a broad range of political ideologies. For example, Frank Bowe, director of the ACCD, represented a far more moderate and mainstream perspective than ACCD board member and sit-in leader Judy Heumann. Despite political, cultural, and generational differences, the entire disability rights movement accepted the necessity of confrontational direct action to win the fight over Section 504. This unity prevented the Carter administration from "picking off" certain groups and granting them favors in exchange for their support of weakened regulations. The consensus on Section 504 was no accident. All of ACCD's member groups knew the reasons behind each of the regulations, so their organizational commitment did not depend on what other groups had decided was necessary. Knowledge created both power and unity and enabled all groups to feel vested in the ACCD's central demand that Section 504 be signed unchanged.

Disability activists were strategic enough to give the new administration an escape route before putting it under unmitigated attack. Heumann told the press soon after the sit-in began, "We've learned that President Carter is aware of our action and is sympathetic."[37] This assertion may have sounded strange, because if Carter were really sympathetic, he could simply order Califano to sign Section 504 immediately. However, Heumann's statement implied that the disability rights community was willing to protect Carter from the political fallout caused by the sit-in if he would intercede at once. A more skillful politician would have taken the hint and figured out a way to hand a victory to the protesters. Jimmy Carter may go down in history for his mediation skills, but this ability was not reflected in his domestic agenda. The administration did nothing to curtail Califano's political blunder, giving the protesters no choice but to go after the president himself. Judy Heumann told reporters on April 22 that she had worked in Carter's election campaign but now was "ashamed I helped Carter get elected."[38] This statement warned the administration that its conduct on Section 504 was weakening its own political base; administration officials also learned not to expect special leniency because they were Democrats.

In addition to establishing the proper relationship with elected officials, disability activists used the necessary proactive tactical approach to win their struggle. Faced with Califano's decision to allow a task force to review and modify the Section 504 regulations, ACCD had two choices. It could wait for the task force's recommendations to be made public and then attack the changes, or it could take the offensive by imposing its own deadline upon Califano. Although the latter option clearly appears preferable in retrospect, elected officials would not continue to create task forces if they did not have a strong record of success in permanently or indefinitely deferring progressive social change. Indeed, the scenario confronting ACCD was almost perfectly engineered to force acceptance of the task force option. Califano was simply requesting time to "understand" the regulations before signing them; how could ACCD demand that the HEW secretary immediately sign regulations he had no role in drafting—indeed, that had been written when HEW was led by a different political party? Wasn't Califano only acting prudently and responsibly in seeking advice from experts on the implications of the regulations? Didn't the lack of congressional hearings necessitate such an investigation? Many social change activists would have swallowed hard and given Carter and Califano "the benefit of the doubt" at such an early stage of their administration. The task force would then have met until the opponents of the regulations had created the political base necessary for a drastic shift in approach. The disability rights community, having lost control of the agenda, would have been forced to compromise or face political defeat.

ACCD avoided this scenario by putting Califano on the defensive by setting a deadline of April 4 for signing the regulations. HEW had to operate under rules set by ACCD, not vice versa. The activists recognized the importance of forcing Califano to act before the task force recommendations were made public; publication of any proposed changes would have shifted the terms of the debate from the need to sign the regulations unchanged to the merits of the new proposals. By keeping Califano consistently on the defensive, the ACCD left him no choice but to concede. They transformed his delay tactics into a weapon against him; each day that passed without the signing of Section 504 caused greater grief to Califano than to the advocates for the regulations. Califano later acknowledged that he signed the 504 regulations prior to his announced deadline "to avoid another round of demonstrations."[39]

Largely because of the movement's proactive approach, the media consistently framed the dispute in terms set by the protesters. The key motto of the Section 504 protests was, "The federal government is trying to steal our civil rights." HEW could have argued that the rights had never legally taken effect and hence could not have been stolen. The agency tried at the outset to convey its own spin on the story, but its message soon became overwhelmed by the protesters' sheer energy and activity. Although the national media emphasized the "confusion" over the regulations rather than the denial of civil rights, the daily photos of people in wheelchairs engaged in civil disobedience and 1960s protest tactics enabled the civil rights theme to predominate. By characterizing the battle as a civil rights issue, the disabled activists put HEW in a trap from which it couldn't escape.

The Section 504 organizers also skillfully used the media. As discussed in Chapter 5, social change organizations should strive to put the media in a position where they become vested in the group's success. This process involves more than having a sympathetic issue; it entails giving the media a role in the remedying of the particular injustice and providing a stream of newsworthy events. It became obvious early on that the local media supported the protesters and would help their case as much as possible. The strong local media backing helped maintain protesters' morale and no doubt influenced HEW's decision not to starve out or otherwise forcibly end the sit-in. But the protest organizers recognized that even the strongest local media support could not decide a national battle. Califano and the Carter administration woke up to the *Washington Post* and the *New York Times,* not the *San Francisco Chronicle.* The *New York Times* favored HEW in the Section 504 dispute. The *Post,* then the country's most influential newspaper, only three years removed from bringing down Nixon, also supported Califano. Although the *Post's* initial news coverage of the April 5 protests was sympathetic, its lead editorial on April 7 concluded that Califano was "absolutely right" to refuse to sign the Section 504 regulations. The *Post* described the regulations as "terrible, confusing, complicated, fuzzy, and bound to do far less for the disabled citizen than for the lawyer seeking a guaranteed annual income." After falsely claiming that the regulations would require employers to hire drug addicts, the *Post* lectured the disability rights activists, explaining that they were fighting for the "right principle but the wrong set of regulations."

After giving Califano all the backing he needed to justify his refusal to sign the regulations, the *Post* then failed to cover the ongoing sit-in by the San Francisco protesters and the vigil outside Califano's home. The protesters later held a day-long vigil in front of the White House. That vigil followed the meeting with Cranston and coincided with the release of a strong letter from the senator urging Califano to sign the regulations immediately. The same day, the activists also had their meeting with Stuart Eizenstat, Carter's chief domestic counsel. The activists, having combined direct action, written support from the senate sponsor of Section 504, and a White House meeting, simply created too much news for the *Post* to continue its silence. On April 23, 1977, the *Post* provided a sympathetic story on the Section 504 protest, quoting at length from Cranston's letter and detailing the local protest activities. The story included no quotes from Califano or any opponent of the regulations. Neither did the coverage mention any of the strong objections to the regulations voiced in the *Post's* lead editorial of April 7. By taking their fight to the *Post's* home turf, the disability rights activists ultimately succeeded in obtaining media coverage that increased the pressure on Carter and Califano to cave in to ACCD's demands.[40]

PUBLIC ATTITUDES AND DIRECT ACTION

It is important to examine the contrast between the public's response to direct actions by disability rights activists and those by AIDS activists. Disabled people naturally generated more sympathy than AIDS activists, who had to contend with widespread homophobia and right-wing assertions that AIDS was God's vengeance on gay people. Also, the disability rights activists never sought to inconvenience people going about their everyday business, as ACT UP and its affiliates sometimes did. Although the disability rights activists caused more than $5,000 in property damage at the San Francisco HEW office, they discomfited only bureaucrats and may have gained sympathy for doing so. They faced no media criticism for their sit-in, although it was no less stubborn an act than many ACT UP actions that received unfavorable coverage. Nor did local or federal police forces treat the disability rights protesters with any of the brutality that typified their response to ACT UP sit-ins. Behavior viewed negatively when carried out by ACT UP activists was identified with courage and commitment in the Section 504 protest. Politicians regularly tried to keep their distance from ACT UP, but San Francisco mayor George Moscone showed his support for the disability rights sit-in by bringing a shower attachment to help make up for the lack of bathing facilities at HEW's San Francisco office.

Social change organizations considering direct action tactics must therefore analyze in advance how the public perception of their constituency will impact the response to their conduct. For example, ACT UP never would have been allowed to take over a federal office for nearly a month. Conversely, 15,000 Hasidic Jews could halt traffic on the Brooklyn Bridge for a march to protest an incinerator without being accused of wrongly targeting commuters. Would the same march by welfare recipients demanding cost-of-living increases have met with similar acceptance? Of course not. The public and media would demand to know why the welfare recipients were not out looking for jobs rather than marching to increase their public support.

Social change organizations are often unable to alter the media's double standard and unfair bias against their exercise of direct action. The group Earth First! was founded in April 1980 by environmentalists opposed to what they perceived as weak compromises by major environmental groups over the future of roadless national forest lands. Earth First! prided itself on its deliberate disorganization, which allowed different chapters to remain formally unconnected to illegal direct-action activities undertaken by various members. The group blockaded logging roads to save old-growth forests and protect habitat for the spotted owl in the Pacific Northwest. It also temporarily prevented campers at Yellowstone National Park from reaching a campground that interfered with a bear habitat. Earth First! members were amazingly courageous, willing to climb giant trees to protect them from being cut and subjecting themselves to the risk of being run over by trucks. Earth First!'s use of direct action to stop clear-cutting and preserve ancient redwoods would seem to represent the type of good deeds that would garner mainstream media support. Instead, as former Earth First! activist Mitch Friedman stated, "Earth First! was never portrayed as Robin Hood, it was portrayed as terrorists. Society doesn't want a crisis dealt with through crisis tactics."[41] Society also doesn't want activists with the "radical" view that humans have no greater claim on natural resources than do other species. Media coverage of Earth First!'s civil disobedience against the timber industry came almost exclusively to dwell on its most controversial tactics, such as tree spiking.[42] When two prominent Earth First! activists, Judy Bari and Daryl Cheney, were injured by a bomb explosion in their car, police and the media falsely alleged that the nonviolent victims had built the bomb themselves to fulfill the agenda of their "terrorist" organization.

The hostile media coverage of Earth First! contrasts sharply with the respect given to anti-abortionist zealots on Ted Koppel's *Nightline* on December 8, 1993. Paul Hill, who less than a year later was convicted of murdering a doctor and another man outside an abortion clinic in Pensacola, Florida, appeared on *Nightline* to debate whether doctors performing abortions should be killed. He argued that they should. Koppel asked, "If a parent would be justified in using violence, even deadly force, to protect a one-day-old infant, why is that same parent not justified to use the same kind of force to prevent the abortion of a five-month-old child?"[43] Koppel's sympathetic treatment of Hill's advocacy of murder, juxtaposed with the media's hostility to civil disobedience by environmentalist "zealots," illustrates that the media can be far more concerned over who is doing the direct action than over what is being done.

Sometimes tactical activists can choose whether to try to overcome or accommodate built-in biases that impact public attitudes toward direct action. Such decisions involve thinking about what type of participant can best convey the necessary message of a particular act. For example, a squatters' organization planning a public squat of a vacant flat can attempt to house a single working mother with two kids, or it can try the same thing with three young male adults with long hair. Public support for squatting will be greater if it results in housing for the mother and children, even though the three men also need homes. In fact, some would argue that the latter trio would better establish the real value of squatting, because public sympathy for the children would obscure the squatting's underlying rationale. My own view is that it is difficult enough to prevail on an issue like squatting without using unsympathetic people as public examples. The most militant direct-action tactics, or those that blatantly seek to defy public attitudes, are not always the best.

If the family succeeds in winning public acceptance for squatting, less sympathetic individuals will benefit from greater opportunities for private occupation. Given the wide-ranging obstacles to achieving social change, activists should utilize tactics that build, rather than impede, public support for their cause.

Although the identity of direct-action participants can be critical, the public's sympathy toward disabled persons does not detract from the significance of their victory on Section 504. Public sympathy can only get a movement so far; on other key issues, such as the fight to make public buses more easily accessible for wheelchairs, the disability rights community lost. It is typically money, not sympathy, that attracts political support. Disability rights activists were not large contributors to political campaigns, whereas their opponents on Section 504, including prominent hospitals and educational institutions, had far more political clout. When this high-powered opposition won the support of Califano, did anybody outside the disabled community believe that Section 504 really would be signed unchanged? The tactical activism of leaders such as Kitty Cone and Judy Heumann brought a victory that never would have been achieved on public sympathy alone. The use of local direct action to win a national political fight is almost unheard of; yet this is precisely what disabled people did when the government tried to steal their rights.

8

Getting Started

AGENDA SETTING AND
ACTION PLANS

In a perfect world, readers of this book who wish to reexamine their organization's tactical approach could sit down with their fellow members, staff, board of directors, or friends and discuss the issue informally. Informal discussions can be the most effective method of persuasion and productive debate because they do not lead people to stake out hard positions or feel defensive about potential change. In most cases, however, social change activists working toward a common goal are not organized according to friendships or affinity groups. As a result, efforts to redirect organizational tactics, strategies, or priorities will typically take place within formal decisionmaking settings. These include retreats, board meetings, staff meetings, community forums, and organization- or constituency-wide conventions. An activist may have a great strategic analysis but still fail to enlist the support of the broader constituency necessary for the strategy to prevail. To avoid this problem, activists must equally understand the tactics necessary to reorient their organizations toward a more effective system for achieving their goals. Of the settings listed above, the open convention holds great but untapped potential for redirecting social change activism. The convention's democratic process, the "start from scratch" philosophy inherent in its structure and approach, and its ability to enable participants to understand the links between proactive strategies and goal achievement makes it a critical forum for enhancing tactical activism in both local and national movements for social change.

RETREATS AND BOARD MEETINGS

Many social change organizations formally adopt their policies and goals at annual retreats or board of directors meetings. The making of the most significant decisions in forums that generally exclude grassroots participation is an unfortunate product of the nonprofit organizational structure through which many social change movements operate. Anyone who has been connected to a nonprofit is familiar with the refrain: it is the board's job to set policy. Although many board members serving nonprofit groups recognize their inability to keep up with the organization's day-to-day work and lack the time or expertise to develop well-thought-out policy, the nonprofit organizational structure assigns them this task. Many boards focus on nuts-and-bolts decisions at their monthly meetings; discussions of systemic issues such as organizational mission or priorities are left to an annual meeting or retreat.

David Brower, who spent seventeen years as the executive director of the Sierra Club and sixteen years as a board member (he resumed board service in 1995), noted in his autobiography that retreats essentially are "executive sessions in which, at times, a few others are allowed to listen, and, at fewer times, to participate." Brower wryly observed how retreats are friendly sessions involving "good humor, even some good jokes, and all this can happen with minimum interference from the telephone—or the members, representatives (lower in echelon) of the club's grassroots."[1] Brower also observed how regular board meetings mirror the anti-democratic nature of retreats: "Some of the decisions made are voted upon in the open. But some are implicit decisions, governing subsequent action but not voted upon in the open. Votes in the open are pro forma. The audiences does not know what the pro and con arguments were." Brower did not become the leading conservationist of the post–World War II generation by fearing the open exchange of ideas. His opposition to policymaking via retreat and board meeting may sound heretical, but it reflects a commitment to an open process that is critical for achieving social change. Even nonprofit staff members who share misgivings about the board's formal control over policy often feel they can do nothing about the problem because of the laws governing nonprofit corporations. In truth, however, the board's legal control of social change organizations operating as nonprofits does not mean board members should set priorities or policies without extensive staff, constituency, or membership input.

Activists who belong to or are employed by nonprofit organizations should encourage their boards to forgo policymaking by retreat or board meeting. Instead, the board should be urged to participate in open membership meetings or conventions at which agendas and strategies for the constituency's needs can be established. Of course, the board will not be legally bound to accept these decisions for the organization, but most people who voluntarily serve on nonprofit boards do so out of a commitment to serve the constituency's interests. Having the board witness an open pro-and-con exchange of ideas among those on the front lines produces far greater results for the organization than getting the board bogged down in butcher paper and mission statements at a retreat. An alternative strategy when board participation at such events is impractical is to have the board agree to ratify the membership's or the constituency's decisions. Both approaches are preferable to confining policy and strategic discussions to the anti-democratic settings of the board meeting or retreat.

REDIRECTING TACTICS AND STRATEGIES THROUGH STAFF

In many nonprofit organizations, the board adopts policies recommended by staff members. Staff can therefore play a critical role in developing tactics and strategies. In most of the successful social change struggles discussed in the preceding chapters, staff members played a central role in developing proactive tactics for their constituencies to consider and, ultimately, implement. In the Tenderloin rezoning battle, the staff of local community organizations understood that the continued risk of development and gentrification necessitated a proactive response. Tenderloin residents had to discuss, approve, and mobilize behind the rezoning strategy for it to succeed, but the community could not have fulfilled its agenda without staff support. The anti-incinerator coalition, CAFE, also relied heavily on the tactical activism of organization staffers Rabbi David Niederman and Luis Garden Acosta. And Kitty Cone and Judy Heumann, staff members for the nonprofit Center for Independent Living in Berkeley, played a central strategic role in the fight by disability rights activists to preserve Section 504 unchanged. Staff members made the logistical arrangements enabling the sit-in to proceed indefinitely, the tactic most critical to the eventual success of their campaign. As in the other examples, the success of the sit-in depended entirely on the constituency's discussion of and agreement to the strategy.

Conversely, staff members who fail to apply the principles of tactical activism contribute to their constituencies' defeat. The "Big Green" initiative on California's November 1990 ballot (Chapter 4) was authored by staff members of prominent environmental organizations who failed to recognize the measure's strategic shortcomings. Memberships of the sponsoring organizations had no input into the text of the measure, which, with broader constituency involvement, might have been rewritten or not placed on the ballot. Valuable resources and volunteer energies were wasted in a campaign that resulted in a lopsided and foreseeable electoral defeat. Similarly, as discussed in Chapter 2, staff members can damage their constituencies' interests when they fail to create the appropriate relationship with elected officials. Individual members of organizations usually lack the media access and political clout to create problems for wayward politicians, who may also be skilled at convincing complaisant staff members to prevent membership protests.

Staff members' primacy in implementing tactical activism flows from several sources. First, organization staff members are often influential constituency leaders—witness the critical leadership roles played by Niederman, Garden Acosta, Heumann. ACT UP is a notable exception among social change organizations, as the group prides itself on its nonhierarchical, anti-leadership approach. The anti-nuclear "affinity" groups that spread throughout the country in the 1980s also successfully operated without staff leadership. It is not absolutely necessary for social change organizations to have paid staff in leadership roles. In practice, however, staff members often exert such a tremendous influence within their constituencies that reorienting an organization's approach requires their approval.

Staff members also are typically trusted and relied upon for tactical and strategic advice by their organization's constituency or membership. This reliance exists even in organizations such as the Gray Panthers, whose membership includes many seasoned political activists and whose staff people do not offer opinions on issues unless requested by the board. Many members relate to their organizations through interaction with staff, who become identified as the organization's voice. There is certainly nothing wrong with staff members' having significant influence over strategic decisions, because they often are hired for their experience as savvy tacticians. Unlike board members, staff members know the day-to-day realities of the organization and the social and political environment confronting it. However, staff members of social change organizations can prevent their group's success, either through incompetence or recalcitrance. Activists do not like to face up to staff incompetence, because people working for nonprofit salaries to further a good cause are presumed to be virtuous, hardworking, committed, and capable. Not all nonprofit staff members display these characteristics, however, and nonprofit executives, board members, and the membership or constituency they represent must be willing to replace staff members who cannot implement organizational decisions competently. An organization can have all the strategic and tactical wisdom in the world but fail to achieve its goals because of incompetent staff. Activists must always remember that social change organizations exist to serve a constituency or cause; they are not a charity for ineffective employees.

Staff recalcitrance, or the refusal to carry out organizational decisions, poses even greater obstacles to a group's success. Social change organization staff members play much the same role as the school district bureaucrats confronting the Neighbors for a New Fratney (Chapter 2)—they are responsible for implementing organizational decisions. Just as the school district's central office tried to hobble the new Fratney proposal through faulty implementation, staff of social change organizations can prevent agreed-upon tactics and strategies from achieving success. Staff can be fired for refusal to discharge group decisions, but, as with the school administrators, proving such insubordination is never easy. For example, a staff person's failure to make timely contact with a key constituency group can be seen as evidence of staff's personal opposition to working with the group, but it can easily be explained away as an innocent case of unsuccessful phone tag. Determining whether an impropriety took place would require a time-consuming inquiry that few groups want to undertake. Staff's role as implementer of decisions makes its support of new tactical and strategic approaches critical.

In social change organizations whose paid staff wield significant influence, the staff meeting can serve as a forum for reexamination of the organization's agenda, strategy, and tactics. Under ideal circumstances, a staff meeting can precipitate a lengthy analysis of the group's successes and of the tactics or strategies that could have been used to avoid its failures. For example, did the unsuccessful campaign arise as part of a proactive strategy for social change or as a defensive response to the opponent's agenda? Did the organization miss an opportunity to create a coalition with other groups that might have altered the outcome? Was the proper media strategy designed and implemented? Were direct actions effectively used? Could elected officials have been used differently to achieve the goal? By fully analyzing these and other issues raised in this book, the entire staff can avoid repeating tactical errors in the future. The process usually takes time and requires discomfiting assessments of what might have been, but the staff and organization emerge with a clearer understanding of how to achieve social change.

Unfortunately, some staff-dominated organizations have little patience for internal questioning of strategies and tactics. Social change organizations exhorting people to question authority often do not want this precept to apply to their own organizations. Rather than being heralded for their initiative, staff members who raise questions about strategic or tactical decisions may open themselves to criticism. They can be charged with second-guessing or with causing "internal problems" in the organization. Those who consistently dispute organizational strategies may well be divisive and their criticisms may entirely lack merit. Some staff members may even have perceptive critiques but not be in sync with what the membership and other staff members feel comfortable with implementing. For example, an activist who believes his or her organization needs to rely more on direct action and confrontation may be entirely correct; if the members are unwilling to take such steps, however, the activist must relent or risk alienation from the group. The fear of getting into trouble by legitimately questioning tactics impedes many committed staff members from raising such concerns. This reluctance is heightened by the scarcity of employment opportunities in progressive social change organizations; to avoid the risk of being fired (and of getting a bad reference for future prospective employers), many staff members prefer to watch impending failure quietly while seeking new employment. This explains why strategically weak organizations often have high staff turnover. Despite these risks, activists earning a living working for social change should not remain silent in the face of poor senior staff leadership. Doing so puts the interests of paid staff over the organization's progress and the interests of the organization over the needs of the constituency or movement it claims to represent. Further, staff members of social change organizations are presumably motivated by values and ideology rather than the assurance of a steady job. Devoting one's talent and abilities to tactically and strategically defective campaigns provides only the illusion of meaningful work; social change is not accomplished through exercises in self-deception.

COMMUNITY FORUMS

If opposition from fellow staff prevents the staff meeting from becoming a vehicle for reorienting tactics and strategies, activists can circumvent their colleagues by holding community forums as issues arise. For example, suppose a broad-based social change organization learns of plans for a toxic waste facility in a low-income, predominantly minority community. Assume that staff leaders have a history of supporting the elected officials responsible for the site decision and have been unwilling to attack them for consistently placing environmental hazards in poor, disenfranchised neighborhoods. A tactical activist working for this organization should not hesitate to work directly with the constituency to prevent the staff leadership from subordinating the group's agenda to the needs of "friendly" politicians. The approach can be as subtle as ensuring that members of the community have the opportunity publicly to discuss strategies before the organization decides its course of action. In this case, community forums may give the organization the constituency support necessary to create a new, nonsubservient relationship with the elected officials supporting the project. Although these forums are capable of being sidetracked or manipulated, it is usually obvious which speakers have credibility with the constituency. The constituency's prevailing sentiment is also usually clear. It is my experience that people who are not political insiders are most willing to support the proactive, confrontational tactics often necessary to prevail. Although a community forum does not guarantee that the best strategic approach is adopted, it does ensure that all alternatives are analyzed.

As a vehicle to steer an organization toward a more strategic approach, the community forum has obvious advantages over the board meeting, retreat, or staff meeting. The process is more democratic and provides for broad discussion and analysis of tactical considerations. Although most forums are unstructured, such meetings give people experience in evaluating proposals for addressing particular issues or problems. They also allow organization staff members to get their group on a successful track without the risks associated with raising strategic concerns at a staff meeting. Because the ideas emerge from the constituency rather than dissident co-workers, staff members opposed to the chosen approach are less likely to feel defensive. As a result, they work more diligently to fulfill the forum's decisions.

Community forums, however, have their limitations. Chief among them is their ability to give a misleading view of the constituency's priorities. We all know from our own experience that we attend events whose subject interests us and skip those that do not. Our attendance at a particular event does not necessarily mean that the subject matter is of great concern to our neighbors, constituency group, or fellow organization members. This is true regardless of the intensity of views expressed over the issue. Thus, a forum to discuss the proposed toxic dump might produce a spirited discussion resulting in the development of excellent strategies to defeat the project. But the forum would not establish that the issue is the constituency's chief concern or even of interest to a significant percentage of members. Sometimes a conclusion on this issue can be drawn from the size of the turnout or the presence (or absence) of particular community leaders. In many communities, however, there are so many forums on diverse issues that the relative importance of an issue cannot be determined by meeting attendance. Further, community forums generally focus on specific issues—such as crime, a planned library closure, or a proposed development project—and do not involve an assessment of the resources that should be spent on the issue within the constituency's or community's overall priorities. This narrow focus can result in a campaign that uses correct tactics but does so over an issue of little interest to most of the constituency. Squandering energy on nonpriority issues is not the way to meet a constituency's needs. Community forums have the potential to redirect tactics, strategies, or priorities, but they fall short as vehicles for broad debate leading to development and achievement of a successful, proactive agenda.

CONVENTIONS

The vehicle with the greatest promise for implementing tactical activism is an open convention. This vehicle, discussed in Chapter 4 in the initiative context, can effectively establish a constituency's priorities, particularly where no formal membership base or organizational structure exists or where there is a multiplicity of such organizations. The latter scenario requires a convention to unify the diverse groups behind a common agenda and strategic approach. Saul Alinsky pioneered the use of conventions to establish common agendas and strategies among already organized groups, and such conventions have become a trademark of contemporary organizations affiliated with Alinsky's Industrial Areas Foundation.

Where there is no undisputed broad-based membership organization representing a constituency, a convention is a critical vehicle for implementing tactical activism. The process can begin as follows. A group of activists learns of or identifies an issue that significantly affects their constituency. The activists may not have a specific issue in mind but rather may want to increase overall community empowerment. The initiators of the process can be staff members of organizations working with the constituency, influential residents, religious leaders, business owners, or representatives of other entities that have sufficient credibility to make the convention a meaningful reflection of a constituency's interest. This latter requirement is crucial, because a convention organized and attended by people lacking credibility among the affected constituency will not make an impact.

The convention is typically scheduled for a Saturday to ensure that the greatest number of people can attend. Notices are posted where members of the target constituency are likely to see them and distributed through the mailing lists of participating institutions or organizations. The agenda should focus either on the specific issue of obvious concern or on a broader theme of definite interest to the community. In the latter case, make it clear that an action plan will be developed at the event. People avoid nonstop talkathons masquerading as political action. If the convention publicity relies on broad messages such as "Our community deserves a fair share of resources," "We want jobs," or "Stop environmental racism," the event organizers must have concrete steps in mind to accomplish these goals.

The convention should be structured to funnel input into the creation of an achievable proactive agenda. Constituency members take the discussions leading to the approval of the agenda more seriously if they focus on realistic objectives than if people are simply throwing out pie-in-the-sky goals they could not possibly attain. Our Tenderloin tenant conventions in 1982 and 1983 demonstrated the importance of having achievable aims. The first event approved an agenda of specific goals and created an action plan that led to the fulfillment of nearly every goal. That convention's agenda served as a blueprint for an entire year of community activism. The second event focused on the more vague concept of a "Tenants' Bill of Rights." Though it was helpful to get tenants thinking about housing issues as civil rights, there was nowhere to go with the agenda after the event. Participants need not be discouraged from creating bills of rights or calling for action on such comprehensive goals as ending poverty, ending hunger, or promoting world peace; raising such issues helps the convention understand where and how their own action can or cannot produce success. But people facing serious problems in their lives are more interested in campaigns likely to make a concrete difference; low-income people are tired of being beaten by the system and want to participate in struggles that will benefit them and that they can win.

Although the process of creating a proactive agenda must include a general discussion of tactics, there may be insufficient time at the convention to develop an agenda and undertake a lengthy strategic dialogue. People may also become so excited about reaching agreement on a realizable action plan that they are psychologically unable to plunge then into tactical analysis. This practical reality can cause the type of divorce between agendas and tactics that I have criticized throughout this work. To avoid this division, the convention should resolve the larger tactical questions that are necessarily associated with the chosen agenda. Thus, if the convention decides that its top priority is the passage of a particular law, it must also reach agreement on the extent of pressure people are willing to exert on the applicable lawmakers. If half the convention is willing to use confrontational direct action against any lawmaker opposing the law whereas the other half is unwilling to wage all-out war on lawmakers over the issue, then no real agreement on the agenda may exist. Social change activists should not start a campaign in which people are clearly divided over tactics.

It could be argued that a campaign can be launched despite these tactical divisions, because a nonconfrontational approach might be able to achieve the group's goals. Such a position is indicative of tactical recklessness. Suppose that midway in the struggle for the law's passage a roadblock emerges that cannot be hurdled without direct action. Those who opposed using such tactics would give up the fight, whereas those eager to proceed would be weakened by the division of their base. The end result, as many activists know, is not simply a crushing defeat; it is defeat accompanied by dissension and recrimination. The groups unified at the convention vow never again to work together, and their once-promising agenda lies in tatters. Weighed against this dangerous but likely scenario is the remote prospect that no roadblocks or tactical disputes emerge, enabling the organization to fulfill its agenda. This raises the question: does the ultimate success of a strategy vindicate its use? The answer is a resounding no. Even the most foolish strategies can result in success. Does the fact that somebody always wins the lottery mean that buying a ticket is a good strategy? Unfortunately, the adverse consequences of reckless social change tactics are not as trivial as the loss of a few dollars playing Lotto. Campaigns plagued by strong divisions over tactics at the outset should not proceed in the hope that prompt success will prevent the dispute from emerging.

Tactical divisions can readily be avoided. In the example of a constituency that seeks the passage of a law, the convention should not discuss the goal in isolation. Participants must discuss the tactics necessary to win a legislative campaign; if constituents are unwilling to resort to these tactics, then a different agenda should be selected. Agreement on the central tactical thrust does not forestall subsequent disputes over details or the type of response that should be made to the opposition's tactics. Disputes of this type, however, do not undermine the assumptions people held when they voted to work on behalf of the agenda. Such tactical debates assist the decisionmaking process and are not divisive. Once the convention has reached agreement on means and ends, discussion of how to implement convention decisions can be left for subsequent meetings. Committees address specific areas, and some form of steering committee replaces the full convention as the ultimate decisionmaking body. The committee can establish formal approval procedures or, preferably, will require each action to have the consent of every key constituency group. This latter approach was successfully used by such groups as the Tenderloin's Luxury Hotel Task Force (Chapter 1), by the Community Alliance For the Environment (Chapter 3), and by the American Coalition of Citizens with Disabilities (Chapter 7). The convention's public agreement on means and ends establishes the playing rules at the outset, endowing the campaign with a sense of trust.

Conventions have an extraordinary ability to get unaffiliated individuals involved in social change. In August 1992 the Tenderloin Housing Clinic sponsored an event for low-income tenants aptly described by the media as a "poor people's convention." Participants included some people affiliated with organizations, but most came because they saw a meeting notice on the street or in the lobby of their residential hotel. Nearly everyone attending either lived on a fixed income, was homeless, or had a low income (or no income at all). Most had no previous experience with the process of establishing agendas and strategies for social change. The sight of a large group of people who were primarily strangers to one another arguing openly about strategies, tactics, and goals was amazing to behold. Television news coverage favorably compared the passion and principle in our convention's speeches to those witnessed earlier in the year at the Democratic and Republican national conventions. This social phenomenon also was seen in a previous, all-day event for low-income tenants in a particular neighborhood. The majority of the goals agreed upon during these all-day conventions were acted upon and fulfilled. The action agenda adopted by the conventions achieved almost biblical status with some participants; people felt they should not work on other issues until the convention's action plan was completely fulfilled. Undoubtedly, the convention process successfully channeled diffuse grievances into a proactive and realizable agenda for progressive social change.

Conventions have their limitations. They are not a permanent substitute for an ongoing social change organization that operates proactively and with tactical know-how. The fulfillment of the convention's agenda can leave the future direction unclear; should another convention be scheduled, or should the people who actively worked to implement the first convention's agenda decide what, if any, future efforts to take? The convention strategy may result in the formation of a new activist organization, which will then set its own agenda, or it may simply resolve certain organization or constituency problems. The unaffiliated people who become active through conventions are primarily interested in problem solving, not organization building. Some unaffiliated people become motivated to join existing organizations, but a convention not expressly set up to create a new organization is unlikely to achieve this goal. If a new entity must be formed to ensure continued participation after the convention goals are achieved, this agenda should be openly discussed and approved at the initial event.

There is also the question of convention size. A convention works best with a few hundred participants. If more than a thousand people must attend, organizers may have to replace direct democracy with representative democracy. It simply can be too difficult to make individual participants feel important to the decisionmaking process when they are sitting with a thousand other people in a large hall. Some organizations, however, can successfully manage such events, which require a significant amount of volunteer or staff coordination. Large events may also require a homogeneous constituency that has discussed the proposed agenda, strategies, and tactics ahead of time in smaller groups. It is quite a difficult task to bring together more than 1,000 diverse and primarily unconnected individuals to develop specifically achievable agendas and agree upon tactics in the course of a one-day event. Events that are too large must sacrifice critical analysis to ensure that everyone has had a chance to put a proposal on butcher paper or a video screen. As a result, the meeting reaches "agreement" on a list of laudatory "priorities"—such as "supporting more affordable housing" or "enhancing employment opportunities"—that may not enable the constituency to a) engage in specific work toward goals that are b) reasonably achievable through c) proactive tactics and strategies d) accepted by the group.

A constituency that can draw more than 1,000 people to a convention probably includes representatives of social service or advocacy organizations. Such constituents are better off engaging in internal group discussions of agendas and tactics, then appointing representatives to a smaller, more manageable convention. The choice is between having a large crowd attend an event that primarily serves to ratify individual group decisions or a smaller audience of organizational representatives that itself engages in the tortuous but necessary discussions on agendas and tactics. Either approach is effective, and the correct choice depends on the nature of the constituency.

NATIONAL CONSTITUENCY CONVENTIONS

Conventions have proven to be successful in reorienting, uniting, and reinvigorating local constituencies toward more effective means of achieving social change. Can they also play this role at the national level? I believe they can. Social change activists got a taste of the potential tactical value of national constituency conventions during the Reverend Benjamin Chavis, Jr.'s term as executive director of the National Association for the Advancement of Colored People (NAACP). The mainstream media did such an effective job of confusing the public over Chavis' agenda, however, that the larger strategic meaning of his efforts has been lost. Prior to his selection to lead the NAACP, Chavis was best known as a member of the Wilmington 10, a group of African-American activists whose wrongful imprisonment in 1972 for setting fire to a grocery store during racial strife in Wilmington, North Carolina, became a national and international scandal. After a federal appeals court ruling freed Chavis from prison in 1980, he became executive director of the Commission for Racial Justice, a project of the United Church of Christ. There he focused on the issue of environmental racism, helping to organize the First National People of Color Environmental Leadership Summit in October 1991 to unify activists involved in environmental justice campaigns. Chavis's long record of activism and success as a bridge builder made him a top candidate to fill the vacancy at the head of the NAACP in 1993. His main competitor was the Reverend Jesse

Jackson. The NAACP apparently feared that Jackson would be too controversial or would use the organization for his own purposes; both charges were eventually leveled at Chavis.

Chavis became head of the NAACP in April 1993, at a time when the organization was widely viewed as irrelevant by the constituency it claimed to represent. A 1993 *Detroit News and Free Press* poll found that most blacks viewed the NAACP as "out of touch" with their main concerns.[2] Although the NAACP had been seen as irrelevant for years prior to 1993, it was not until Chavis's selection that the traditionally staid organization took specific action to reorient its approach. Because Chavis had openly campaigned for his position, vowing to revitalize the organization, his selection appeared to reflect the NAACP's openness to new agendas, tactics, and strategies. Chavis, the perfect model of a tactical activist, seemed capable of redirecting the cautious organization toward a more productive approach to social change activism.

Chavis faced a staggering challenge. The conditions of African-Americans living in urban areas worsened dramatically in the 1980s. By 1993 African-American neighborhoods were beset by high unemployment, poverty, record high rates of impoverished single-parent families, and the drug abuse and crime that flow from these conditions. African-American men were entering prison in unprecedented numbers, gang violence was epidemic, and the federal government had abandoned what small commitment it once had to funding programs that would improve the lives of African-Americans living in urban neighborhoods. Chavis did have the "benefit" of a newly elected Democratic president, but Bill Clinton abandoned his urban assistance package before Chavis had a chance to get started. Nor could the presence of forty African-American congress members stave off the prompt defeat of what little economic stimulus Clinton sought to direct toward low-income African-American communities.

In the face of these tremendous obstacles, Chavis did something historic: he initiated contact with all of the diverse strands within the African-American community. Rather than rounding up only the usual suspects, Chavis brought the outcasts and untouchables of the community into the process. These included such groups as the "street gang truce" movement, which, whether the general public likes it or not, plays a major role in some African-American communities, particularly among young people.[3] (The current and former gang members who are publicly advocating an end to inner-city gang warfare often have criminal records, and law enforcement is especially critical of their efforts.) Chavis also met with African-American intellectual radicals, whose forefather,

W.E.B. DuBois, had been ousted from the NAACP nearly fifty years earlier. Chavis even brought the Nation of Islam into his orbit, thus attempting to link the long-antagonistic factions of the civil rights movement: the integrationists and the nationalists. This connection posed
Chavis's greatest risk, as many people feel the anti-Semitism, homophobia, and staunchly patriarchal vision of the Nation of Islam's leader, Louis
Farrakhan, undermines whatever positive benefits his organization has
brought to urban low-income African-American neighborhoods. Although
media attention focused on Chavis's outreach to gangs and the Nation of
Islam, Chavis also led the NAACP into strong public support for gay
rights. He also announced plans to work more closely with Latino and
Asian communities, so that the National Association for the Advancement
of Colored People would, in fact, include all "people of color."[4]

After reaching out to every corner of the African-American community and beyond, Chavis needed a vehicle to get these diverse groups behind an agreed-upon action plan. The answer: a national convention.
Dubbed the "African-American Leadership Summit," the convention
brought representatives of all of the factions of the African-American
community to Baltimore on June 12, 1994. Chavis intended for the first
summit to address the basic issues unifying all groups, with a second
event in August to develop an agreed-upon agenda and action plan. The
convention could have been seen as the most significant effort in more
than two decades to address the ongoing crisis in the African-American
community. Editorials could have praised Chavis for his willingness to
bring together longtime adversaries to resolve problems affecting Americans of all races. The NAACP could have been seen as the driving force
behind efforts to reignite a national commitment to address inner-city
concerns. Political conservatives forever preaching self-help to African-
Americans could have favorably interpreted Chavis's convention as a victory for community introspection over demands for more direct government aid. However, none of these potential angles interested the
mainstream press. For the national media, controlled by white editors
and boasting few African-American reporters, there was only one angle
on Chavis's summit: the invitation of Farrakhan. The basic theme was
that Chavis was leading a distinguished organization into the gutter by
associating with an outspoken, gay-bashing, white-hating anti-Semite.
The media were careful to quote African-Americans to support their
analysis, protecting themselves against claims that their slant reflected
white fears of African-American unity. Thus, Michael Myers, a former
NAACP assistant director, became a minor celebrity for claiming that

the NAACP had been "hijacked by black nationalist radicals."[5] Myers became a popular media counterpoint to Chavis, used to show mainstream African-American opposition to the NAACP's new approach. Denton Watson, a former NAACP public relations director, echoed Myers, arguing that Chavis was transforming the organization into a "separatist movement that will only further confuse youths and strengthen their enemies."[6]

Although African-American leaders with mainstream media acceptance, such as Cornel West, attended the convention and defended Chavis's "big tent" approach, their views were overshadowed by the publicity and street protests surrounding Farrakhan. Chavis attempted to distinguish between inviting a constituency group to the table and agreeing with its views, but the media were not interested in any explanation for Farrakhan. The media also were unwilling to examine the strategic need for the convention to be all-inclusive rather than exclusionary.

The disputes over Farrakhan made Chavis's summit a springboard for public controversy rather than a buildup to the second, more focused event. Because of Chavis's remarkable success at obtaining broad and diverse representation at the convention, however, the NAACP accomplished its initial goal. Prior to the event, few would have believed that a conservative group like the NAACP could serve as the unifying agent for the African-American community. Drawing broad attendance at one event is not the same as achieving unity, but Chavis's convention strategy clearly set the process in motion. Those present at the summit, along with NAACP members, strongly supported Chavis's approach.[7] He and his supporters were undaunted by the Farrakhan controversy, and Chavis's strategy was affirmed at the NAACP's annual conference, held a month after the summit. This show of support, however, may well have represented the proverbial "vote of confidence" often given to leaders just before they are fired. Shortly after the NAACP annual meeting, Chavis was charged with committing $332,400 in organization funds to settle a sexual harassment complaint brought against him. Chavis's explanation for the arrangement was vague and contradictory, and his expenditure of association funds to settle a personal matter without board knowledge or approval was indefensible. Key financial backers of the NAACP, such as the Ford Foundation, Mobil Oil, General Motors, and Philip Morris, now had the perfect excuse for conditioning future funding on his termination. These groups needed a way to find a nonpolitical motive for demanding Chavis's resignation, and his financial malfeasance provided this opening.

The NAACP voted to fire Chavis at an emergency board meeting on

August 20, 1994, and immediately canceled the second African-American Leadership Summit, scheduled to begin the next day. Little attention was paid to the relationship between these two decisions. If Chavis was fired for financial malfeasance and not for his political tactics, then the NAACP should have proceeded with the second summit. If Chavis was essential to the event, he could have been fired upon its closure. The NAACP's summary and unilateral end to a year-long process of creating a blueprint for African-American unity and action renewed skepticism about its true commitment to this difficult goal. Chavis's pursuit of black "operational unity" through the convention process could not overcome the NAACP's longstanding hostility to black nationalism.

Following his dismissal, Chavis sought to continue the summit process by creating the National African-American Leadership Summit as an independent organization. He then developed an alliance with Farrakhan, who had raised the idea of a million-man march during the June 1994 Summit. Chavis joined with Farrakhan to hold summits in August and December 1994 and June 1995 to advance this goal. While these summits were ignored by the NAACP, mainstream media, and prominent elected officials, such luminaries as Jesse Jackson and Cornel West continued their participation, and grassroots momentum for the march steadily built.[8]

On October 16, 1995, the summit process culminated in the historic Million Man March. Although the march included nearly all of the summit's original constituency groups, the mainstream media focused primarily on Farrakhan's influence on the event. The Nation of Islam leader did nothing to squelch this perception, but participants emphasized the march's expression of racial pride and solidarity rather than Farrakhan's rhetoric.

Benjamin Chavis's numerous faults—his sexual harassment scandal, his alliance with corporations seeking to undermine Superfund environmental laws, his role in creating or ignoring the NAACP's financial problems, and his attempt to blame Jews and Jewish organizations for his discharge from the NAACP—should not cause activists to dismiss his diligent adherence to a strategic principle for obtaining a potential unity among the black community's historically divergent integrationist and nationalist strands. It is clear that Chavis successfully used the convention process to tap into the longstanding desire for unity and social change activism among African-Americans who wanted to repair the breakdown in their community life.

It remains to be seen whether post-march events lead to the creation of a broad-based agenda that unifies all African-American constituencies (including women, who were excluded from the march). Much will be determined by Farrakhan's willingness to relinquish the Nation of Islam's socially and morally unacceptable perspectives in favor of an inclusive, progressive African-American agenda. The convention strategy, at a minimum, has reawakened a vital public debate about the strategies and tactics necessary to revive African-American communities. Where this dialogue leads will reveal much about the future of national social change activism in the years ahead.

THE CASE FOR A NATIONAL ENVIRONMENTAL CONVENTION

One of the exciting features of the African-American summit was the prospect that a new, unified, and strategic assault on the terrible problems confronting urban African-American communities would emerge. Activists who diligently, democratically, and in good faith try to make positive things happen are preferable to those who only complain about the status quo. Environmental activists could also benefit from a convention strategy. Although environmental hazards threaten the health and safety of millions of Americans, polls taken in 1994 found that fewer than 5 percent of Americans see such problems as among the country's most pressing.[9] Membership in national environmental organizations declined sharply in 1994, a trend that only reversed in response to unprecedented attacks on environmental protection by the newly ascendant Republican Congress. Although the loss of "paper" members does not necessarily translate into a decline in activism, environmentalists' national political failures during a period of Democratic Party control of Congress and the presidency has led many to conclude that national environmental politics desperately needs an overhaul. The question "Who lost the environment?" has become today's progressive activist version of the "Who lost China?" debate that filled right-wing periodicals for decades.

Many grassroots environmental groups have already recognized the value of a national convention process. In October 1991 in Washington, D.C., environmental justice groups held the First National People of Color Environmental Leadership Summit. At the conference more than 600 activists from a diverse range of ethnic groups and geographical areas adopted "Principles of Environmental Justice" to guide their burgeoning movement.[10] A regional follow-up event held by the Southern Organizing Conference for Social and Economic Justice in December 1992 brought together more than 1,500 people from eight southern states. Local groups and Greenpeace organized the event. In addition, Lois Gibbs's Citizens Clearinghouse for Hazardous Wastes (CCHW) regularly holds national conferences for its network of more than 7,000 grassroots groups. The CCHW's tenth anniversary convention in May 1993 in Washington, D.C., was highlighted by the arrival of the Greenpeace "Putting People First" bus tour drawing attention to the Clinton administration's flip-flop on the East Liverpool incinerator (Chapter 2).

These conventions were primarily designed for activist networking rather than as vehicles for bringing new people into environmental organizations. As essential as these types of events are, they do not provide the high-profile publicity burst necessary to create a national environmental agenda capable of capturing the public's focus. Nor are such events designed to mobilize unaffiliated environmentalists behind a national environmental campaign. These successful precedents are a good sign, though, that larger conventions involving both grassroots activists and mainstream groups could produce positive results.

Distrust between local grassroots and national mainstream environmental organizations has become so strong over some issues that trying to assemble everyone in one convention may seem a fanciful and even dangerous notion. The political, cultural, racial, class, and geographical divisions among people who call themselves environmentalists may also forestall the creation of a common environmental agenda. Nevertheless, the idea of a national environmental convention is worth exploring in what is clearly an untenable status quo. As the African-American summit showed, the convention process entails a commitment to open and democratic decisionmaking that can encourage participation and the creation of an agenda and action plan. Local grassroots organizations would have an opportunity to confirm their claims that they, and not the national groups, best reflect the rank-and-file position on issues. A convention would also increase local activist control over national environmental issues. Some national organizations may balk at an event that gives local groups equal power over strategic decisionmaking and establishing national environmental priorities. Their attendance is not required, however, because a convention's credibility does not depend on the presence of organizations that are not effective advocates of progressive environmental change.

A national convention could accomplish several goals. First, it could help create a specific national environmental agenda. Most of the public does not really understand what environmentalists want at the national level. Confusion over the specifics of environmentalists' demands weakens political accountability; it is not always clear to the public when a betrayal has occurred. For example, even people sympathetic to the environmentalist position on the spotted owl would have had a difficult time learning the "true" pro-environment position (if one existed). Such a position could have become widely known through adoption by a convention. If the convention voted that the only pro-environment position on the spotted owl was a total ban on harvesting in the owl's habitat, politicians who supported weaker restrictions would be seen as opposing rather than supporting environmentalists. This clarity would still not prevent groups like the Wilderness Society from hailing weaker restrictions as a great environmental victory, but the public would know (and sympathetic media would point out) that the weaker restrictions violate the national environmental platform. The frequent charge of a mainstream sellout on environmental issues would have greater resonance if the public could clearly recognize that the "victory" was inconsistent with the democratically adopted, majority environmentalist position.

The convention's creation of a specific national environmental agenda would also build grassroots activism around national environmental issues. Many mainstream environmental organizations do little to encourage individual involvement in national campaigns. Some critics have attributed this complacency to national groups' fear of having to deal with a real constituency base that could hold them accountable. A more charitable explanation is that leaders of such organizations do not know how to mobilize people around national issues. Local organizations attract activist participation because stopping an incinerator or toxic dump directly affects area residents' own lives. Federal environmental legislation and administrative action also directly impact people's lives, but these issues lack the sense of imminent crisis that typifies local campaigns. Grassroots environmentalists mobilize around specific action agendas; mobilizing people on national issues requires a specific national agenda. Thus, Greenpeace's effort to link local activists in a national campaign against waste incinerators would greatly benefit from a national convention that adopted this issue as part of its specific agenda. Democratic approval of this agenda would no doubt stimulate the participation of people who do not live near incinerators but who are concerned about the cause. As it stands now, Greenpeace's nationwide campaign is seen as the goal of one organization rather than the product of a national consensus-building process.

A convention would also end the terrible underutilization of environmental activist energy. Unfortunately, some environmental leaders suffer from the media-fed illusion that people today do not really want to become passionately involved in campaigns for social, economic, or environmental justice. For example, in late 1994 a representative of the National Resources Defense Council explained declining environmental activism by noting that people recycle or buy "green" products and "no doubt feel they are doing their bit and don't need to do any more."[11] This viewpoint is interesting for two reasons. First, the only activity the NRDC and similar groups ask of people is that they write a check; it is the decline in this sort of "activism" that is blamed on recycling. Second, community organizers know that people who have already shown a willingness to do something are the best candidates to take on additional tasks. As the saying goes, "If you want something done, give the task to a busy person." Some people's activism begins and ends with recycling; but many others would like to do more but do not know where to begin. The millions of people who now recycle could well be a national base for enhanced environmental activism.

Constituencies cannot be effectively mobilized when there is no clearcut issue, cause, or agenda to mobilize around. Likewise, people do not know how to hold organizations accountable when they have no clear idea of the organizations' specific goals. When they are confused about issues or worry that they might be boondoggled, people have little enthusiasm for mobilizing or contributing money. People for the Ethical Treatment of Animals (PETA), the national animal rights group, illustrates the benefits of having a clear-cut organizational agenda. PETA built a tremendous grassroots base at the same time that environmental organizations experienced a decline in support. The sentiments underlying animal rights advocacy are not so distant from those of environmentalism, and the two movements have many opponents in common. Why has PETA succeeded where environmental groups have faltered?

PETA's goal, to prevent abuse of animals in any setting, is large and simply stated, but the organization gives its members a wide variety of specific ways to get involved. PETA's bimonthly publication, "Animal Times," is chock-full of specific ways for people to help animals. The actions are listed under the heading, "You're Making a Difference if You . . . ." Suggestions range from calling corporate chiefs to protesting traveling animal acts. Most of the targets are national or even international. PETA understands—as the founders of ACT UP understood—that people want to have an impact and manages to demonstrate to its members month after month how they can do so. Environmentalists have largely failed at this tactic. Although there are at least "50 Ways to Save the Earth," as a recent best-selling book notes, environmentalists have not been nearly as successful as PETA in harnessing and channeling activist energy, in part because they have not developed a means for measuring progress toward specific goals. A few years ago, PETA had the aim of getting cosmetics labeled "cruelty-free" when their development involved no animal testing. Thanks to the actions and support of its members, the group succeeded. PETA's constituents could thus point with pride to a clear victory on a well-defined national issue. By contrast, environmental goals are diffuse, largely unprioritized, and often formed without widespread consensus. Many of those seeking to save the earth understand the urgent need for environmental activism but are playing in an orchestra with no conductor, not even an agreed-upon score. To use another analogy: the difference between PETA's approach and that of environmentalists is like the difference between organizing firefighters into a line to stop a fire at a certain point, on the one hand, and randomly sending out individuals with buckets to dump wherever they see flames, on the other. The first action is purposeful and orchestrated; the second, hit-or-miss and, ultimately, demoralizing.

Environmental organizations can (and sometimes do) use PETA's mobilization tactics without participating in a national convention, but a convention represents the best means for creating an agenda in support of which nationwide, purposeful, and orchestrated activism could occur. People want to do more to protect the environment and are awaiting the call. The convention would represent a symbolic break from the past and send a signal that a national mobilization on an agreed-upon political agenda was about to begin. This was one of the purposes of the original Earth Day; however, the lack of a specific political agenda at Earth Day's twentieth anniversary celebration in 1990 allowed it to become a milestone in the corporate appropriation of environmental issues.

A national environmental convention would require the following elements. First, a national leader having the type of stature in the environmental community that Ralph Nader holds among consumer advocates or Jesse Jackson has among African-Americans would have to serve the "convener" role (played by Chavis for the African-American summit). Second, funding from a national foundation or wealthy individual unaffiliated with any particular "agenda" must be obtained to stage the event, to cover travel and lodging costs for grassroots activists, and to do advance planning. Once the convention begins and an agenda and action-plan are agreed upon, the participants will have to decide who is responsible for ensuring its implementation. The convention may decide to create a new national organization to work toward achievement of the convention agenda and to represent grassroots activists in the Washington political arena. Lois Gibbs of the Citizens Clearinghouse on Hazardous Wastes, among others, has recognized the need for such an entity. Alternatively, the convention could set up a steering or implementation committee, bodies that neighborhood conventions have used successfully. The entity created, whatever form it takes, must understand how to mobilize the nation behind a specific environmental agenda.

The convention's success would also require environmental groups to reassess their emphasis on organizational sovereignty. The environmental movement comprises small and large organizations that typically seek to differentiate themselves from one another. Those with paid staff are particularly attentive to creating a market niche so they can attract funds and resources. A national convention transcends individual organizations. Its decision to emphasize a particular issue could thus be threatening to organizations that work on unrelated matters or that prefer to exercise control over the chosen issue in the manner that they, and not the convention, see fit. Because many environmental groups are nonprofit corporations, deviation from the convention decisions could be rationalized as a board of directors decision. National organizations might also fear that empowering local groups could reduce their influence and even render them irrelevant. Despite these concerns, environmentalists must focus on advancing *issues*, not organizations. A convention that emphasizes unity over differentiation would itself further the cause.

As problematic as a national environmental convention appears, even the worst-case scenario for such an event may well be preferable to the status quo. A televised broadcast of a national environmental convention would at least put environmental issues in the spotlight. Such attention might inspire the next generation of environmental leaders and activists to get involved. The event would have value even it got bogged down in procedural fights, policy disputes, or boring speeches; both the public and members of environmental organizations would see clearly how far the once-ascendant environmental cause has deteriorated. A national convention could provide the spark necessary to redirect environmental activism toward a more confrontational, constituency-led, and strategic approach that would lead to victory rather than defeat in the national arena. Modern American environmentalism began at the start of the twentieth century. The twenty-first century should mark the resurgence, not the demise, of environmentalists' political power.

PROCEEDING PROACTIVELY

There is no simple formula for achieving progressive social change. Tactics that have regularly proven successful in a particular context are not guaranteed to work under other circumstances; even objectively foolish strategies have achieved their desired ends. Tactical activists must therefore be open to creativity, innovation, and provocative, controversial, or even dubious ideas. Remaining silent for fear of being laughed at or criticized is not the path to progressive change. The activists portrayed in this work have all been attacked by the media, politicians, or even traditional allies for their commitment to achieving their agendas. Tactical activism is not for those overly sensitive or easily intimidated.

For more than two decades, right-wing Republicans have offered a barrage of national blueprints for change. Although their prescriptions largely seek a return to the policies that governed the pre–New Deal, pre–Great Society America, the mere existence of a seemingly comprehensive program gives the right-wing agenda a scholarly patina not justified by its content. A public looking for answers turns to the only plan on the table; thus does a hodgepodge of three decades of right-wing proposals stapled together become a "Contract with America" and the chief focus of national political discussion for 1995. Social change activists have succeeded at the local level by creating positive agendas, but there has not been a progressive agenda-setter in the White House since Franklin Delano Roosevelt, the most popular president of this century. It has been said that Roosevelt's greatest success as president lay not in the ultimate success of the programs he designed. Rather, what made him the most admired president of this century was his constant experimentation, his development and implementation of plans and agendas for social change, his instilling of confidence that if one tactic did not work, something else would, and his attitude that he would never give up the fight. The Roosevelt generation developed faith in the government's ability to solve problems even though FDR's program as a whole never achieved significant economic results. Today's progressive political constituencies are not in straits as dire as those of the Depression, but the obstacles to social and economic justice, and to a fairer distribution of wealth, may be even more powerful today than they were in the Roosevelt era. Not the least of these obstacles is a national Democratic Party with no clear agenda. By proceeding proactively and consciously analyzing what tactics and strategies can best advance our goals, social change activists can inspire, mobilize, and ultimately move public sentiment in a progressive direction.

9

Conclusion

**ACTIVISM FOR THE
TWENTY-FIRST CENTURY**

In Frank Capra's classic film, *It's a Wonderful Life,* Jimmy Stewart plays George Bailey, a character who comes to feel he has accomplished nothing in life and stands over a bridge contemplating suicide. In the nick of time, an angel appears and shows him how poorly his town and family would have fared had he never been born. Stewart, realizing that he has made a positive impact on his world, renews his spirit and embraces life in a finale that has brought tears to viewers for generations.

One does not have to accept fully the premises of Frank Capra to recognize that far too many activists have become distraught George Baileys bemoaning their perceived inability to make a difference in the world. I have tried to dispel this attitude by showing how activists can prevail in their campaigns by using specific tactics and strategies. Without tactical activism, the Brooklyn Navy Yard incinerator would be operational, federal AIDS funding would continue to be flagrantly misused, and the Fratney School would have been converted to a teacher training center instead of a multicultural bilingual school. The opposition's success in any of these struggles would have lent further credence to the notion that the activists ran aground against insurmountable barriers to social change.

Of course, activists will often fail regardless of the tactics or strategies used. But a campaign that has maximized its potential for success should not be castigated because of a disappointing outcome. Activists who create proactive agendas, establish fear-and-loathing relationships with elected officials, seek coalitions with ideologically diverse constituencies when necessary, strive to align the media with their cause, and understand how to use direct action and the courts have succeeded regardless of the results they achieve. Tactical activism maximizes the potential for victory; it does not guarantee success.

The Republican Party's seizure of Congress following the November 1994 elections led many progressives to despair about the future; one gets the sense that many are lining up next to George Bailey on the bridge. But people whose energy and talent can enhance local, state, and national struggles for social change must not now abandon their dreams. As the late, legendary folksinger Lee Hays put it, following the election of Ronald Reagan and a Republican Senate majority in 1980, "I've had kidney stones, and I know this, too, will pass."

The 1980s did pass, but the decade's legacy continues to haunt social activism. In essence, the Reagan-Bush years led progressive constituencies to seek political support by emphasizing the extremism of their opponents' agenda rather than the merits of their own. Rather than offer alternative blueprints for society or use strategies and tactics necessary to expand the constituency base for progressive reform, activists focused on the anti-environmental ravings of Secretary of the Interior James Watt, the proposed definition of ketchup as a vegetable for school lunches, and the platform of Jerry Falwell's Moral Majority. This strategy enabled the Democratic Party to achieve short-term goals, but it did not increase political support for an agenda that went beyond defending the status quo. When this essentially reactive approach helped elect a Democratic president and Congress in 1992, the fatal flaw of organizing around anti-Republicanism became clear. Neither the Clinton administration nor the Democratic-controlled Congress saw the election as mandate for implementing a progressive agenda, and both increasingly took issue with the demands of the progressive constituencies whose grassroots efforts were responsible for the 1992 results. Bill Clinton took pains to distance himself from social change activists and their organizations; it soon became clear that the people to be put first by Clinton were not those who actively worked in his campaign. Without a Republican bogeyman, the Democratic president and Congress had no agenda or affirmative message to offer voters in the next election; thus was the opening created for the 1994 Republican sweep.

Activists and their constituencies at the local, state, and national levels do not need to be told what issues should constitute their agendas. Social change advocates have argued for years for the need to redirect military spending to social needs, increase aid to cities, improve public transit, enact universal health care, strengthen penalties against violators of clean air and water laws, require public financing to ensure poor women's right to abortions, impose a higher minimum wage, mandate public campaign financing, and carry out a whole laundry list of other proposals. The failure to implement them so far does not mean they should be abandoned. Portions of the right-wing agenda have been pushed consistently for more than fifty years and remain unrealized; progressives often act as if their failure to initially prevail requires a whole new agenda rather than new strategies and tactics to mobilize broader support.

Social change activists' constant search for new ideas, proposals, and agendas could well be a reflection of fertile and creative minds. It could also signal a pervasive insecurity spawned by a media culture that views attacks on New Deal programs as "innovative" but labels proposals for public investment in human needs as a return to the failed "tax-and-spend" policies of the past. Right-wing activists do not get intimidated by media depictions of their issues, and their steadfastness has brought many issues once thought untenable—from the elimination of welfare to the abolition of HUD—into the political mainstream. Progressive activists must also maintain confidence in their social prescriptions and not follow every election defeat with a rethinking of their basic goals. Activists and their constituencies know what policies must be pursued to increase social and economic justice; patience, and a renewed focus on strategies and tactics for broadening support for these policies, have been missing.

I have tried to demonstrate that progressive change is won by activists and their constituencies, not simply by elected officials. Those who believe in social change must fully accept their own leadership role in the process and recognize that neither politicians nor political parties are the prime movers of progressive change.

Winning political power is like building a field of dreams: if activists and their constituencies build a strategically sound campaign or movement for social change, the elected officials will come. The Democratic Party wanted nothing to do with the civil rights movement for nearly a decade after Rosa Parks's refusal to change seats; the creation of the movement was a necessary prerequisite before politicians gave their support.

The character of George Bailey was created more than a decade before the famous bus ride of Rosa Parks. Had Bailey known the ramifications of Parks's act, he might never have doubted the value of his own life. Today's activists must also recognize that their participation in public life will make a critical difference in their world. By acting proactively and with tactical and strategic wisdom, social change activists can bring a degree of social and economic justice to the next century that has for too long been deferred.

Notes

CHAPTER 1

1. The VISTA program became an early target of the incoming Reagan administration transition team's plan to "defund the left." By 1982, VISTA-funded community-based organizing for social change had been nearly eliminated.

2. In the late 1970s, when the city briefly had district elections, the Tenderloin was split over two districts, with no progressives objecting. In 1987, when progressives attempted to restore district elections, there was a consensus that the Tenderloin should not be split, because it was seen as a distinct neighborhood.

3. *San Francisco Chronicle*, "The Squeeze" and "Tenderloin Tango," February 4–5, 1981.

4. Tactical use of ballot initiatives is further discussed in Chapter 4.

5. Alice Baum and Donald Burnes, *A Nation in Denial* (Boulder, Colo.: Westview Press, 1993), pp. 82, 170, 29, 129, and 130.

6. Ibid., p. 135. Christopher Jencks, who concedes that everything he knows about homelessness has come from reading books, also fails to appreciate the obvious link between rising rents and homelessness (see acknowledgments, pp. 85–89, in Jencks's *The Homeless*, Cambridge, Mass.: Harvard University Press, 1994).

7. *A Nation in Denial*, pp. 186–187. Contrary to the authors' claims, thousands of formerly homeless persons now live in SROs rehabilitated and upgraded through funds earmarked for the homeless.

8. Baum and Burns, *A Nation in Denial*, pp. 186–187.

9. *San Francisco Chronicle*, March 11, 1994, "Networks Boost Crime News," p. C18.

10. Janine Jackson and Jim Naureckas, "Crime Contradictions: U.S. News Illustrates Flaws in Crime Coverage," *Extra!* (May–June 1994), pp. 10–13. The Tyndall Report is published by ADT Research, 135 Rivington, New York, New York 10002. Phone (212) 674–8913.

11. Ibid.

12. Ibid. Also see *New York Times*, November 13, 1994, "No Crystal Ball

Needed on Crime," and *San Francisco Chronicle,* October 31, 1994, "Violent Crime Jumped in '93, Survey Shows," p. A1. According to the FBI, the number of serious crimes reported to law-enforcement agencies fell 3 percent in the first half of 1994, as cited in the *New York Times,* December 5, 1994, "Serious Crime Is Still Declining, But Fears Remaining, FBI Reports." The nation's homicide rate fell 8.2 percent from 1993 to 1994, with even greater declines in such high pro-file crime areas as south Los Angeles (22 percent drop) and New York City (48 percent fewer killings in 1994 than in 1990). *New York Times,* October 24, 1995, "U.S. Says Murder Rate in 1994 Fell for Third Consecutive Year," p. A12.

13. Richard Moran, a professor of sociology and criminology at Mount Holyoke College, has noted that no study has ever convincingly demonstrated that adding police lowers crime rates. *New York Times,* February 27, 1995, "More Police, Less Crime, Right? Wrong," p. A15.

14. Brochure produced by Berry and Muller Campaigns, Inc., 1592 Union St., #477, San Francisco, CA 94123.

15. The removal of a bus shelter on one of the Tenderloin's worst corners did more to eliminate drug trafficking in the area than thousands of arrests.

16. *San Francisco Chronicle,* May 19, 1994, "600 Citizens Blast Jordan on Crime, Softly," p. A15.

17. Robert Fisher, *Let the People Decide: Neighborhood Organizing in America* (Boston: Twayne Publishers, 1984). This book provides an explanation for the seemingly contradictory ideological approach of neo-Alinsky groups like those in the PICO networks. Fisher observes that such groups focus on organization-building skills and deemphasize political education and ideology. Their obsession with scoring "victories" leads them to avoid potentially divisive positions; moreover, by deemphasizing ideology, such populist organizations can and have become supporters of right-wing causes such as anti-abortion or anti-integration (pp. 140–141). Fisher's analysis makes it even more imperative that progressive secular and religious groups directly confront congregations about the ideological misconduct of their anti-crime efforts.

18. *San Francisco Free Press,* November 7, 1994, "Can Brown Top Wilson's Comeback?" p. 1. This newspaper was produced sporadically by *Chronicle* and *Examiner* reporters during the San Francisco newspaper strike of November 1–12, 1994. Article by Robert B. Gunnison and Steven Capps, referring to a speech made by Wilson in Orange County in early November 1994.

19. *San Francisco Chronicle,* June 11, 1994, "State Crime Down in Major Offenses," p. A17. Story by Robert Gunnison, citing a California attorney general crime report.

20. *New York Times,* September 25, 1994, "Star Appeal or Not, Governor Richards Faces Tough Campaign in Texas," p. 1.

21. Elliott Currie, *Reckoning: Drugs, the Cities and the American Future* (New York: Hill & Wang, 1993), pp. 204–212.

22. In *Let the People Decide,* Robert Fisher notes that "organizers bring an ideology, skills, experience and perspective to their work; they owe it to neighborhood people to share this with them openly and honestly. Not to do so will in the long run increase suspicion" (p. 163).

23. Mount Holyoke professor Richard Moran "(More Police, Less Crime")

shares my assessment that community policing is "mostly public relations" and notes that the most thorough analysis of police beats ever done showed that foot patrols had virtually no effect on crime rates.

CHAPTER 2

1. Mary Beth Rogers, *Cold Anger: A Story of Faith and Power Politics* (Denton, Texas: University of North Texas Press, 1990), p. 27.

2. Ibid., pp. 169–170.

3. Harry Boyte, *Community Is Possible: Repairing America's Roots* (New York: Harper & Row, 1984), p. 128; quote from Sonia Hernandez.

4. The Clinton administration's April 1994 "Continuum of Care" homeless plan required cities and counties seeking federal homeless funds to develop their own long-range and strategic homeless plans. Thus does one homeless plan beget yet another and another. A new president will no doubt require that every government entity start plans from scratch as a funding prerequisite.

5. William Greider, *Who Will Tell the People: The Betrayal of American Democracy* (New York: Touchstone/Simon & Schuster, 1992), pp. 12, 101–107, 113, 124.

6. Ibid., pp. 107, 130, 132–133, 215–216.

7. Ibid., p. 215.

8. Joel Bleifuss, "Talk of Politics and Toxics," *In These Times* (March 21, 1994), pp. 12–14.

9. Greider, *Who Will Tell*, pp. 214–215.

10. Bleifuss, "Talk of Politics," March 21, 1994.

11. Greider, *Who Will Tell*, pp. 215–216, quoting Curtis Moore, former counsel for the Senate Environmental Affairs Committee. Similar sentiments expressed by Richard Ayres, chairman of the Big Ten's Clean Water Coalition.

12. Greider, *Who Will Tell*, citing Lois Gibbs, p. 215.

13. Cited on Greenpeace flyer for the "Put People First, Not Polluters" bus tour.

14. Albert Gore, *Earth in the Balance: Ecology and the Human Spirit* (New York: Plume, 1993).

15. *New York Times*, December 6, 1992, "Gore Says Clinton Will Try to Halt Waste Incinerator," p. D9.

16. Browner subsequently disqualified herself from decisions about the project because of her husband's employment with a national environmental group whose Ohio affiliate was "involved" in the dispute (*New York Times*, May 19, 1993), "For Crusader Against Waste Incinerator, a Bittersweet Victory."

17. Will Nixon, "Up in Smoke," *In These Times* (March 21, 1994), p. 16.

18. Conversation with Rick Hind, October 21, 1994.

19. *Washington Post*, May 18, 1993, "Clinton's Smoke Blows Stacks," column by Mary McGrory.

20. *New York Times*, May 18, 1993, "Administration to Freeze Growth of Hazardous Waste Incinerators," p. A1.

21. Margaret Kriz, "Slow Burn," *National Journal* (April 3, 1993), p. 811.

22. The bill's enactment was motivated by Democratic senators' concern over retaining control of the Senate, because the Desert Protection Bill had become a litmus test for Feinstein's ability to "get things done" in Washington.

23. *Los Angeles Times,* September 21, 1994, "Environmental Movement Struggling as Clout Fades."

24. See Chapter 7 for further discussion of Clinton's relationship with AIDS activists. Although it should be obvious that Bill Clinton epitomizes the politician who only respects those he fears, some critics "on the left" have argued that progressive opposition to Clinton will pave the way for a right-wing resurgence in the 1996 election. The idea that constituencies should remain silent while Clinton betrays commitments to them is a strange strategy for achieving progressive social change. (See *The Nation,* May 30, 1994, "The Left and Clinton: As Bill Goes, So Do We," pp. 744–746, and responses in the June 13, July 25, and August 1, 1994 issues).

25. *San Francisco Examiner,* October 14, 1994. Letter to the editor from Carl Pope, p. A22.

26. Quote is from Kramer's 1989 book, *Report from the Holocaust: The Making of an AIDS Activist* (New York: St. Martin's Press, 1989), cited in Robert M. Wachter, *The Fragile Coalition: Scientists, Activists and AIDS* (New York: St. Martin's Press, 1991), p. 169.

27. The Green Party candidate received 10 percent of the vote as the Republican defeated the incumbent Democrat.

28. For a discussion of the Greens' New Mexico campaign, see *The Nation,* October 24, 1994, "The Greens Climb in New Mexico," pp. 453–458.

29. I am indebted to Robert Peterson's article in *Public Schools That Work: Creating Community,* edited by Gregory A. Smith (New York: Routledge, 1993), for much of the material about Fratney.

30. Parent despair over bureaucratic control of schools has reached the point where some communities are seeking drastic results. In West Pikeland, Pennsylvania, located in a semirural area west of Philadelphia, parents are using grassroots organizing tactics to support their drive to have the district's only high school secede and join a neighboring district. The secession movement is a response to school-district plans to double the number of students in the school. Such plans run counter to parent preference for smaller schools, decentralization, and greater local control. (See *New York Times,* October 24, 1994, "Beyond the PTA: Parents Seek More Power," p. A1).

31. Ibid., citing a study by the Center for School Change at the University of Minnesota.

CHAPTER 3

1. Greider, *Who Will Tell,* p. 234.

2. Ibid., p. 235.

3. Unless otherwise noted, the events and chronology of the Brooklyn Navy

Yard incinerator fight were provided by Larry Shapiro, Arthur Kell, and Martin Brennan of NYPIRG in various conversations and correspondence during 1994 and from fact sheets prepared by NYPIRG.

4. *New York Newsday,* "Brooklyn Sunday" supplement, February 20, 1994.

5. Conversation with Luis Garden Acosta, November 20, 1994.

6. Both the Satmars and the Latinos of Williamsburg supported Dinkins in 1989, so people openly wondered at the time about Dinkins's political wisdom in sacrificing their support for a project chiefly advocated by Wall Street and the *New York Times*. The Satmars strongly supported Rudolph Giuliani in 1993, and Dinkins's narrow defeat is partially attributable to his switch to a pro-incinerator position.

7. A fifty-ton-per-day medical waste incinerator had been built in the south Bronx in recent years. The opening of the North River Sewage Treatment Plant in West Harlem in 1986 was soon followed by complaints of foul odors and respiratory problems from the area's predominantly African-American residents. The plant was built in Harlem after the affluent, mostly white Upper West Side organized succesfully to defeat construction in that neighborhood.

8. The *New York Times* never forgave Holtzman's strong opposition to the Brooklyn incinerator. In both the 1992 US. Senate primary and her 1993 re-election bid, the *Times* editorialized against Holtzman for her incinerator stand. The *Times'* strong pro-incinerator position may explain Mayor Dinkins's support of the project.

9. Correspondence with Arthur Kell of NYPIRG, July 28, 1994.

10. *New York Daily News,* March 24, 1992, "Dinkins Cools on Incinerator."

11. Ibid.

12. Conversation with Garden Acosta, November 20, 1994.

13. *New York Times,* May 7, 1992, "Co-op Effort Worsens a Rift in Williamsburg"; also *New York Newsday,* Brooklyn edition, May 15, 1992, "Patched Rift Threatened."

14. *New York Times,* May 7, 1992, "Co-op Effort."

15. *Newsday,* Brooklyn edition, October 6, 1992, "Race to Pollute."

16. Ibid.

17. Ibid.

18. *Staten Island Advance,* October 30, 1992, "Activists Attack Incinerator, Co-generation Plant," p. A7, quoting Shapiro of NYPIRG.

19. *New York Times,* December 27, 1992, "Grave Site May Be Under Proposed Incinerator," p. 32.

20. Photos of the march are included in the *Brooklyn Heights Courier,* July 12–July 25, 1993, "Paying Tribute to Heroes of Revolutionary War."

21. *New York Newsday,* January 15, 1993, "Incinerator Burns Marchers."

22. Ibid.

23. *New York Times,* January 15, 1993, "Environmental Concerns Unite a Neighborhood," photo caption.

24. All quotations in this paragraph are from *The Legislative Gazette* of Albany, New York, June 14, 1993, "Groups Want Hearings on Navy Yard Incin-

erator." Garden Acosta later learned the incinerator was actually a fifty-five-story monstrosity (conversation with Garden Acosta, November 20, 1994).

25. *New York Newsday,* Brooklyn edition, June 23, 1993, "City Trashes Albany Pollution Bill."

26. Correspondence with Larry Shapiro, June 10, 1994. The *New York Newsday* "Brooklyn Sunday" supplement of February 20, 1994 ("There's the Rubbish") says that in 1989 Giuliani considered incineration projects "a necessity."

27. *The Phoenix,* September 27–October 4, 1993, "No-show by Mayor Angers Those at Fort Greene Forum."

28. *New York Times,* February 27, 1994, "Incinerator Again Testing New Mayor."

29. *New York Newsday,* Brooklyn Sunday supplement, February 20, 1994, "There's the Rubbish."

30. *New York Times,* February 27, 1994, "Incinerator Again Testing New Mayor."

31. Ibid.

32. *New York Newsday,* Brooklyn edition, March 8, 1994, "Turning Up the Heat."

33. *New York Daily News,* Brooklyn edition, March 8, 1994, "Incinerator Move Called State Cop-out."

34. Ibid. The oft-repeated theme of a "railroad job" first appeared in *New York Newsday* on October 30, 1992, "Group Sues to Stop Navy Yard Incinerator."

35. All quotations in this paragraph are from the *New York Daily News,* March 20, 1994, "State Ignores Navy Yard Toxins."

36. *New York Times,* September 18, 1994, "Hasidic and Hispanic Residents in Williamsburg Try to Forge a New Unity."

37. Conversation with Garden Acosta, November 20, 1994.

38. *New York Times,* September 18, 1994, "Hasidic and Hispanic Residents in Williamsburg Try to Forge a New Unity."

39. Conversation with David Niederman, November 11, 1994.

40. *New York Times,* September 18, 1994, "Hasidic and Hispanic Residents in Williamsburg Try to Forge a New Unity."

41. Conversation with Garden Acosta, November 20, 1994.

42. Ibid.

43. Correspondence with Arthur Kell of NYPIRG, July 28, 1994.

CHAPTER 4

1. *New York Times,* August 20, 1994, "Paying a Question in Ballot Initiatives."

2. *San Francisco Chronicle,* September 10, 1994, "Hiram Johnson Please Call Home."

3. Ibid.

4. For example, the state of Washington used the initiative process to increase

the minimum wage for workers. Corporate opposition to such an obvious step for reducing poverty had prevented legislative efforts to accomplish this goal.

5. See Margaret Brodkin and Coleman Advocates for Children and Youth, *From Sand Boxes to Ballot Boxes: San Francisco's Landmark Campaign to Fund Children's Services,* p. 90. The book was funded by the Charles Stewart Mott Foundation and is available from the author.

6. Saul Alinsky, *Rules for Radicals* (New York: Vintage, 1972), pp. 12–13.

7. In fairness to Zimmerman's tactical acumen, Proposition 167 was partially developed to direct corporate funds away from an anti-welfare initiative on the same ballot backed by Republican governor Pete Wilson. The tactic succeeded, as business interests primarily focused on defeating Proposition 167 and Wilson's measure went down to defeat.

8. Official opposition ballot argument, California Voter Handbook, November 1990.

9. *New York Times,* October 22, 1994, "Defying Omens, Health Care Drops From Campaign Stage," p. 1.

10. Ibid.

11. *San Francisco Chronicle,* September 20, 1994, "Prop 186 Backers Try New Tactic," p. A1.

12. The ballot measure was technically a referendum put on the ballot by landlords after it was signed by the mayor into law. Everyone knew that legislative passage of vacancy control would become subject to a referendum. By pushing to enact vacancy control in early 1991, tenant advocates were, in essence, choosing to put an initiative on the November 1991 ballot. Tenant advocates were in no different a position than if they had used the initiative route directly.

13. Our opposition's campaign manager, Jack Davis, had never previously lost a rent-control-related campaign. Davis received the lion's share of credit for masterminding Frank Jordan's upset victory over Art Agnos in the 1991 San Francisco mayor's race.

14. Alinsky, *Rules for Radicals,* p. xviii.

15. Thomas Ferguson and Joel Rogers, *Right Turn: The Decline of Democrats and the Future of American Politics* (New York: Hill & Wang, 1986).

CHAPTER 5

1. Ben Bagdikian, *The Media Monopoly,* fourth edition (Boston: Beacon Press, 1992), pp. 15, 47–48.

2. *San Francisco Chronicle,* December 6, 1982, "Our City's Shame," p. A1.

3. I no longer attempt to pressure people to talk to the press; media coverage is not worth driving a wedge between the person and the organization. An equally effective story can be told without subjecting people to undesired stress.

4. I dealt extensively with the producer on a story in which he sought to support his thesis that there was enough low-cost housing available for all of the homeless staying in shelters. It became obvious that his commitment to his the-

sis overshadowed any journalistic obligation to report the facts. The resulting two-part series was so confusing that its message was lost.

5. City Hall-, statehouse- or Capitol-based reporters often do such favors for the executive branch in exchange for priority access on major stories.

6. An Orange County legal-aid attorney who made the tactical error of responding to this columnist saw her position on an issue unfairly depicted. Although given space on the editorial page, the response was half the length of the offending piece and had been so extensively edited that the purpose of the response was lost.

7. Fairness and Accuracy in Reporting (FAIR), 130 West 25th Street, New York, NY 10001.

8. Jonathan Eagleman, Carolyn Francis, and Doug Henwood, "The Way Things Aren't: Rush Limbaugh Debates Reality," *Extra!* (July–August 1994), pp. 10–18.

9. Douglas Crimp and Aden Ralston, *AIDS Demographics* (Seattle: Bay Press, 1990), pp. 108–109.

10. Ibid., pp. 108–113.

11. Jonathan Kwitny describes the facts surrounding the Kolata story in detail in *Acceptable Risks* (New York: Poseidon Press, 1992), pp. 302–306. Kwitny concludes that Kolata's story "violated professional standards." Kolata wrote similar attacks on AIDS activists' drug-testing agenda on November 21, 1989 ("Innovative AIDS drug plan may be undermining testing") and on March 12, 1990, when a front-page story again charged activist critics of the FDA with "placing patients at great risk of being harmed by experimental drugs." The *Village Voice* followed the latter story with a blistering attack on Kolata's coverage of AIDS (Kwitny, *Acceptable Risks,* pp. 328–329).

12. Ken Silverstein, "DLC Dollars," *The Nation,* June 20, 1994, p. 858.

13. Jude Wanniski. *The Way the World Works: How Economies Fail—and Succeed,* third edition (Morristown, N.J.: Polyconomics, Inc., 1989).

14. Ibid., p. xii.

15. Susan Faludi. *Backlash: The Undeclared War Against American Women.* New York: Crown, 1991.

16. Dinesh D'Souza. *Illiberal Education: The Politics of Race and Sex on Campus.* New York: Vintage, 1992.

17. David Brock. *The Real Anita Hill: The Untold Story.* New York: Maxwell Macmillan, 1993.

18. Christina Hoff Sommers, *Who Stole Feminism? How Women Have Betrayed Women* (New York: Simon and Schuster, 1994).

19. Katie Roiphe. *The Morning After: Sex, Fear and Feminism on Campus.* Boston: Little, Brown, 1993.

20. For an excellent analysis and media survey of the anti-feminist backlash, see "The 'Stolen Feminism' Hoax," *Extra!* (September–October 1994), pp. 6–9, and "Campus Feminists: The Media's New Bogeywoman," *Extra!* (March–April 1994), pp. 5–6, both by Laura Flanders. Some of Katha Pollitt's essays are compiled in *Reasonable Creatures: Essays on Women and Feminism* (New York: Knopf, 1994).

21. Susan Faludi, "I'm Not a Feminist But I Play One on TV," *Ms.* (March/April 1995), pp. 31–39.

CHAPTER 6

1. The "loss" is often financial. The federal judiciary's attempt affirmatively to suppress social change activism has been repeatedly demonstrated in the issuance of large fines against civil rights litigants whose claims are viewed as "frivolous." Reagan's appointees to the federal bench in the South have exhibited a hostility toward civil rights cases akin to that displayed in southern state courts in the 1950s.

2. Self-identified progressive elected officials often prefer using delaying tactics, rather than casting a publicly recorded vote against a progressive constituency, to kill legislation. A vote for further "study" of an issue allows the public clamor essential for social change to evaporate.

3. The case title is *Whitfield v. Board of Supervisors* (1991) 227 Cal. App. 3d 451; 277 Cal. Rptr. 815.

4. Gerald Rosenberg's *The Hollow Hope: Can Courts Bring About Social Change?* (Chicago: University of Chicago Press, 1991, pp. 132, 340–341) discusses the resource issue by examining the entire question of whether social change movements can really achieve their goals through litigation. Rosenberg demonstrates that most African-American civil rights activists of the 1950s and 1960s had little faith in litigation and that even the Supreme Court ruling in *Brown v. Board of Education* caused little reaction in the African-American community. He concludes that successful grassroots efforts like the Montgomery bus boycott may have increased donations to the NAACP for litigation, funds that could have been more effectively used in direct-action and legislative strategies. Rosenberg makes this point even more strongly in chronicling how environmental litigation drained movement resources without accomplishing significant social reform.

5. This state court decision was subsequently accepted for review by the U.S. Supreme Court.

6. The defeat of anti-gay ballot initiatives in Oregon and Idaho in November 1994 followed local referenda earlier that year in Austin, Texas, and Springfield, Missouri, where laws protecting gay rights were overturned by overwhelming margins. Voters who oppose attacks on gay rights appear less likely to support affirmative protections.

7. Taylor Branch, *Parting the Waters: America in the King Years 1954–63* (New York: Simon and Schuster, 1988).

8. Friction also occurred because the success of King's Montgomery bus boycott meant that Alabama officials punitively "outlawed" the NAACP in their state, costing the organization a large segment of its dues-paying membership. See Branch, *Parting the Waters,* pp. 186–187.

9. Miles Harvey, "Shades of Green," *In These Times* (July 11, 1994), p. 10. Quote cited from the *Portland Oregonian.*

10. Alexander Cockburn, "The Green Betrayers." *The Nation* (February 6, 1995), p. 157.

11. Quoting directly from lawsuits also enables reporters to publish controversial allegations without risk of a libel suit. Attorneys have traditionally enjoyed similar immunity, although at least one court has ruled that attorneys' immunity ends if lawsuit allegations are included in a press release or otherwise disseminated outside the legal system.

12. The California Supreme Court ruling in *Tobe v. City of Santa Ana* (1995) 95 Daily Journal DAR 5239 in April 1995 dealt a major blow to opponents of these measures. The decision, following the reversal in the Miami case (*Pottinger v. City of Miami* 40 F. 3d 1152 [11th Cir. (Dec. 7) 1994]) and the San Francisco ruling in *Joyce v. City and County*, U.S.A. Ct. No. C 93 4149 DLJ/JSB, may deter legal advocacy organizations from expanding significant resources on similar litigation.

CHAPTER 7

1. The following summary of the conditions giving rise to ACT-UP is included in several books on the subject. I have relied primarily on the following: Bruce Nussbaum, *Good Intentions: How Big Business and the Medical Establishment Are Corrupting the Fight Against AIDS* (New York: Atlantic Monthly, 1990); Wachter, *The Fragile Coalition;* Crimp and Ralston, *AIDS Demographics;* Kwitny, *Acceptable Risks;* Randy Shilts, *And the Band Played On: Politics, People and the AIDS Epidemic* (New York: St. Martin's, 1987); and Larry Kramer, *Reports from the Holocaust* (New York: St. Martin's, 1989).

2. Nussbaum, *Good Intentions,* pp. 129–130, 139–140, and 142–143.

3. Wachter, *Fragile Coalition,* p. 59.

4. Crimp and Ralston, *AIDS Demographics,* pp. 26–27.

5. Crimp and Ralston, *AIDS Demographics,* pp. 14–15.

6. Nussbaum, *Good Intentions,* p. 187.

7. Conversation with ACT UP member Laura Thomas, June 7, 1994.

8. Nussbaum, *Good Intentions,* pp. 204–206; Crimp and Ralston, *AIDS Demographics,* pp. 76–77 and 80–81.

9. *San Francisco Chronicle,* February 1, 1989, "AIDS Blockade Halts Morning Commuter," p. A1.

10. *San Francisco Examiner,* February 1, 1989, "Read This or Else," p. A3.

11. *San Francisco Chronicle,* February 1, 1989, "AIDS Blockade Halts Morning Commuters," p. A1.

12. Wachter, *Fragile Coalition,* pp. 62–63.

13. Crimp and Ralston, *AIDS Demographics,* pp. 131–141.

14. *San Francisco Chronicle,* December 18, 1989, "AIDS Protests at Churches," p. A4.

15. Crimp and Ralston, *AIDS Demographics,* p. 137.

16. Wachter, *Fragile Coalition,* p. 20.

17. Nussbaum, *Good Intentions,* pp. 278–279.

18. HR 4370, introduced in 1993, would have cost $2 billion over five years. It won only twenty-one co-sponsors in the House and went nowhere.

19. Crimp and Ralston, *AIDS Demographics*, p. 141.

20. Ibid.

21. Ellen Cooper, staff of FDA, quoted in Nussbaum, *Good Intentions*, p. 204.

22. *East Bay Express* (Berkeley), August 5, 1994, "AIDS Vaccine," p. 1.

23. Ibid.

24. *San Francisco Chronicle*, January 16, 1995, "Kansas City ACT-UP Chapter May Shut Its Doors for Good," article citing figures from the U.S. Public Health Service.

25. *New York Times*, January 12, 1995, "Larry Kramer's Roar Turns to Contented Purr," p. B1.

26. Unless otherwise noted, the events and chronology of the Section 504 struggle were provided by disability rights activists Kitty Cone and Judy Heumann in various conversations and correspondence during 1994.

27. *New York Times*, April 11, 1977, "Handicapped Use Protests to Push HEW to Implement '73 Bias Law," p.12, and May 1, 1977, "Equity for Disabled Likely to Be Costly."

28. Joseph A. Califano (*Governing America: An Insider's Report from the White House and Cabinet*, New York: Simon and Schuster, 1981) later claimed that Mathews was "sympathetic" but felt Section 504 was "one of the most irresponsible and thoughtless acts of the Congress" (p. 258).

29. Califano, *Governing America*, p. 260.

30. *Washington Post*, March 30, 1977, "Handicapped Plan Protest at HEW Offices in 10 Cities."

31. *San Francisco Chronicle*, April 6, 1977, "HEW Protest by Handicapped."

32. *San Francisco Chronicle*, April 7, 1977, "Handicapped Call Off D.C. Demonstration," p. 9.

33. The only change made to the original version of Section 504 was an attorney general's opinion clarifying that alcoholics and drug addicts were covered by the act as long as they were otherwise qualified for the job or program involved (Califano, *Governing America*, p. 261).

34. *New York Times*, May 1, 1977, "Equity for Disabled Likely to Be Costly."

35. Ibid.

36. *Washington Post*, January 8, 1977, "Carter Broke Promises, Say Handicapped," p. A3.

37. *New York Times*, April 11, 1977, "Coast Sit-in Wins Some Gains," p. 12.

38. *Washington Post*, April 23, 1977, "Handicapped Protest Turned Away at HEW."

39. Califano, *Governing America*, p. 261.

40. The *Post*'s May 1, 1977, editorial, "HEW and the Handicapped," following the signing of the regulations, reflected its grudging shift in position. Though still maintaining that the regulations would create a "welter of lawsuits" and involve "cumbersome coercion," the *Post* concluded that it "would like to

think that the positive values in the drive to end discrimination will prevail." The editorial also tried to defend its pro-Califano stance by noting that the secretary's revisions to Section 504 had "cut down substantially on the paperwork" requirements—as if objections to retaining Section 504 unchanged had been about paperwork, not civil rights.

41. William Dietrich, *The Final Forest: The Battle for the Last Great Trees of the Pacific Northwest,* New York: Simon and Schuster, 1992.

42. Ibid., p. 154.

43. "Koppel Covers for Limbaugh's Rumor-Mongering," *Extra!* (July–August 1994), p. 17.

CHAPTER 8

1. David Brower, *Work in Progress* (New York: A Peregrine Smith Book, 1991), pp. 214–215.

2. Salim Muwakkil, "Advancement?" *In These Times* (September 5, 1994), p. 6.

3. In Chicago, a street gang known as the Gangster Disciples set up the 21st Century Voices of Total Empowerment (VOTE) project. The organization has drawn large crowds to protests against school cutbacks and health-clinic closures and works to ensure that its 30,000 gang members vote. Rather than praise these positive actions, the Chicago Crime Commission considers the gang's work as cause for "worry." The redirection of African-American youth from activities leading to prison to those increasing their community's political clout is clearly seen by many as a threat to the existing political order (*San Francisco Chronicle,* October 10, 1994, "Chicago Gang is Cleaning Up Its Act," p. A8).

4. Salim Muwakkil, "NAACP Follows Chavis' Lead," *In These Times* (July 25, 1994), pp. 7–8.

5. Ibid.

6. Ibid.

7. Ibid.

8. Chavis's second and third summits are discussed in Salim Muwakkil's "Closing Ranks," *In These Times* (December 12, 1994), pp. 20–21. On the link between the summit and march, see Muwakkil, "Face the Nation," *In These Times* (October 30, 1995), pp. 15–18.

9. *Los Angeles Times,* September 21, 1994, "Environmental Movement Struggling as Clout Fades."

10. Jim Schwab, *Deeper Shades of Green: The Rise of Blue Collar and Minority Environmentalism in America,* San Francisco: Sierra Club Books, 1994. The "Principles" are set forth in Appendix C, pp. 441–443. Schwab discusses the summit on pp. 383–393.

11. *Los Angeles Times,* September 21, 1994, "Environmental Movement Struggling as Clout Fades."

Index

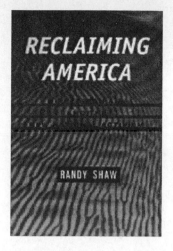

RECLAIMING AMERICA

NIKE, CLEAN AIR
AND THE NEW NATIONAL ACTIVISM

Randy Shaw

"An inspiring look at how idealistic citizens can shake the power structure and bring about progressive change."
  San Francisco Chronicle & Examiner Book Review, front page

"Shaw provides the definitive account of the historic national campaign to reform Nike's labor practices. *Reclaiming America* is a must read for everyone seeking to achieve greater social and economic fairness in the 21st Century."
  Medea Benjamin, Co-Director, Global Exchange

"Enormously valuable in depicting how grassroots activism can still overcome big money in the national arena."
  Gene Karpinski, Executive Director, U.S. PIRG

Have activists taken the bumper-sticker adage "Think Globally, Act Locally" too literally? Randy Shaw argues that they have, with destructive consequences for America. Since the 1970s, activist participation in national struggles has steadily given way to a nearly exclusive focus on local issues. America's political and corporate elite has succeeded in controlling the national agenda, while their adversaries—the citizen activists and organizations who spent decades building federal programs to reflect the country's progressive ideals—increasingly bypass national fights. The result has been not only the dismantling of hard-won federal programs but also the sabotaging of local agendas and community institutions by decisions made in the national arena. Shaw urges activists and their organizations to implement a "new national activism" by channeling energy from closely knit local groups into broader causes. Such activism enables locally oriented activists to shape America's future and work on national fights without traveling to Washington, D.C., but instead working in their own backyards.

$16.95 paperback ISBN 0-520-21779-9
at bookstores or order 1-800-822-6657

University of California Press
www.ucpress.edu

Compositor: ComCom
Text: 10/13 Sabon
Display: Franklin Gothic Demi
Printer: Maple-Vail Book Mfg.
Binder: Maple-Vail Book Mfg.